# Working in the global film and television industries

# Working in the global film and television industries: Creativity, systems, space, patronage

edited by *Andrew Dawson and Sean P. Holmes*

BLOOMSBURY ACADEMIC

First published in 2012 by

Bloomsbury Academic

An imprint of Bloomsbury Publishing Plc
50 Bedford Square, London WC1B 3DP, UK
and
175 Fifth Avenue, New York, NY 10010, USA

CIP records for this book are available from the British Library and
the Library of Congress.

ISBN 978-1-78093-020-6 (hardback)
ISBN 978-1-78093-023-7 (paperback)
ISBN 978-1-78093-021-3 (ebook)

This book is produced using paper that is made from wood grown in managed,
sustainable forests. It is natural, renewable and recyclable. The logging and manufacturing
processes conform to the environmental regulations of the country of origin.

Printed and bound in Great Britain by the MPG Books Group, Bodmin, Cornwall

Cover image: Aimee Corrigan/This is Nollywood

**www.bloomsburyacademic.com**

For Alicia Brooke Robinson and Marjorie Wood Dawson, with love.

# Contents

# List of contributors

**Andrew Dawson** teaches film studies at the University of Greenwich in London. He has a long-time research interest in the political economy of work. In 2004, he wrote *Lives of the Philadelphia Engineers: Capital, Class and Revolution, 1830–1890* (Aldershot: Ashgate). More recently, he has focused on the motion picture industry, especially in the United States, with studies of runaway production, strike patterns and African American entry to Hollywood during the civil rights era. He is collaborating with Sean Holmes and the BECTU History Project on a number of oral history initiatives. His course, Working for Hollywood, addresses themes raised in this collection of essays, available at http://w3.gre.ac.uk/~dao7/index.html.

**Galina Gornostaeva** is a self-employed researcher. She works on issues of the film and television industry, cultural clusters and quarters and cultural governance. She has participated in several research projects including the Economic and Social Research Council (ESRC)-funded project on production chains in the film and television industry in the United Kingdom (LSE), the INTERREG-funded project on functional urban regions in Europe (LSE) and so on. She also has a long-standing connection with the School of Humanities at the University of Greenwich.

**Olof Hedling** is an associate professor in film studies at Lund University, Sweden. For some years, he has worked on the phenomena of European film policy, regional film funds and regional film and television production. Of late he has co-edited the collection *Regional Aesthetics: Locating Swedish Media* (Stockholm: Royal Library, 2010) and co-guest-edited a *Film International* special issue on the subject of *Making Movies in Europe: Production, Industry, Policy* (2010).

**Sean P. Holmes** is deputy head of the School of Arts at Brunel University and teaches in the Film and Television Studies programme. He has published extensively on the history of trade unionism in the American entertainment industry in journals such as the *Journal of American History* and the *Historical Journal of Film, Radio and Television.*

His book, *Weavers of Dreams, Unite!: Actors' Unionism in Early Twentieth-Century America*, will be published next year by the University of Illinois Press.

**Linda Marchant** is a senior lecturer in photography at Nottingham Trent University. Her research interests centre on the links between photography and celebrity culture. She has presented work on topics ranging from 1930s and 1940s Hollywood portraiture to ideas around contemporary 'visual gossip'. She is currently undertaking her PhD studies in the Department of Culture, Film and Media at the University of Nottingham.

**Ikechukwu Obiaya** is a lecturer at the School of Media and Communication of the Pan-African University, in Lagos, Nigeria. His research is based on the Nigerian film industry with particular focus on the role of the National Film and Censors Board in the establishment of a distribution framework for the industry. He is also interested in audience analysis, and some of his work on the audience of Nigerian video films has been published.

**Richard Paterson** is currently head of research and scholarship at the British Film Institute and senior research associate of the Centre for Cultural Policy Research at the University of Glasgow. His research continues to focus on the film and television industries with a particular interest in the sociology and economics of audiences and organizations, and he has published widely on these topics.

**Katrien Pype** is currently a postdoctoral researcher (Marie Curie IOF) at the Science, Technology and Society Program at the Massachusetts Institute of Technology and the Institute of Anthropological Research in Africa at the K.U. Leuven (Belgium), where she is working on a project that studies the dialectics between ICT and the lifeworlds of old people in contemporary Kinshasa. She is an anthropologist, with a particular interest in media and popular culture. She has published in academic journals such as *Africa*, *Journal of Modern African Studies* and *Journal of Southern African Studies*. Her book on the production of television serials in Kinshasa is forthcoming with Berghahn Books (expected June 2012).

**Alison Smith** is a lecturer in French and subject head of European Film Studies at the University of Liverpool. She has published books on the politicized French cinema of the 1970s and on major Nouvelle Vague directors Agnès Varda and Jacques Rivette, as well as articles on various aspects of post-New Wave French cinema. Her current research is on representations of the multilingual in European cinemas.

**Clare M. Wilkinson-Weber** is an assistant professor of anthropology at Washington State University Vancouver. She was educated at Durham University, England, and the University of Pennsylvania, where she received her PhD in anthropology. Her research interests include material and visual culture, gender and media production. Her work has been centred in India, where she has been chiefly concerned with local conceptions of creativity and skill in artistic practice, and shifting aesthetic and social patterns in the Hindi film industry. Recent publications have focused on dress, fashion and the processes of film production, with questions of the co-option of commodities in media industries, the making of film costume and fashion and performance in film to the fore. Her articles have appeared in *Visual Anthropology Review*, *Anthropological Quarterly* and *Journal of Material Culture*. A book, *Embroidering Lives: Women's Work and Skill in the Lucknow Embroidery Industry*, was published by SUNY press in 1999, and she is currently working on another book titled *Fashioning Bollywood: The Making and Meaning of Hindi Film Costume*.

# Acknowledgements

The editors would like to thank all the contributors to this volume, especially those who took part in the 'Working for the Film and Television Industry' session at the European Social Science History Conference in Ghent in April 2010. We would also like to thank the University of Greenwich and the School of Arts at Brunel University for providing the funding that allowed us to attend the conference.

# New perspectives on working in the global film and television industries

chapter

# 1

ANDREW DAWSON AND SEAN P. HOLMES

## Introduction

This collection is the first of its kind to grapple with the diverse experiences of women and men who work in the many film and television production centres scattered across the globe. The essays it contains, all of them specially commissioned, offer unique insights into the lives of media workers.[1] They focus on different groups of workers at various points in time and at a range of geographical locations, shedding new light on their experiences in an industry characterized by a complex spatial and hierarchical division of labour and assessing the imprint they have made, both individually and collectively, on the creative process. They also explore broader shifts in the organization of production and the changing role of the state. From its inception in 1895, film-making has straddled national boundaries and crossed continents. Though Hollywood has long dominated the global marketplace, its hegemony has not gone unchallenged and, in terms of total output, it now lags behind both the Indian film industry and the Nigerian film industry. Unlike most of the existing scholarship, our collection acknowledges this and harnesses the expertise of scholars working in a range of national and transnational contexts – Africa and India as well as North America and Europe.

Film and television as cultural commodities have tended to work in such a way as to obscure the conditions under which they are produced and thereby to deny the various groups involved in the production process an identity as workers. Film and Television Studies as a discipline has generally reinforced this tendency by defining films and television shows as cultural texts and, as such, something that can be studied largely without reference to the workers who produce them. This collection of essays takes as its starting point the premise that film and television are the products of human labour and that a full critical review of the operation of the film and television industries must, as film historian Michael Nielsen put it almost thirty years ago, 'merge dispassionate analysis of structures with the real-life stories of ... the workers themselves' (Nielsen 1983: 47–8). Multidisciplinary in its orientation and international in its scope, it explores the experience of working in the film and television industries in a variety of social, economic and political contexts. Not only does it provide detailed analyses of specific systems of production and their role in shaping the experience of work both above and below the line in the film and television industries, but it also engages with a number of important theoretical and methodological questions that attach to the study of working in the film and television industries.

## Scope of the study

We have arranged the essays in such a way as to highlight what we see as the key themes that emerge out of them, each of which we will explore in greater depth later on in our introduction. Section I focuses on systems of production, juxtaposing Andrew Dawson's work on 'flexible specialization' and the free-market paradigm as exemplified by contemporary Hollywood against Galina Gornostaeva's examination of the Soviet film industry in the wake of the Khruschev-era thaw and Olof Hedling's analysis of government sponsorship of the creative industries in contemporary Sweden. Section II brings together three articles that engage with the efforts of workers in the film and television industries to carve out what film theorist Barry King has termed 'manoeuvrable space' in the workplace: Sean P. Holmes's piece on silent movie star Jetta Goudal, Richard Paterson's examination of the experience of freelancers in the contemporary British television industry and Ikechukwu Obiaya's overview of working practices in Nollywood. Section III is based around the theme of patronage and clientelism. It encourages readers to consider the parallels between the experiences of film workers in Kinshasa as recounted in Katrien Pype's piece on the production of teleserials in the Democratic Republic of Congo (DRC) and those of female cinematographers in France as set out in the Alison Smith article on the contemporary French film industry. Section IV draws together two pieces of scholarship that look at the issue of creative agency in the context of film production from markedly different disciplinary perspectives: Linda Marchant's historical study of stills photographers in the British film industry in the 1950s and Clare M. Wilkinson-Weber's anthropological analysis of hairdressers and make-up artists in contemporary Bollywood.

In their mature form, the global film and television industries have generally been characterized by a highly stratified labour force. This is a consequence – in part, at least – of the efforts of employers to control expenditures by establishing a clear distinction between creative talent and technicians, a project that found its clearest expression in the line that accountants in studio-era Hollywood inserted into their budget sheets to indicate where one set of labour costs began and another ended. Where precisely the line of demarcation is located has varied over time and according to national and institutional context, but it has played a central role in shaping employment practices in every major centre of film and television production. In most production centres in North America and Europe, there is a clear division between above and below the line, in addition to a well-developed job hierarchy extending from top to bottom. But in many newer centres of film and television production, especially in Africa, where the industry is not so well capitalized, the division of labour is not so minute, and the workforce draws upon religious and familial cultural traditions from outside the industry – the division is blurred and the hierarchy flatter. In its most common usage, the term 'above-the-line' is applied to workers who are able to exercise a degree of creative control over the production process (writers, directors, editors, cinematographers and leading actors, for example), differentiating them from 'below-the-line' workers, a large and amorphous group that might include technical specialists of one kind or another, craft workers, ancillary staff and supporting actors. This collection includes studies of workers in both categories. As editors, however, we have tried to problematise the practice of drawing rigid distinctions between the two, acknowledging its role in constructing workplace hierarchies but questioning its utility in terms of making sense of creative practices in the film and television industries.

## Theorizing systems of production

Contributions to this volume range from studies of individual crafts to analyses of the wider political economy of film and television production. Underpinning them all is an assumption that work and the labour processes that create commodities lie at the heart of modern capitalism (including the Soviet Union, where the state assumed the role of capitalist). Making film and television programming is an arena of social conflict in which owners of media companies advance payment to workers who in return sell a capacity to work but actual production depends on the subsequent actions of the two parties. The quality and quantity of output is, therefore, the source of constant tension, sometimes in the open but mostly hidden. We are not the first to adopt this broad perspective: our claim to originality lies in the adoption of a global perspective. We draw upon the work of political economists, sociologists, industrial relations specialists, historians and anthropologists – all of it either American or European in its focus. While they do not all share our conclusions, they believe in the centrality of work and contribute to our understanding of cultural work in film and television. Hortense Powdermaker is doubly important: first, as a pioneering anthropologist of the movie industry and, second, in the ability of her book's title, *Hollywood, the Dream Factory*, to sum up one of the contradictions at the heart of film production – the creation of imaginative cultural products under modern factory conditions (Powdermaker 1950). Michael Chanan and Michael Nielsen make early theoretical contributions, though they are sadly insufficiently recognized today (Chanan 1976; Nielsen 1985). Murray Ross offers a well-researched and sound institutional study of labour-management relations in the Hollywood film industry that still rewards attention (Ross 1941). Alan McKinlay and Chris Smith reassert the theoretical importance of the labour process and question wild claims as to the uniqueness of the creative industries found in some recent studies (McKinlay and Smith 2009). Richard Florida (2002) offers a thought-provoking assessment of the importance of creative communities which finds support among some contributors to this collection, although he does seem to believe that the hierarchical world of labour management has turned upside down as managers are forced to pursue creative workers who can pick and choose where they locate themselves.

In mapping the structures and processes that underpin global film and television production, we need to be aware of the social and political forces that help construct our theoretical perspectives. While we might want to believe that we are dispassionate observers of social reality and that there is a gap between us and the object of our study, reality is a good deal more complex. Dawson's contribution to this collection draws attention to the continued influence of 1980s Los Angeles urban geographers upon how we understand the motion picture industry, identifying a false dichotomy between the labour system of classical-era Hollywood and new Hollywood which impedes clear understanding of the nature of work in motion pictures. Dawson contends that (like all theoretical constructs) the 'flexible specialization' model elaborated by urban geographers such as Susan Christopherson, Michael Storper and Allen Scott was influenced by the moment of its creation. At the time, the city's older, mass production industries were on the wane, and the movie industry was threatening to leave town. The flexible specialization school addressed the anxieties of industrialists, planners and intellectuals facing the uncertainties of global markets and the dismantling of state regulation by envisioning a bright new future: highly productive movie businesses firmly rooted in Hollywood would offer socially rewarding jobs. Specialist small firms competing among themselves would enhance efficiency, improve working conditions and create closer bonds between capital and labour. Optimistic assurances about the future, at least in part, rested on the creation of a good/bad binary divide between classical and new Hollywood where all that was inefficient, rigid and discordant was associated with the earlier period.

Although the flexible specialization school subsequently modified its view of the industry in response to contrary evidence, the Fordist/post-Fordist dichotomy continues to exert a strong influence on film development agencies and city planning departments as well as film and media studies in higher education. The adoption of the flexible specialization model by regional planners during the 1980s alerts us to the intimate connection between, on the one hand, how we conceptualize the industry's system of production and, on the other, the activities of government in regulating the industry and in pursuing regional development goals. While the state can be seen as a consumer of academic theory, government concerns also powerfully loop back to influence the way academics conceptualize the industry's present, future and past. At the same time, the 2008 banking crisis and the collapse of the neoliberal world view offer us the opportunity to seize the moment and re-conceptualize work in the media industries on firmer ground. The thirty-year-old claim that unfettered markets deliver efficiency and social welfare is, at least for the moment, treated with widespread scepticism.

John Caldwell and the 'production studies' school have offered an exciting new approach to studying media labour that seeks to occupy the intellectual space provided by the collapse of the banking system. In so far as they focus on the practices and beliefs of film and video workers, 'not just the prestige producers and directors but also those of the many more anonymous workers, such as gaffers and grips, in Hollywood's lower castes and crafts', the school shares many of our concerns (Caldwell 2008: 1). Like the scholars whose work is brought together in this collection, Caldwell and his associates assert that media workers are producers of cultural meaning and that creativity is not the preserve of an elite. They draw upon new sources of information – material that is not secreted away 'behind the scenes' but hidden in plain sight, such as the 'making of' additions to DVD releases of movies and the rituals of industry gatherings. As a reflective fieldworker sceptical of industry spin, Caldwell is well aware of his own problematic location as he teases out the meanings of workers' stories and trade customs.[2] For the moment, production studies focuses narrowly on an Angeleno or, at best, Anglo world, although this could easily be remedied. Nevertheless, as far as we are concerned, the production studies model is ultimately flawed. This collection of essays – which looks at the changing division of labour and workers' experiences, beliefs and actions – parts company with production studies at the point where it pursues the study of cultural meaning beyond the industry, wage labour and the social relations of work. '[E]ven the objects of consumption are sites of cultural production as consumers adopt, modify, and re-purpose the cultural meaning of domestic tools and media technologies', declare the editors of Production Studies (Mayer, Banks and Caldwell 2008: 3). Blurring the real distinction between production and consumption means that for scholars in the field of production studies, media workers, fans and audiences are all producers of culture. But if we are all producers of culture, what makes media workers distinctive? While media workers do author texts – at least collectively – they have many other social relations not shared by fans or by audiences. They deploy varying degrees of skill, struggle to stay in an industry with a superabundance of labour, work closely with colleagues, and have cooperative or antagonistic relations with their managers. For the moment at least, production studies has little to say about management-labour relations, conflict and conciliation, and collective action. As theorists from Marx onwards point out, workers are alienated from that which they produce, neither owning the tools of the trade nor the finished article. This is as true of hula-hoop manufacture as it is of Hollywood, despite the latter's glittering visual attractions. Production studies, with its emphasis on tracing the meaning of cultural products, runs the risk of fetishizing films and television programmes by obscuring the social relations of production in the film and television industries behind an analysis of the meaning of commodities in circulation.

## Methodologies

To engage fully with the past and present of movie workers' lives, and to explore the interplay between the shifting division of labour and work culture and creativity, this collection needs to draws upon a wide range of disciplines and methodologies. Holmes uses his historical training to dissect the career of 1920s star Jetta Goudal in an industry only just assuming its modern shape. He draws upon popular magazines, newspapers and hitherto largely ignored archival sources in Los Angeles to explore

Goudal's efforts to wrest control over her star image from her employers. Dawson, also a historian, deploys a reflexive historiographical approach in his assessment of the impact of 1980s Los Angles urban geographers upon our understanding of Hollywood's labour process since the 1920s. Most contributions to this volume deal with the modern period and look to the disciplinary traditions of anthropology, sociology and film studies. Wilkinson-Weber and Pype, building upon a scholarly tradition established by Hortense Powdermaker in the early 1950s, craft finely detailed anthropological studies of media workers based on extensive fieldwork in Mumbai and Kinshasa. Other contributors locate themselves within the discipline of sociology, or draw upon its methods. Gornostaeva frames the careers of leading Soviet directors Grigori Chukrai and Andrei Tarkovsky within Soviet political and bureaucratic structures. Paterson's study of the attitudes of freelancers in the British television industry utilizes a major longitudinal industry study carried out between 1994 and 1998, while Hedling's essay on Swedish workers and regional policy harvests invaluable information from interviews with business leaders and policy makers. Ikechukwu Obiaya similarly conducted invaluable interviews with Nigerian film workers. Even Film Studies, a discipline that has rarely concerned itself with the issues raised in this volume, offers ways of exploring the interrelationship between creativity and the social division of labour. Marchant combines an aesthetic assessment of the artistic achievements of studio photographer Cornel Lucas with a clear analysis of the 1950s British studio system. Smith's familiarity with the artistic achievements of French women directors and editors drew her attention to the glaring absence of women cinematographers in the film industry in contemporary France.

## Systems of production

Contributors to this volume point to the range of systems of production under which media workers are employed. Dawson and Holmes, for instance, look at an industry that has operated from its inception on free-market principles. Gornostaeva, in contrast, focuses on an industry in which the state took on the role of producer, while Hedling concentrates on an industry that occupies the middle ground between these two extremes, offering valuable insights into the role of the state in stimulating regional film and television production in contemporary Sweden. The Hollywood studios of the 1920s, explored by Holmes in his study of Jetta Goudal, are markedly different from the late-Soviet-era production units described by Gornostaeva and from the regional production hubs described by Hedling. While some industry centres, especially those in North America, Western Europe and South India are well established and very large, others, such as Kinshasa in the DRC, are of more recent origin and considerably less well capitalized.

As Paterson demonstrates, and Dawson corroborates, the character of film and television production in Britain and America has changed materially since the 1980s. Competition created by the emergence of new media outlets such as cable, DVD and the internet, and government-initiated deregulation of broadcasting, spread the impact of direct market forces across the industry. Hollywood studios contracted out production to smaller, nominally 'independent' companies, whilst in Britain, the BBC was forced to buy programming from smaller outside firms. In both industries, new commercial relations between media companies encouraged management to pass on the uncertainties and competitive pressures they faced in the marketplace to their employees, which had an important impact on labour markets and the social organization of work. Paterson ably documents the emergence of freelance work as the dominant mode of employment in British television following regulatory changes introduced by government. Flexible, short-term contracts – an explicit objective of government policy in the 1980s and 1990s – reduced the proportion of long-term core staff to a minority. Such a change in modes of employment had substantial consequences. Freelancers working on short-term contracts seldom saw themselves as part of the organization. A culture of occupational individualism emerged in which each worker prioritized self above loyalty to the organization or colleagues. Such short-term opportunistic behaviour was also found among employers as well as freelancers. The new system undermined the creative process by encouraging risk aversion, while freelancers found themselves developing new programming ideas in their own time. When asked, most freelancers complained about insecurity and expressed a strong preference for staff employment. Nevertheless, Paterson shows that attitudes were polarized, with some freelancers expressing an aversion to longer contracts. With the collapse of traditional notions of promotion, new career strategies emerged, and cynicism replaced optimism among many older workers ejected from staff jobs. While full-time employment with the BBC, or similar organizations, remained the goal for many, successful freelancers maintained the currency of their reputation by accumulating social capital. The new system created job uncertainty and shifted the power balance towards employers, no longer counterbalanced by trade unions. This, combined with persistent oversupply of labour, depressed wages. While the goal of the new structure was to create a more efficient system with lower costs of production, it could only do so by creating a massive contradiction between, on the one hand, encouraging workers to think and act individually and, on the other, creating cooperative work in a highly complex industry.

While Africa's film industries face some of the commercial pressures of their European and American counterparts, their historical development and modern characteristics are substantially different. But, as Pype warns, care needs to be taken in making broad generalizations as there is relatively little research on the political economy of television production in Africa. Both Obiaya's study of Nigeria and Pype's examination of Kinshasa point to a system of production built upon video and churning out low-budget films, soaps, serials, talk shows and commercials. In economies where capital is in short supply, production and exhibition infrastructure limited, and skilled labour scarce, then an industry based on cheap and easy-to-use video cameras turning out large numbers of films makes real sense. Obiaya suggests that low capital requirements facilitate easy entry into the industry and thereby help to democratize the film-making process. At the same time, compared with Europe and America, industry boundaries are differently drawn. In Kinshasa, social and religious networks that are formally outside the industry are, in reality, an integral part of labour recruitment and television production.

Pype reveals the extent to which Pentecostal churches in the contemporary DRC act to recruit television industry personnel and help generate large audiences. The key unit of production is the acting troupe, linked to the church, and Pype provides detailed analysis of the social composition of the group placing particular emphasis on kinship bonds. In turn, a troupe is dependent on a local television station. As most members of the troupe lack previous artistic experience, junior artists are introduced gradually, initially in commercials. Experienced members of the troupe write scripts using a multiplicity of themes, images and storylines drawn from local culture, including Kinshasa's popular paintings. To create investors and generate income for the troupe, large and small businesses are incorporated into the film narrative, including local breweries, telecom providers, boutiques and supermarkets. Revenue is also boosted through advertising commodities linked to Western consumer culture.

## The role of the state

The state has always played a vital role in overseeing and, in some instances, determining systems of media production. Our studies of industries under quite different political regimes, in varieties of geographical and historical contexts, demonstrate this centrality. Directly or indirectly, government has a powerful impact on structure and work experience. From the beginning of the twentieth century, strong government regulation and sometimes direct control was a feature of media industries both on economic and ideological grounds. More recently, the direction of government policy has supported a neoliberal agenda by dismantling trade barriers and reducing state regulation.

Gornostaeva's close examination of the stormy relationship between the Soviet state and the talented director Andrei Tarkovsky reveals not only important differences but also significant similarities between the film and television production systems of the USSR and the West. While in all areas of the globe, the state is important in regulating film industries, Gornostaeva understands the particular importance of focusing attention on the character of the Soviet state because it carried out many of the functions commonly associated with film studios and media corporations in Western film industries – especially script selection, financing, marketing and distribution. The arrogation of administrative and commercial control within the Soviet state apparatus created a different division of labour from that of the West. In the USSR, the roles of movie mogul, studio executive and producer were carried out by what Gornostaeva calls 'kino bosses' in the state apparatus which, paradoxically, made the director supreme within the film production unit. At the same time, the state's strict ideological control of media politicized the role of director.

Andrei Tarkovsky found working in the USSR irksome, but once removed to Italy he soon discovered that the economics of the marketplace were just as restrictive as the directives of the Soviet state. While Gornostaeva pinpoints the distinctive qualities of Soviet film production, she also draws important parallels between the Soviet system and Hollywood. In both instances, film-making was governed by the extent to which finance and channels of distribution were made available. In the West, it was media corporations' relations with the marketplace that determined what films were produced, while in the USSR, the state assumed the roles of individual capitalists. Also, in both East and West the state exerted strong ideological control. Cold War pressure encouraged the Soviet Union and the United States (through the interventions of the House Committee on Un-American Activities in the late 1940s and 1950s) to limit political debate in their respective industries.

By the time the USSR finally collapsed in 1991, and with it all-enveloping state control, Western governments had already advanced along the deregulation path. The rise of the freelance worker that Paterson and Dawson document in their studies of Britain and the United States was facilitated by the deregulation strategies adopted by their respective governments. But, paradoxically, as film and television production relies more and more upon marketplace commands, so the state continues to play a crucial role. Media companies look to governments to defend them against commercial threats from elsewhere (for example, in relation to piracy and copyright enforcement), nation states and municipalities seek to grab footloose film shoots, while weaker industries seek protection from a stronger American industry through bodies such as Nigeria's National Film and Video Censors Board. At the same time, many governments, particularly in Europe, see media industries as a useful spur to national economic growth.

As Hedling shows in his study, the Swedish state supports the film and television industry and uses it as a vehicle to regenerate depressed regions, which then has an impact on media workers' lives. Highlighting regional film policy, particularly in relation to the town of Ystad, he shows how tax incentives establish specific locations as regional production hubs. By acting as co-producers, regional film authorities hope to attract production companies, thus creating ideal spaces for what Richard Florida terms 'the creative classes' and 'creative communities'. Ystad, home to the 'Wallander' television series, has benefited substantially from increased business revenues, film-induced tourism and new employment opportunities for film workers. Whether such a strategy can disperse film production, create new cities or offer a serious challenge to the hegemony of the US motion picture industry is doubtful. While these policies have brought some benefits to film workers, the prevalence of freelancing means that actors, directors and skilled technicians are often reluctant to relocate to the town. As Hedling points out, there are inherent limitations in the kind of films that can be shot in regional locations, and Ystad is seen by media workers as too dependent upon a single brand. Most prefer to locate in major cities where the range of alternative employment opportunities mitigates against job insecurity. Reluctance to move to new centres also fosters tensions between experienced film workers travelling from Stockholm and immobile 'non-professionals' in the regions. State action can have other, more indirect, effects as in the case of the Indian government's switch from protectionism to free trade. As Wilkinson-Weber demonstrates, this dismantling of tariffs resulted in the flooding of local markets with cheap Western beauty products which, perhaps unintentionally, had a corrosive impact on working practices among Mumbai's film hairdressers and make-up artists. While most governments have, as in the case of India, acted as cheerleaders for neoliberalism, the Nigerian state, as Obiaya's article demonstrates, has taken the lead in regulating professional standards in the country's expanding industry, though whether this will benefit industry workers remains to be seen.

## Patronage and clientelism

Another theme that we have tried to foreground in this collection is the role that patronage and clientelism have played in determining the experiences of workers in the film and television industries. In her essay on film-making in the Soviet Union, Gornostaeva argues that these interlocking phenomena were an inevitable corollary of Soviet-style totalitarianism (or, more specifically, of the economic and artistic stagnation of the Brezhnev era) and, by extension, something that was unique to the Soviet system of production. What emerges from the other articles in this collection, however, is that networks of patronage and clientelism in one form or another have been recurrent features of film and television production, flourishing in a wide range of national and historical contexts.

The most carefully theorized analysis of how such networks function is Pype's piece on the production of television serials in the DRC, which borrows the concept of 'wealth-in-people' from anthropological treatments of slavery and welds it to notions of patronage that derive from the anthropology of art. Pype argues that Kinshasa's nascent television industry is underpinned by multiple networks of patronage and clientelism, all of them quasi-familial: the links between the 'big men' who own the television stations and the acting troupes who rely upon them for funding, the ties that bind together individual troupe members under the authority of a charismatic leader who functions both as an artistic director and as a spiritual father to his performers, and the bonds that structure the relationship between the troupes and the Pentecostal churches under whose auspices they operate. In other contexts, the lines of patronage and clientelism may be less clearly drawn than they are in contemporary Kinshasa, but they are certainly no less significant. As Holmes's article on the regulation of actors' labour in silent-era Hollywood makes clear, continued success for star performers like Jetta Goudal was at least as dependent upon cultivating good relations with studio heads, producers and directors as it was upon talent or popular appeal. As Paterson explains, freelancers in the contemporary British television industry must embed themselves in the informal networks of potential employers if they are to have any chance of finding regular employment. And as Wilkinson-Weber demonstrates in her article on the Indian film industry, make-up artists and hairdressers in contemporary Bollywood are locked in an unequal relationship with the stars who use their services and must always be looking to cultivate new patrons in case they should find themselves cast aside by their present employers.

# Gender

What is also clear from this collection of essays is that the ways in which networks of patronage and clientelism operate are often highly gendered. This manifests itself most visibly in the context of the film industry in contemporary France where, as Smith explains, most aspiring female cinematographers have to serve a *de facto* apprenticeship under an established director of photography who, given pre-existing gender imbalances in the industry, will almost certainly be a man. Even after they have established themselves in the industry, admission to the prestigious *Association Française des Directeurs de la Photographie Cinématographique*, a body in which women remain significantly under-represented (just as they are in equivalent professional associations in the United Kingdom and the United States), requires the support of a patron. Though what Smith terms *marraines* – that is, female patrons – are by no means unknown, *parrainage*, or male patronage, remains very much the norm.

Not surprisingly, the gendering of networks of patronage and clientelism has manifested itself in different ways in different national and historical contexts. In the DRC's burgeoning television industry, for example, female performers often struggle to find patrons because if they solicit favour from one of Kinshasa's 'big men' by throwing his name into a script (a key strategy for male performers), they risk compromising their respectability and alienating their fans, a group whose collective sense of morality is rooted in Pentecostalism. If Jetta Goudal's experiences in silent-era Hollywood are any indication, the best hope for female workers looking for a measure of respect and equality in the cinematic workplace has lain in stepping out of patron-client relationships that subordinate them to male authority whenever the opportunity presents itself. The happiest period of Goudal's Hollywood career came when she was able briefly to cast off the yoke of her chief patron, Cecil B. De Mille, and to work in a unit headed by screenwriter and sometime director Frances Marion. As a woman working in a field that was dominated by men, Marion was acutely sensitive to the gender biases at work in the motion picture studios. Rather than seeking to impose her will upon Goudal as De Mille and others had done, she opted to draw her into a collaborative relationship, an arrangement that worked to the advantage of both parties.

# Manoeuvrable spaces

A key concern for several of the contributors to this collection is the process by which workers in the film and television industries carve out 'manoeuvrable spaces' in the workplace. The concept of 'manoeuvrable space' is borrowed from Barry King's work on stardom as an occupation, a body of scholarship that redrew the boundaries of the sub-discipline of star studies in the 1980s by shifting attention away from the screen actor as object of consumption to the screen actor as labourer (King 1984, 1985, 1987). Rather than situating his analysis at the level of the individual star, King focuses on the role of the star system in structuring labour-management relations in the Hollywood film industry and explores the ways in which economic practices have combined with film as a technology to transform actors' labour into its commodity form. At a purely theoretical level, his Marxist account of what he terms 'the particularities of performance as a labour process and the relations of production in which such a process occurs' (King 1987: 145) works very well. Where it falls short is in its ahistoricism and its failure to get to grips with stardom as a lived experience.

One of King's central assertions is that stardom as an economic and cultural institution invests stars with a degree of autonomy in their relations with their employers – manoeuvrable space, as he terms it – that is simply not available to performers further down the occupational hierarchy. In his article on the now almost forgotten screen siren Jetta Goudal and her efforts to exercise a degree of control over the construction of her star persona, Holmes sets out to test this contention in the context of the Hollywood film industry in the 1920s. What he concludes is that whilst the position of stars is, indeed, a privileged one compared to that of lesser performers, manoeuvrable space is not a property that is inherent in the institution of stardom. Rather, it is something that has had to be staked out and defended by individual stars, often at considerable personal cost. Even though the court case that marked the culmination of Goudal's lengthy battle with Cecil B. De Mille over the terms of her commodification vindicated her position and established the right of Hollywood stars to a say in how they are represented on screen, it effectively ended her career in the movies and condemned her to obscurity.

Detached from the institution of stardom, the concept of manoeuvrable space takes on a wider relevance in terms of helping us to make sense of the collective experiences of other groups of workers in the film and television industries. Within the parameters set by a system of production that required creative workers to strike a balance between standardization and innovation, Cornel Lucas, a prominent stills photographer at Pinewood Studios in the 1950s, was able to carve out a great deal of manoeuvrable space for himself – considerably more, in fact, than a silent-era Hollywood star like Jetta Goudal. Even so, if his work fell short of the high standards that were expected of him, he was answerable not only to his employers but also to the stars that he photographed, as evidenced in 1952 when he delivered what was adjudged to be a substandard set of images of actress Yvonne de Carlo and felt obliged to tender his resignation. As Marchant's article makes clear, moreover, Lucas's position was an anomalous one in that, even though he was engaged in what fell into the category of technical work, his distinctive visual style marked him out as an artist and, as such, a key member of the creative team at Pinewood. Workers who fall below the invisible line that divides technicians from the so-called 'talent' in the film and television industries have generally struggled, by comparison with relatively privileged individuals like Lucas, to find any room for manoeuvre.

## Labour relations and unionization

Denied manoeuvrable space and its attendant benefits, workers both above and below the line have often sought collective solutions to the problems they encounter in the workplace. After producers placed her on an unofficial blacklist in the late 1920s, Jetta Goudal, a supreme individualist in so many respects, threw herself wholeheartedly into the ultimately abortive efforts of the New York-based stage actors' union, the Actors' Equity Association, to organize the movie industry. Trade unions have long been a feature of the film and television industries in the United Kingdom. Stills photographers at Pinewood in the 1950s, for example, were represented by the Association of Cinematograph Technicians, a union founded by technicians at the Gaumont-British Picture Corporation in 1933 which played a key role in defending its members against the threat posed by non-specialized labour. As Richard Paterson points out, however, the emergence over the past thirty years or so of freelancing as the dominant mode of employment in the British film and television industries has undercut the position of organized labour by fostering insecurity within the workforce and a culture of individualism that is at odds with the mutuality of trade unionism. As Clare Wilkinson-Weber demonstrates, trade unions continue to figure prominently in the political economy of film production in India even in the face of the economic liberalization that has transformed Bollywood over the past twenty years. Though the privileges that now accrue to top hairdressers and make-up artists have opened up divisions between workers at the top of the occupational hierarchy and workers at the bottom, the Cine Costume, Make-Up Artistes and Hair Dressers' Association remains an important player in the Bollywood studios, monitoring working conditions on behalf of its members and regulating entry into the industry.

In centres of production where the film and television industries are still, relatively speaking, in their infancy, organized labour is a far less visible presence than it is in North America, Europe and India. Amongst workers engaged in the production of teleserials in the DRC, for example, the organizational impulse has yet to manifest itself at all. Whether it will begin to do so if a system of production that is, as Katrien Pype acknowledges, essentially pre-industrial gives way to something that is more institutionally complex and more heavily capitalized – which, it should be noted, is by no means a given – remains to be seen. In the Nigerian film industry, collective action in one form or another is on the increase as below-the-line workers look to fashion as a response to what make-up artist Elfrida Ehonwa, quoted in Obiaya's piece on the hidden face of Nollywood, has described as 'housemaid treatment' at the hands of their employers. Even here, though, the organizational impulse is inhibited by the high level of competition for jobs and employment practices that encourage Nigerian film workers to think of themselves in individualistic rather than collective terms.

Where trade unions have managed to establish themselves as more or less permanent features of the film and television industries, their effectiveness has often been undercut by the reluctance of different groups of workers to unite in pursuit of a common set of goals. In Hollywood, for example, workers are organized along craft rather than industrial lines, and the history of organized labour has been punctuated by frequent bouts of internecine warfare, usually triggered by jurisdictional disputes or, as in the 1930s and 1940s, ideological differences. As Dawson points out, moreover, the relationship between workers above and below the line in the Hollywood studios has long been a troubled one, largely because the former are inclined to see themselves as artists rather than labourers and, as such, somehow set apart from the latter (although it is interesting to note that actors and screenwriters, not technicians, led the Hollywood battle against media corporations in the post-war years). That concerted action by different groups of workers remains both feasible and potentially very effective, however, is demonstrated by recent events in Mumbai. As Wilkinson-Weber explains, the undercutting of union-negotiated wage scales, the refusal of many employers to pay wages promptly, and unapproved extensions to the working day have long been problems in the Bollywood film industry. When workers responded towards the end of 2008 by staging a three-day strike, they did so under the aegis of the Federation of Western India Cine Employees, an umbrella organization that brings together unions representing a wide range of occupational categories. By pooling their collective resources, they succeeded in forcing major concessions from their employers.

## Creative agency

What does this collection of essays tell us about creative agency, a concept closely linked to manoeuvrable spaces? The discipline of film studies, which places great emphasis on the filmic text, has tended to define creativity as the preserve of above-the-line workers such as producers, writers, directors and actors. Four of the contributors to this collection – Holmes, Gornostaeva, Wilkinson-Weber and Marchant – challenge this way of thinking about productive processes in the film and television industry, arguing that the practice of drawing sharp distinctions between above-the-line and below-the-line workers needs to be interrogated and that we need other ways to understand creativity in an industry with a complex social division of labour involving large numbers of people working cooperatively.

Holmes' treatment of actress Jetta Goudal shows that creativity is not just demonstrated by on-screen performance. He points out that while stars in the early studio system had little control over their public persona, Goudal was determined to represent herself as a serious and dedicated cultural worker. When shooting *Paris at Midnight* (1926), for example, she convinced director Frances Marion to allow her to design her own costumes. Gornostaeva's study of Soviet-era director Andrei Tarkovsky points to different considerations. For her, artistry is not determined by personality and ego but by location within a specific system of production. It was directors like Tarkovsky who stood on the fault line between, on the one side, state-controlled finance, distribution and film censorship and, on the other, the production team that shot and edited the film away from official scrutiny. At the same time, the Soviet practice of utilizing workers lacking industry-specific skills but who were, nevertheless, highly trained created directorial challenges but also opportunities for men like Tarkovsky. For example, Moscow actors migrated between live theatre and screen as demand dictated, and classically trained musicians alternated between writing concert music and film scores. It was the role of the all-powerful director to meld this often disparate labour force together into an effective creative unit. While directors were accountable to those above, it also opened up immense creative opportunities within the closed space of the production unit. Gornostaeva sees as contradictory the role performed by Soviet-era directors – they were privileged rebels, simultaneously being insiders and outsiders. While Tarkovsky possessed considerable individual ability, it was his specific location with a system of production that allowed demonstration of that creativity. While Gornostaeva reveals the irritations faced by Tarkovsky under Soviet close financial, ideological and aesthetic control, she tells us little about the impact of his directorial powers upon the creativity (and job satisfaction) of colleagues occupying lower rungs of the production unit's occupational ladder.

Wilkinson-Weber's study of the Mumbai industry's hairdressers and make-up artists reveals that imagination clearly exists among groups that Hollywood accountants deem below-the-line and, therefore, without talent. Just like Gornostaeva, Wilkinson-Weber also shows that creativity exists under specific material and historical circumstances. Until the early 1990s, hairdressers and make-up artists relied heavily on their own resources and creative initiative in producing desired effects for both actors and stars. Drawing upon the traditions of the theatre – improvisation, illusion and skilful bricolage with limited materials – they created everything from a desired skin tone or the latest hairstyle to a nasty-looking war wound. A flood of imported beauty products undermined existing skills and shifted the locus of creativity outside movie studios to hair and beauty salons. While a new generation emerged with fresh skills, the intimate relationship between artist and star dissolved as cosmetic companies sought stars' endorsement of beauty products. Marchant's detailed study of the career of studio photographer Cornel Lucas, head of the pool studio at Pinewood in the 1950s, similarly invites us to consider creativity beyond existing conceptual boundaries. Needing to work to deadlines imposed by the British equivalent of Hollywood volume production, photographers like Lucas had to demonstrate innovation by offering novelty to the viewing public whilst, at the same time, maintaining audience familiarity and corporate recognition. Studio-imposed style constraints appear at first glance to act in opposition to artistry: producing formulaic images implies a lack of professional choice and a restriction on the ability of the photographer to deploy imagination. While Marchant recognizes the tension between creative autonomy and organizational demands in Lucas's work, she also points to the creative benefits of him working as part of a team in a large organization. Surrounded by a network of supportive and skilled personnel working to common goals and assisted by dedicated laboratory staff, Lucas produced photographs of the highest quality. On one level, Marchant's study makes only a modest proposal that some studio photographers should be admitted to the privileged status of above-the-line, creative occupations. But on another level, by recognizing that Lucas's originality was only possible through collaboration with other workers both inside and outside his department, she highlights the social dimension of the creative process. Creativity, then, is not a quality possessed by individuals but a characteristic determined by the social nature of production.

These studies point to new ways of conceptualizing the production process in the film and television industries that make the accountants' dividing line between creative and non-creative workers redundant. If, as some contributors suggest, the possession of artistic distinction is part of a collective social process determined by proximity to others and more broadly by the division of labour, and not an individual attribute, then where does creativity end? What impact does the collective expertise of assistant directors, grips and gaffers have on the finished product? Nevertheless, shrill and insistent claims that creativity is an attribute located in the uniquely talented individual are likely to intensify if the freelance and individualized work practices identified by Paterson persist. Perhaps the accountants' line will continue to arbitrarily separate industry workers for many years to come.

## Final word

This volume has aspirations to global coverage but the reality is somewhat different. If we are quick to draw attention to the strengths and uniqueness of this volume in uncovering the lives of industry workers, it is our duty to be honest in pinpointing weaknesses. In these pages, there is excellent coverage of major centres of production in North America, Europe and India as well as smaller centres in the Soviet Union, Scandinavia and Africa. But we are missing, as readers will notice, contributions dealing with media workers in Latin America, Australasia and the Far East. Believe us, it was not through want of trying. At the same time, we as editors had aspirations to range widely over the industry's elongated occupational hierarchy. This goal has only been partially achieved: while we do include studies of an American actor and a Soviet director, we also have significant treatments of ignored or little-studied groups, such as Mumbai hairdressers and make-up artists, British studio still photographers, women camera operators in France and the charismatic film-makers of Kinshasa. We make no apology for including actors and directors in this volume, but we do regret not bringing to your attention the working lives of other marginalized or forgotten industry crafts. We would have liked to include, for example, studies of gaffers, sound operators, runners, second assistant directors, security guards and clerical labour. Some occupations such as laboratory worker and film editor are gone for good, but a record of their lives and struggles should still be made. We anticipate that others who chafe at what they read in this volume will want to do better, fill gaps or take completely new directions. If you are one of them, the contributors and editors salute you; there is much to be done. We look forward to your effort with eager anticipation.

## Notes

1  Katrien Pype's essay, 'Fathers, Patrons and Clients in Kinshasa's Media World: Social and Economic Dynamics in the Production of Television Drama', also appears in her forthcoming *The Making of the Pentecostal Melodrama. Religion, Media and Gender in Kinshasa*, New York: Berghahn, 2012.

2  See also Vicki Mayer (2011).

# Bibliography

Caldwell, J. T. (2008), *Production Culture: Industrial Reflexivity and Critical Practice in Film and Television*, Durham, NC: Duke University Press.

Chanan, M. (1976), *Labour Power in the British Film Industry*, London: British Film Institute.

Florida, R. (2002), *The Rise of the Creative Class: And How It's Transforming Work, Leisure, Community and Everyday Life*, New York: Basic Books.

Goldsmith, B. and O'Regan, T. (2005), *The Film Studio: Film Production in the Global Economy*, Lanham, MD: Rowman & Littlefield.

King, B. (1984), 'Stardom as an Occupation' in P. Kerr (ed.), *The Hollywood Film Industry*, London and New York: Routledge & Kegan Paul.

King, B. (1985), 'Articulating Stardom', *Screen*, 26 (September-October): 27–50.

King, B. (1987), 'The Star and the Commodity: Notes towards a Performance Theory of Stardom', *Cultural Studies*, 1 (2): 145–61.

Mayer, V. (2011), *Below the Line: Producers and Production Studies in the New Television Economy*, Durham, NC: Duke University Press.

Mayer, V., Banks, M. J. and Caldwell, J. T. (eds) (2008), *Production Studies: Cultural Studies of Media Industries*, New York: Routledge.

McKinlay, A. and Smith, C. (eds) (2009), *Creative Labour: Working in the Creative Industries*, Basingstoke: Palgrave Macmillan.

Nielsen, M. (1983), 'Towards a Workers' History of the US Film Industry', in V. Mosco and J. Wasko (eds), *The Critical Communications Review, Volume I: Labor, the Working Class, and the Media*, Norwood, NJ: Ablex Publishing.

Nielsen, M. (1985), *Motion Picture Craft Workers and Craft Unions in Hollywood: The Studio Era*, PhD dissertation, University of Illinois, Urbana, IL.

Powdermaker, H. (1950), *Hollywood, the Dream Factory: An Anthropologist Looks at the Movie-Makers*, Boston, MA: Little, Brown.

Ross, M. (1941), *Stars and Strikes*, New York: Columbia University Press.

# Systems of production

# Labouring in Hollywood's motion picture industry and the legacy of 'flexible specialization'

chapter

# 2

ANDREW DAWSON

In the 1980s, a group of economic geographers in Los Angeles – Susan Christopherson, Michael Storper and Allen Scott – proposed a radically new way of understanding the movie industry, a paradigm that still affects us all today. Observing the contemporary scene, they pointed to the emergence of small, specialist firms clustered in Hollywood operating with great efficiency across the film, television and music industries. This new system of 'flexible specialization' (FS), they argued, was separated by a clear industrial divide from earlier, 'Fordist', mass production that dominated the industry until the years following the Second World War. The new structure, replacing the monopoly of the major studios with the competition of small production firms, not only offered greater productivity but it also promised to enhance labour welfare: while Fordism was characterized by rigidity, managerial hierarchy and deskilling, FS assured those who worked in the industry of meaningful work and closer bonds between capital and labour. 'In many respects', declared Susan Christopherson and Michael Storper, 'the strong social network of the motion picture industry resembles aspects of craft communities in cities in early industrial Europe and the 19th century United States' (Christopherson and Storper 1986: 317). If the details remained to be mapped out, nevertheless, the promise of a bright future for those working in Hollywood helped allay fears that the industry might succumb to runaway production and decamp to new locations and also rebutted the charge of pessimists who believed that global capitalism would bring cheap labour and meaningless, subdivided work into its competitive race to the bottom.

Hollywood's FS theorists looked for inspiration to the ideas of Michael J. Piore and Charles F. Sabel, particularly as set out in *The Second Industrial Divide* (1984). Drawing upon the experience of the industrial districts of Third Italy, they detected a fundamental restructuring taking place across the globe as manufacturing shifted from once-dominant Fordist mass production to small-scale, cooperative manufacture with firms located close to each other reaping the benefits of external economies of scale (Piore and Sabel 1984; Sabel and Zeitlin 1997). Christopherson and Storper were excited at their discovery because not only was the movie industry of major global importance, but they also believed it was the first example of a whole industry making the transition from mass production to FS; all previous transitions were from craft production to FS.

Theorists also closely identified themselves with an emergent scholarly trend much closer to home – the Los Angeles school of urban development. In what proved to be a heady mixture of avant-garde social philosophy and Angeleno chauvinism, city intellectuals announced their hometown to be the world's first postmodern, post-Fordist city of the future. Understanding the motion picture industry's trajectory, FS practitioners believed, offered them a strategic role in mapping out the economic future of Los Angeles and understanding global industrial development.

Drawing upon the powerful intellectual currents represented by Piore and Sabel and the Los Angeles school, FS theory still attracts a following in academic circles, particularly among planners, sociologists, and media and cultural studies scholars. At one level, the theory offers a clear and plausible model of Hollywood's industrial development – 'a sustained and ambitious attempt to explain the transformation of Hollywood beyond its "Golden Age"', according to two of its most effective detractors (Aksoy and Robins 1992: 5). At another level, it resonates closely with the 1980s zeitgeist. For want of a better paradigm, it is also what our students are often taught.

A prominent feature of FS theory, especially in its early years, was its promise of a better future for Hollywood labour: through the operation of the marketplace and the power of local agglomeration, FS secured a place for labour in the new media landscape; at the same time, FS theorists contrasted the benefits of the present with the failings of Fordism as a further means to highlight labour's future prospects. Such faith in the marketplace, combined with restorationist fantasies that a pre-industrial system of artisan labour can be revived, can only be seen as utopian.

This speculative reading of the industry's present and future also seriously distorts our understanding of the past. Uncritical faith in the positive impact of the marketplace, combined with a dogmatic insistence on inserting an industrial divide between classical and new Hollywood, fails to adequately comprehend the historical development of motion pictures and the industry's labour processes. What we need is a comprehensive theory of labour's place in twentieth- and twenty-first century Hollywood. What is offered here is a critique of FS theory – and an explanation for its longevity – rather than an alternative framework in which to understand media labour; nevertheless, a more comprehensive model is indicated.

FS theorists have responded to the weight of criticism and conceded on a number of points – they now grant, for example, a far more prominent role to the large corporation and to the impact of runaway production. Crucially, they have qualified their wildly optimistic assessment of media labour's prospects. Nevertheless, supporters have yet to reflect on what impact these changes have had on the overall veracity of their theory.

Given the substance of the criticism and subsequent modifications to the FS position, it is surprising that the school continues to attract support. Yet, what this paper suggests is that, ultimately, the strength of FS theory rests not so much on its ability to comprehend modern Hollywood and the role of labour within it as upon the much flimsier foundation of its capacity to offer reassurance about the future prospects of motion pictures and the industry's place within the city of Los Angeles. As a result, what we need to understand is why such a theory emerged in 1980s Los Angeles and why it still finds support today. Taken cumulatively, the impact of the theoretical and empirical assault on the FS model suggests that we must jettison the flawed paradigm. The protracted global financial crisis and the subsequent willingness to re-evaluate the infallibility of free markets in intellectual and government circles offer a suitable opportunity to reconsider a theory that has been with us for a quarter of a century.

## Flexible specialization

In a series of three key articles published between 1986 and 1989, Michael Storper and Susan Christopherson elaborate all the key elements of Hollywood FS theory (Christopherson and Storper 1986, 1989; Storper and Christopherson 1987). As a result of the twin shocks to the system of the 1948 Paramount Decision and the rise of TV competition, mass cinema audiences disappeared. The studios, forced to divest themselves of cinema ownership, no longer had a guaranteed market for each movie. At the same time, the dwindling number of spectators, seduced away by the attractions of TV, eliminated the mass family-oriented market and replaced it with a more fragmented audience. The Hollywood studios responded by producing a series of expensive blockbusters that relied upon novelty and variation, something that the studios, with their commitment to house style and adherence to genre, were less capable of fulfilling. Without a large, captive market, or a standard product, mass production ended with the studios shifting movie making to small, highly specialized independent companies turning out a more differentiated product. As a result, the large, vertically integrated businesses of classical Hollywood crumbled, eventually to be replaced in the new Hollywood of the 1980s by independent production companies subcontracting work to small specialized firms. As Christopherson and Storper put it, 'The industry is vertically disintegrated and its production process is nonroutinized and designed to maximize variability of outputs and flexibility with respect to inputs' (Christopherson and Storper 1986: 305). Management of the film-making process shifted from the hands of corporate executives and departmental heads under the old studio system to deal-making entrepreneurs networking with other business owners in the new Hollywood marketplace. To survive, firms needed to increase efficiency, which in turn created new structures:

> [T]hose firms providing services to producers have become smaller and more specialized. These specialized subcontractors reduce their own risks by marketing their services to other entertainment industries, including recording and television. As a result of these combined processes of vertical disintegration and cross-industry subcontracting, an entertainment industry complex has developed. (Christopherson and Storper 1986: 305)

Within this system of production, each firm is specialized but the complex as a whole remains flexible. Small firms in this transaction-intensive entertainment industry needed to respond quickly to market changes. Engaging in frequent non-routine deals encouraged firms to congregate close to each other in order to reap external economies of scale, such as access to specialist information, capital, labour and suppliers. The entrepreneurial and technical skills necessary to sustain high levels of transactions were maintained and reproduced by social and family networks. Higher education institutions, such as the film schools of the University of California, Los Angeles, and the University of Southern California, also nourished the transmission of expertise within this industrial community.

The transition from the old to the new, post-Fordist, system proved a long and drawn-out process. Fordist structures disintegrated first in pre-production as direct market relations increasingly governed salaries, heralding the end of the star system, which tied talent to studios through long contracts. In future, a star's salary was determined by their ability to attract audiences to each of their pictures. Changes also occurred in the production phase of film-making as location and overseas markets became important for box-office success, encouraging film shoots outside Los Angeles and outside the United States. With the peeling away of each successive stage of the process, vertical disintegration became unstoppable such that by the late 1960s the old system lay in ruins, ripe for a process of re-agglomeration in the building of new Hollywood.

The vertical collapse and the agglomeration effects of small, deal-making production companies clustering near each other led to spatial relocation. In the classical era, large studios needing plenty of land located in a broad arc from the San Fernando Valley to Santa Monica, away from built-up areas, around but not in Hollywood; Hollywood was more a locus of activity and a place to meet. By the 1980s, pre- and post-production and much of the workforce was concentrated in Los Angeles, with shooting taking place across a much wider field; now 65 per cent of contracting production companies were located in Hollywood.

Critics were quick to point out that the model lacked adequate explanation for the initial emergence of the industry in Hollywood and that there was no place in it for the large media corporation and the state (Pollert 1991). The FS school – despite its roots in economic geography – failed to account for the industry's location in Hollywood. For Scott, 'a mature motion picture industrial complex might have sprung up virtually anywhere in the United States in the early years of the twentieth century' (Scott 2005: 24). Thus, agglomeration theory is able to explain why a specific location has competitive advantage only at the point where firms first appear and exhibit that competitive advantage. As James Curry and Martin Kenney perceptively note, the arrival of the industry 'seems as much a historical fluke as evidence of paradigmatic importance' (Curry and Kenney 1999: 3).

Emphasizing the economic significance of small, independent firms leaves out the crucial role of large media conglomerates that commission, finance and buy films for national and international distribution. As Asu Aksoy and Kevin Robins point out, the history of the major producers' domination of the industry is one of continuity, not rupture. According to them, the impetus to monopolization and control distribution is at the heart of the industry because making a film is costly, yet audience tastes are fickle. Thomas Edison first tried to bring order to chaos with his Motion Picture Patents Company, but it was nickelodeon proprietors who, by 1920, had successfully established their own large-scale, monopolistic film production in Los Angeles. The Great Depression of the 1930s acted to powerfully reshape the majors, but their dominant role remained. In new Hollywood, multimedia conglomerates, the successors to the majors, controlled the activities of the independent production companies. Following the 1948 Paramount Decrees, ending ownership and control of theatres, the majors restructured themselves and through the use of financial muscle, control of film distribution, rental of studio space and the colonization of new media, maintained the upper hand with independent producers. In the late 1980s, for example, all the majors – Warner Brothers, Buena Vista/Disney, MCA/Universal, Paramount, Columbia and Fox – with the exception of Disney, had existed as majors since the Paramount case. In 1990, the majors controlled 69 per cent of total box-office receipts, leaving the independents to compete for ten to fifteen (Aksoy and Robins 1992: 7–9). Competition among independents and the bargaining power of the conglomerates enabled the latter to drive down picture costs, which in turn reduced demands upon their capital.[1] Thus, if the majors remained a powerful force in the industry, surely they continued to influence the lives of those working in independent production companies.

According to the FS model, the state plays no significant role in new Hollywood, even though, as Helen Blair and Al Rainnie point out, the Supreme Court's Paramount case was crucial in shifting the industry across the industrial divide from classical-era Fordism to the new regime of small independent producers. The state is exogenous in the FS model (Blair and Rainnie 2000: 190). Yet all the evidence points in a different direction: from the 1920s onwards, the studios maintained close links with the US government in order to regulate and protect their interests, both nationally and internationally. In the 1980s, the federal government aided deregulation by reversing the Paramount Decision and relaxing TV network financial interest and syndication rules (before abolishing them in the early 1990s); it also enhanced the strength of multimedia corporations by aggressively supporting the enforcement of copyright abroad.

While FS theory emphasizes the corrosive impact on Hollywood of swarms of small production firms, taking a wider perspective it is equally true that after a number of years of uncertainty the industry reintegrated within globalized and localized media markets. While pre-production and post-production are highly concentrated in Los Angeles, other semi-independent centres, notably in Canada, have opened up while financing, administration of production and distribution are firmly in the hands of monopolistic multimedia corporations with national and international reach.

## Politics of production

FS, according to Christopherson and Storper, 'has generated new types of jobs, employment relations, and processes of wage determination' (Christopherson and Storper 1989: 331). Following Piore and Sabel, Christopherson and Storper were convinced that agglomeration's external economies created and sustained a highly skilled labour force and that the marketplace offered the promise of liberating labour from the tyrannies of mass production. They felt that just as in the early industrial revolution, when small masters, journeymen and apprentices worked together, so in modern-day Hollywood a skilled and adaptable workforce would shift easily between projects under the watchful but largely benevolent gaze of media entrepreneurs (Christopherson and Storper 1986: 317). The rigid and hierarchical studios of old Hollywood would be transformed from oppressive factories into artisanal communities populated by small enterprises, similar in character to the nineteenth-century cutlery trade in Sheffield or textile manufacture in Philadelphia.

Precisely how a vision of harmonious communities of skilled workers could be grafted onto the existing pattern of work in motion pictures was never articulated. Most media commentators recognize that the new commercial relations between big and small firms have allowed risks of production to be passed down the subcontracting chain. Exactly how much proprietors would hand on to their workforce remained unclear, but an equally plausible *a priori* argument would suggest that flexible production far from advancing labour welfare actually increased the rate of exploitation, further distancing capital from labour and undermining cordial relations. In addition, the world of film and TV production has always been, and still remains, highly stratified by income and status. Although wages in the industry are popularly perceived as good, the distribution of income is highly skewed towards executive and celebrity remuneration. In 1997, the average weekly earnings in motion pictures were US$1,233, but the median income stood at only US$370, suggesting wide variations in rates of pay and hours of work.[2]

Christopherson and Storper soon dropped their commitment to imagined artisan communities: 'The notion of a new era in labor relations, one based on the mutual respect of employers and workers, is implicit in much of the literature on flexible specialization. Our study does not bear out this prospect' (Christopherson and Storper 1989: 346). What could be viewed as a dramatic *volte-face* neither made mention of their responsibility for propagating such notions in the first place nor offered any explanation as to why they changed their mind, or what impact this had on the consistency of the theoretical model. Nevertheless, quite how far FS theory had shifted as a result of this recanting remains in doubt. Theorists still believed that Hollywood labour held an advantage, compared with workers elsewhere, since they could claim a share of the benefits of agglomeration when they bargained with their employers. At the same time, the debilitating belief that the labour system of new Hollywood was in some ways superior to Fordist managerialism remained implicit or explicit in FS writings.

Casting aside the vision of artisan utopias, FS theorists came to accept that the short-life, project-based activities of flexible companies could be responsible for employee uncertainty, labour market instability and widening divisions among workers. Christopherson and Storper now detected the existence of a privileged group of core workers, consisting of about two-thirds of the workforce, who through networking activity worked full-time and earned up to 45 per cent more than their compatriots. They were surrounded by a less privileged third who, although paid the same rate, worked fewer hours. It should be remembered that divisions and inequality are not new but are also found in mass production and are integral to the capitalist process of production. While this evidence provides a welcome step forward in our understanding of modern media labour, there is a danger that FS has created a static dualism between privileged core workers, on the one hand, and a disadvantaged periphery, on the other – rather than seeing boundaries between groups of workers as permeable and constantly shifting. Although FS has identified this core group, its precise character remains unclear: does it, for example, see itself as privileged, and what relationship does it have with employers? Not only do FS supporters see divisions among technical and craft occupations but they also believe that the gap is widening between talent and other workers as actors, screenwriters and directors accept additional entrepreneurial roles, in contrast to production workers who become more specialist. Overall, Christopherson and Storper consider that 'flexible specialization is associated with a qualitative redefinition of skills, rather than de-skilling or up-skilling'. The massive over-supply of labour, growing divisions within the skilled trades and the estrangement between talent and technical labour led to a decline in the 'commonalities of experience', contributing to the breakdown of older patterns of labour solidarity and a reduction in the bargaining power of trade unions (Christopherson and Storper 1989: 340).

More recently, the FS school has looked beyond the confines of Hollywood production companies to explore the wider operations of the global industry. But, in doing so, supporters undermine their original theoretical position. Christopherson, particularly, has made important contributions to our understanding of the impact of runaway production upon media labour and the role played by transnational conglomerates. She argues that, since the 1990s, increasing competition between regional media centres enables corporations to foment conflict between local alliances of workers and government. Faced with rivalry between regions and the threat of job losses, unions moderate wage demands and dilute work rules, while municipal governments offer sweeteners to companies. Unions lobby for local or national subsidies believing that this will help create a 'level playing field', while all the time playing directly into the hands of media corporations only too willing to gobble up subsidies from whatever source.[3]

Looking beyond the confines of film and TV companies, FS theorists are also increasingly aware of the dystopian implications of 'flexible capitalism' on the social fabric of Los Angeles. They note the spread of gated communities and a widening gap between haves and have-nots – between professionals, engineers and managers in the high-tech industries, on the one hand, and the poorly paid in the sweated trades, on the other.

While much of what FS theorists point to is valuable in understanding contemporary industry and labour conditions, it forms no part of the original formulation. Nevertheless, the inability of FS theory to comprehend empirical reality has not led to its formal renunciation. If FS supporters no longer believe in an artisan idyll, that the role of government is unimportant, and that the process of agglomeration is a powerful, positive economic force for Hollywood workers, what do we have left? Yet the theory will not wither and die because it is succoured by forces outside the intellectual milieu that created it.

FS theorists pay attention to the impact of economic forces on media labour, but workers themselves, and their actions, do not play an important part in their model. This is not entirely unexpected: FS draws heavily on neoclassical economic theory and as a result is concerned with factors of production, the operation of the firm, competition and markets. But understanding the process of accumulation also involves understanding how the clash of social forces structures the industry's development – a political economy of motion picture production. FS allows no place for the self-activity of workers in determining their own history.[4] Yet, as commentators have pointed out, the power of media labour is important. Since the 1980s, while the American labour movement suffered setbacks, union strength in film and TV remains significant (although it too has suffered relative decline), especially compared to unions elsewhere in the private sector. Since the 1960s, actors and screenwriters have confronted media entrepreneurs in a number of militant national disputes.[5]

## Fordism: classical Hollywood distorted

FS theory is not only unsure of the impact FS has upon contemporary workers and finds it difficult to locate labour within its theoretical framework, but it is also seriously deficient in understanding Hollywood's past. Labelling the studio-era 'Fordist mass production' fails to adequately comprehend the industry's labour process in the years between 1920 and 1950. Many of the analytical problems stem from the deployment of Piore and Sabel's binary 'industrial divide', between mass production (Fordism), on the one hand, and FS (post-Fordism), on the other. Fitting movies into such a rigid template seriously distorts the nature of the industry and its historical development. It may seem harsh and unwarranted to highlight the deficiencies of FS theory in relation to the studio era when the primary purpose of the FS school, and all its empirical data, is to explain development in the years after 1980. But this would be to misunderstand the significance of the earlier period within the FS paradigm: it exists as a theoretical 'other' – the very antithesis of the modern industry – and is therefore integral to any assessment of the validity, consistency and logic of the overall FS model.

In the 1920s, according to Storper and Christopherson, the paternalistic movie moguls 'shaped the production process in the image of the assembly line' (Christopherson and Storper 1986: 306). Oligopolistic producers churned out films for an undifferentiated market – 'film product was sold by the foot rather than on the basis of content' (Christopherson and Storper 1986: 306) – while the shooting script controlled and deskilled studio labour through the separation of the conception and execution of work tasks. Stable employment conditions and a system of recruitment and apprenticeship led to the establishment of an almost exclusively white, male workforce. Note the binaries (see Table 2.1): oligopoly/competition, mass/differentiated production, internal/external economies, managerial/market control, white male/ethnic and gender diversity, stable/uncertain employment and deskilled/skilled workers. Fordism is not only the exact opposite of the FS of new Hollywood, but it is also, for the most part, an inferior system.

Table 2.1  The characteristics of Fordist and post-Fordist Hollywood

| Fordist/Classical Hollywood, 1920–50 | Post-Fordist/New Hollywood, 1980– |
| --- | --- |
| Oligopoly | Competition |
| Mass production | Differentiated production |
| Internal economies of scale | External economies of scale |
| Managerial control of labour | Market control of labour |
| White, male workforce | Ethnic and gender diversity of workforce |
| Stable employment | Short-term contracts |
| Deskilling | Skilled |

But classical-era Hollywood was not organized along mass production lines and was thus not in any meaningful sense 'Fordist'. In the studio era, the process of film-making was fragmented and departmentalized with work sometimes moving sequentially and at other times in parallel between different stages of an industry clearly demarcated by pre-production, production (shooting) and post-production. The early introduction of the shooting script, for example, was a means to try to bring order to a complex, diverse and divided labour process. Mass production industries, such as the automobile industry, have no need to issue such elaborate instructions, as the assembly line or belt provides physical control and determines the pace and order of work. The shooting script is more analogous to machine-shop practice where job cards accompanied components around several factory departments, guiding and directing a labour force accustomed to exercising a degree of control over what and how quickly they produced. This is not to suggest that classical-era Hollywood was organized along craft lines – rather, it was a distinct industry with a complex system of production, embodying elements of old and new industrial practices and processes – but it certainly was not a mass production industry.

Linking classical Hollywood to mass production has a long history, starting with the movie moguls who made such claims because they wanted to be associated with industrial modernity. Coupling mass production with movies is also a useful heuristic device encouraging those teaching film studies, and our students, to explore the contradictions between industrial production, on the one hand, and artistic creativity, on the other – in the same way as Hortense Powdermaker uses the term 'dream factory' (Powdermaker 1950). But neither linkage actually transforms the industry into mass production. The Ford Motor Company turned out an average of over 1 million Model A cars per annum in the early 1930s, while a typical studio produced only forty to fifty feature films. For all the sameness of Hollywood products in the 1930s, feature films were sufficiently differentiated by studio style, genre and cast to convince audiences of their individuality. Accommodating studio-era realities to a Fordist model proved troublesome for FS theorists: uncomfortable with their conceptualization of mass production, they also labelled the studio-era 'routinized batch production', but this created more problems than it solved because batch production was already a defining feature of FS.[6] Of course, understanding a complex production system and how it changes over time is not easy, but the creation of a single industrial divide hinders rather than helps comprehension.

FS theory also offers us a caricature of classical-era studio labour relations. The FS model sees early studios as rigidly organized hierarchies dominated by paternalistic movie moguls. Mass production and intensification of the division of labour raised levels of exploitation and encouraged deskilling. Monopolistic studios hoarded labour, which fostered long-term job security for powerful white, male workers able to keep outsiders at bay and hand down jobs from father to son. At the same time, large-scale organization and an overarching managerialist ethos encouraged set-piece battles as unions confronted larger-than-life studio heads (Christopherson and Storper 1986: 307).

Painting such a picture of classical-era Hollywood – which opens the door to interpreting new Hollywood's FS as a less coercive labour system – can only be done at the expense of seriously distorting the realities of work inside early studios. Far from enjoying stable employment conditions, studio workers suffered from high levels of job insecurity in the classical era. According to Lovell and Carter, '[c]asual employment has typified the industry from the very beginning'. Actors, extras and production workers signed daily and weekly contracts, and moved between studios as production schedules changed. The arrival of sound in the late 1920s, studio bankruptcies and reorganization in the depressed 1930s, and regular seasonal fluctuations, created marked variations in the demand for labour. For example, in May 1934, before the seasonal rush, employment by the majors stood at 7,880; by September it had risen to 13,734 – an expansion of 74 per cent (Lovell and Carter 1955: 4–5). Not only did seasonal demand for employment force the industry to pay a wage premium in order to attract labour at peak times from other employment, but it also exacerbated inequalities as a cluster of more privileged workers, or 'family', able to hold on to their jobs during the seasonal downturn, were surrounded by a floating group of less privileged employees who came and went with the ebb and flow of film-making. Uncertain employment conditions and divisions among workers are not unique to new Hollywood but were commonplace throughout the industry in the twentieth and twenty-first centuries. The operation of the roster system – codified by a 1946 labour-management agreement – mitigated the worst effects of instability in the classical industry. The roster ensured that those who were hired last and worked least were laid off first, and those with the most working days were first to get the call back. This not only ensured the orderly retreat and advance of a seasonal industrial army but also enabled the studios to fully utilize their more experienced hands.[7] This is not to argue that the pattern of employment in classical and new Hollywood was identical simply because labour insecurity existed in both – indeed, it was not – only that the stable/unstable binary presented in the FS model is unable to capture the subtle and gradual shifts in labour cohesion and employment conditions over several decades.

Whether labour's ranks were less permeable under mass production than FS is also open to question. As FS theorists rightly point out, classical-era studios were lily-white, male domains but in new Hollywood there still remained barriers to entry. The positive impact on employment of the civil rights and women's movements, and passage of Title VII of the 1964 Civil Rights Act was disappointing: minority hiring in back-of-camera occupations increased from 8.4 per cent in 1967 to 14.6 per cent in 1975, but this apparent substantial advance was as much a reflection of parallel changes in the ethnic mix of the Los Angeles workforce as a result of changes in industry recruitment practices. In other words, with more minority workers in the city, each worker found it just as difficult to gain entry to lucrative studio jobs as before. Recruitment through word of mouth, or networking, among racially homogenous groups is a major cause of the dearth of black entrants, according to the US Commission on Civil Rights (1978: 3, 11; Dawson, forthcoming). With the increase in networking in new Hollywood, linked to short-term, project-based employment, the barriers to minorities and women new entrants are just as high.

The FS school believes that the conditions of vertically integrated, mass production studios created mass collective labour that 'exhibit high levels of work force solidarity and have contributed to militant industrial unionism' (Christopherson and Storper 1989: 332). Certainly, at times, there was militancy, but studio employees were never a homogenous group nor did industrial unionism take hold in motion pictures. Labour historians have long noted the connection between the technologies of mass production and the formation of industrial unions: the manufacture of automobiles, steel and electrical goods at the beginning of the twentieth century, for example, gave rise to the United Auto Workers, United Steel Workers of America and United Electrical Workers – each claiming to represent all workers in their respective industries. At no stage, though, do we see the creation of a similar union in motion pictures. Throughout the industry's history, workers have divided their loyalties between 'talent', technical and craft unions. Actors, screenwriters and directors formed their own guilds, technicians joined the International Alliance of Theatrical Stage Employees (IATSE), while members of the older crafts brought with them membership of the brotherhoods of carpenters, painters and electricians. Murray Ross called classical-era IATSE 'semi-industrial' (Ross 1941: 8), but it would be just as accurate to call it 'semi-craft'. IATSE organized live-theatre stagehands and cinema projectionists before adding motion pictures to its jurisdiction. In Hollywood, members were split among a number of studio locals according to their craft. The industry's departmental structure and fluid and overlapping job demarcation led workers to spend almost as much time falling out with each other as they did fighting their bosses. As a result, any aspiration to 'one big union', if it ever existed as a major sentiment within IATSE, was thwarted from the beginning by the competing claims and often bitter jurisdictional battles with carpenters, painters and electricians. A protracted civil war broke out within the ranks of studio labour during the 1930s, fuelled by Depression-era ideological divisions, as the Conference of Studio Unions (CSU), representing a disparate group of craft locals outside the industry's collective bargaining structure and dissidents within IATSE, battled against a gangster-led IATSE with corrupt links with studio heads. The CSU might have evolved into an industrial union, but in 1946 it was defeated following a protracted and unequal struggle in which the studios put their weight behind IATSE (Horne 2001). The defeat of CSU paved the way for IATSE's domination of manual and technical trades, and this is the closest it has come to representing all back-of-camera trades but, ironically, this occurred after the demise of the studio system. Labour militancy is neither a constant of the classical era nor did it disappear after the collapse of the studios – contrary to the FS model. As we have seen, a massive wave of industrial unrest occurred during the period 1935–46, but few disputes took place in the period before, while the years since the Second World War have seen high rates of unionism and militancy among actors and screenwriters.

## Theoretical inertia

The FS model makes a concerted, if flawed, attempt to understand the Los Angeles motion picture industry. Never dominant, always with its critics and detractors, it has nevertheless found widespread credibility and authority, particularly in the fields of media studies, media economics, businesses studies, geography and urban planning and development.[8] The reasons for its continued support are not hard to find: it offers what seems to be a clear, simple and plausible meta-narrative for the economic development of the industry; it provides a theoretical framework for those in universities trying to make sense of a complex industry, and it validates the actions of those who give advice to policy makers.

But if, as we suggest here, FS theory is fundamentally flawed in its ability to explain both new and classical-era Hollywood, then we cannot account for the theory's continued attraction primarily in terms of its formal logic, internal consistency and ability to comprehend reality. To explain the popularity of such a model, we need to return to the 1980s, the period in which FS theory first emerged. In an uncertain environment, FS offered intellectual assurance that, as the regulated and state-supported industries of the post-war years finally gave way to deregulation and market-driven global capitalism, there was still a place for creativity, skill and meaningful work. Left-wing thinkers have long doubted late-capitalism's ability to deliver widespread social benefits, but here was a theory that directly spoke to such scepticism. FS placed its faith in petty media capitalism in the hope that smaller firms would replace the hegemony of monopolistic giants. That free markets could, potentially, operate in such a progressive fashion allays anxieties about the direction of modern society and flatly contradicts pessimistic Marxists readings, such as Harry Braverman's *Labor and Monopoly Capital* (1974), which predicts the degradation of work under large-scale, corporate capitalism. As commentators have noted, FS theory attracts widespread support not only among the usual suspects – libertarian and right-wing free-market adherents – but across a surprisingly broad spectrum of right, centre and left-leaning thinkers, including those who style themselves Marxist. At the same time, FS theory neatly chimed with new Hollywood's self-image as a place of entrepreneurial vigour, artistic creativity and the home of independent auteurs (Blair and Rainnie 2000: 188–9). Just as FS theory disguises the continued power of media conglomerates, so Hollywood has a vested interest in emphasizing artistry over mammon.

University planners, economists and urban geographers found in FS theory a justification for their own actions in supporting locally based, free-market capitalism as a viable (i.e. efficient) and socially progressive alternative to corporate capitalism. The supposed example of the motion picture industry – along with evidence from Third Italy, US mini steel mills and Japanese and US machine tools and electronics – suggested to FS theorists that at crucial junctures real technological and organizational choices were possible and that mass production was not the goal or the ultimate stage of industrial development (Christopherson and Storper 1986: 305–19). City planners and business groups, keen to sustain local film industries, drew directly upon FS policy implications. The pioneer work of the Greater London Council (GLC) in the early 1980s looked to Piore and Sabel's writings. In *The London Industrial Strategy*, the GLC claimed to see signs of the emergence of FS in the capital's cultural industries, and a report on Greater Manchester's culture industries referred to the example of Third Italy as a potential route forward (Pollert 1991: xxx, 139).

The wider aspirations of FS theorists have always been linked to the goal of regenerating the Los Angeles economy. Scott, Christopherson and Storper all took up academic posts in Los Angeles during the early 1980s, at a time of intense uncertainty in motion pictures and the local economy, where they were active in the emerging Los Angeles school of urbanism. A wave of deindustrialization swept away many of the city's mass production industries, creating a deep sense of unease about the future. Storper recalled, 'At the time the newspapers in LA were filled with stories about the crisis of Hollywood and how Hollywood was leaving to go to other places to shoot films' (Hoyler, Freytag and Jöns 2004: 73). Their research soon uncovered the good news that the industry, far from leaving town, was thriving as an agglomeration of small, independent producers. The coincidental publication of Piore and Sabel's *The Second Industrial Divide* in 1984 introduced these Americans to the example of northern Italy, crucially providing them with the theoretical underpinning for understanding Hollywood's local success. But the crisis persisted in the 1990s as defence and aerospace declined following the end of the Cold War, which encouraged further intellectual ruminations on the part of FS practitioners.

The Los Angeles school, drawing its support from an iconoclastic band of geographers, regional planners and public policy specialists, gave an additional postmodernist twist to FS theory.[9] Major cities can generate their own intellectual movements – for example, nineteenth-century Manchester and Philadelphia developed their own distinctive schools of political economy – all in their own ways articulating the pride, aspirations and fears of local business and community interests. Supporters of the Los Angeles school believed that the city was ignored and slighted by urban sociology and that now was the moment to proclaim that, far from being an exceptional, deviant or isolated city on the Pacific shore – and, therefore, incapable of supporting a general theory – it was the prototypical city of the future. 'We feel justified', announced Scott and Soja, 'in advancing the claim – with apologies to Walter Benjamin – that the city has now become the very capital of the late 20th century, the paradigmatic industrial metropolis of the modern world.'[10] A good deal of this claim rested on the discovery of 'flexible capitalism', as Scott explained:

> Throughout the era of Fordist mass production, [Los Angeles] was seen as an exception, as an anomalous complex of regional and urban activity in comparison with what were then considered to be the paradigmatic cases of successful industrial development. [Yet] with the steady ascent of flexible production organization, Southern California is often taken to be something like a new paradigm of local economic development, and its institutional bases, its evolutionary trajectory, and its internal locational dynamics as providing important general insights and clues. (Scott 1993: 33)

Often couched in the florid and overblown language of postmodernism – well suited to the needs of thrusting and ambitious academics – the work of the school detected revolution and epochal change round every corner. The city's premier status was assured, so the more pragmatic policy-oriented members of the Los Angeles school believed, as long as it could point to economic or technological developments – or 'technopoles' – as harbingers of future growth. As we have seen, the FS school first promoted motion pictures as a leading sector; at other times it was also aerospace, information technology and, bizarrely, a combination of apparel, furniture and jewellery. In order to accommodate this optimistic future, theorists nimbly reclassified motion pictures as a low-technology craft industry (Scott 1990, 1993: 11; Scott and Rigby 1996).

While this irritating boosterism provides plenty of ammunition for critics, more lasting damage was done to the coherence and integrity of the FS model. It is the school's belief in a new form of industrial organization, flexible capitalism, the constant search for an engine of economic growth (and therefore the city's salvation), and its willingness to speculate about unlikely futures, that fatally undermines FS theory (Miller 2005). Whether Los Angeles is a paradigmatic city is of secondary importance as far as this study is concerned; the fact that FS theorists see their main purpose as defending and promoting the fortunes of the local economy leads them to celebrate 're-industrialization', at the expense of limiting the ability of their model to explain historical and contemporary reality. The jingoism of Angeleno intellectuals fatally compromises the model. Framed in such a fashion, motion pictures simply cannot bear the weight of expectation. The industry is undoubtedly a world leader; nevertheless, it alone cannot be the economic salvation of the city, nor can the FS panacea explain the historical past or the future of the industry.[11]

## Conclusions

The experience of Hollywood labour is determined by a series of disjunctures and complex reorganizations within a broad process covering the full span of the twentieth and twenty-first centuries. It is a history of the intersection of power relations at work, and global media monopolies regulated by local and national states, only partially explained by changes in relations between firms and shifts in spatial location. Those who work in the industry have a central part to play in any rounded account, not just as they are subjected to economic forces but as real social actors. 'The bones of the true history of the U.S. motion picture industry have been unearthed,' Michael Nielson declared nearly thirty years ago, 'but it is up to the workers to flesh out the beast with their own life stories. The bottom up story must be told' (Nielsen 1983: 82). This is a stirring call to arms; nevertheless, we also need to tell the story from the top down.

FS draws upon neoclassical economics and as a result neglects real human beings, agency and consciousness; as a model that stresses equilibrium, it also fails to deal with crisis and class conflict. Any understanding of industrial relations in Hollywood needs to identify active social groups and assess the balance of power between them. Differences between 'talent' and craft and technical workers have certainly widened since 1950, which reduces the power of the guilds and unions. The prevalence of contracting and the spread of project working have played a considerable part in this. While FS theorists see flexibility as potentially beneficial, we also need to recognize that it can equally lead to intensification of labour and the growth of managerial prerogatives even if, at the same time, some workers believe that they are more autonomous.

One of the major contributions of FS theory has been to highlight the existence of a group of small business owners running contracting firms, although they have a shadowy existence within the model. We need to know if this is a distinct class of petty entrepreneurs: does it have its own world view and what relations are there between workers, on the one hand, and executives in large media corporations, on the other? If a new social layer has emerged in Hollywood, are entrepreneurs independent of or integrated within big capital? While it is true that large media corporations have stepped back from direct involvement in production, it could be argued that they continue to exercise control but do so screened behind a decentralized production process and formal contractual relations between worker and small entrepreneur.

As the FS debate dims and social scientists move on to other areas of intellectual concern leaving behind an indelible imprint on the study of the motion picture industry, we should not lose sight of the ideological underpinnings and shortcomings of the theory first formulated in the 1980s. With the crumbling of the certainties of New Deal protectionism and state regulation in the 1980s, questions were raised by those apprehensive at the prospects for industrial society. FS theory offered a comforting answer: the future would be assured by resourceful market-oriented small enterprises run as fraternities of capital and labour. Such has not proved to be the case and FS theorists no longer paint such an optimistic picture of the film and TV industries. These predictions rest on dubious intellectual foundations: that the industry is divided between a gloomy past and a bright flexible future, that the marketplace delivers social welfare, and that large media conglomerates, and local and national states, play no important role in the industry or in workers' lives. Given that the experience of recent years negates the FS paradigm, and that theorists have moved beyond the initial premises, what is left of the theory?

If reality has overtaken FS, should we not jettison the theory? Some commentators, such as regional planners and creative-industry boosters, still rely on it for intellectual succour, and it also finds a place in media textbooks. But beyond these constituencies, its impact is diminished. We need to recognize that the ideological moment creating FS – a point where neoliberalism emerged out of the ashes of the older regulated economy – has passed. We, in the second decade of the twenty-first century, are confronting far more important changes to those of the 1980s. The near collapse of the global financial system in 2008, and the protracted crisis that followed, gives us intellectual space to question the certainties of neoliberalism in a way that has not been possible in the past few decades. In the 1980s, the deregulation of the Reagan and Thatcher eras led to the ascendency of free-market ideas; the near collapse of finance capitalism allows us to challenge these beliefs. While markets can bring social benefits to some, they are also anarchic, despotic and arbitrary. Of course, what new social theories will emerge out of this intellectual turmoil and what light they will cast on the experience of those who work in the motion picture industry remain to be determined.

## Notes

1 For accounts of the film industry that emphasize the continued importance of large corporations, see Wasko (1994, 2003).

2 Pacific Gas and Electric Company quoted in Curry and Kenney (1999: 17).

3 Christopherson (2006). For a different approach to the politics of runaway production, see Dawson (2006).

4 For example, in what appears as an afterthought, Christopherson and Storper call for the creation of new, but unspecified, institutions to protect industry workers against exploitation (Christopherson and Storper 1989: 346).

5 Dawson (2009). For a view that talent-union success came not through labour militancy but as a result of absorbing managerial functions, such as the disbursement of repeat performance fees to members, see Paul and Kleingartner (1994).

6 Storper (1989: 277). David Bordwell, Janet Staiger and Kristin Thompson use the term 'serial manufacture' (Neale and Smith 1998: 92).

7 Curiously, Christopherson and Storper (1989: 335) see the roster system as post-Fordist, a product of the break-up of the studio system, even though it appeared two years before the Paramount case.

8 Recent examples of sympathetic treatments of the FS model are found in Miller (2000), Caves (2000), McGuigan (1996), Caldwell (2008), Holt and Perren (2009), Marti (2008), Goldsmith and Regan (2005), Wayne (2003).

9 The output of the Los Angeles school is voluminous. Titles relevant to the motion picture industry and the economic development of Los Angeles include Soja (1989), Scott and Soja (1986, 1996) and Scott (1993).

10 Scott and Soja (1986: 249). For a questioning of Los Angeles' role as a paradigmatic global city, see Curry and Kenney (1999: 1–28). Allen Scott accuses the authors of mechanically 'counter[ing] what they perceive as the LA School's boosterism with crude proclamations about Los Angeles as an economic has-been' (Scott 1999: 34).

11 The Los Angeles school is a broad and fragmented church and not all its members subscribe to the same ideas. Michael Storper (2001: 164–5), for example, firmly rejects postmodernism for its abandonment of rationality.

# Bibliography

Aksoy, A. and Robins, K. (1992), 'Hollywood for the 21st Century: Global Competition for Critical Mass in Image Markets', *Cambridge Journal of Economics*, 16 (1): 1–22.

Blair, H. and Rainnie, A. (2000), 'Flexible Firms?', *Media, Culture & Society*, 22 (2): 187–204.

Caldwell, J. T. (2008), *Production Culture: Industrial Reflexivity and Critical Practice in Film and Television*, Durham, NC: Duke University Press.

Caves, R. E. (2000), *Creative Industries: Contracts between Art and Commerce*, Cambridge, MA: Harvard University Press.

Christopherson, S. (2006), 'Behind the Scenes: How Transnational Films Are Constructing a New International Division of Labor in Media Work', *Geoforum*, 37 (5): 739–51.

Christopherson, S. and Storper, M. (1986), 'The City as Studio: The World as Backlot: The Impact of Vertical Disintegration on the Location of the Motion Picture Industry', *Environment and Planning D: Society and Space*, 4: 305–20.

Christopherson, S. and Storper, M. (1989), 'The Effects of Flexible Specialization on Industrial Politics and the Labor Market: The Motion Picture Industry', *Industrial and Labor Relations Review*, 42 (3): 331–47.

Curry, J. and Kenney, M. (1999), 'The Paradigmatic City: Post-Industrial Illusion and the Los Angeles School', *Antipode*, 31(1): 1–28.

Dawson, A. (2006), '"Bring Hollywood Home!" Studio Labour, Nationalism and Internationalism, and Opposition to "Runaway Production", 1948–2003', *Belgisch Tijdschrift voor Filologie en Geschiedenis/Revue Belge de Philologie et d'Histoire*, 84: 1101–22.

Dawson, A. (2009), 'Strikes in the Motion Picture Industry', in A. Brenner, B. Day and I. Ness (eds), *The Encyclopedia of Strikes in American History*, Armonk, NY: M.E. Sharpe.

Dawson, A. (forthcoming), 'Challenging Lilywhite Hollywood: African Americans and the Demand for Racial Equality in the Motion Picture Industry, 1963–1974', *Journal of Popular Culture*, 45 (3).

Goldsmith, B. and O'Regan, T. (2005), *The Film Studio: Film Production in the Global Economy*, Lanham, MD: Rowman & Littlefield.

Holt, J. and Perren, A. (eds) (2009), *Media Industries: History, Theory, and Method*, Malden, MA: Wiley-Blackwell.

Horne, G. (2001), *Class Struggle in Hollywood 1930–1950: Moguls, Mobsters, Stars, Reds, and Trade Unionists*, Austin, TX: University of Texas Press.

Hoyler, M., Freytag, T. and Jöns, H. (2004), 'Technology, Organization, Territory: A Biographical Interview with Michael Storper', in M. Storper (ed.), *Institutions, Incentives and Communication in Economic Geography*, Wiesbaden: Franz Steiner Verlag.

Lovell, H. and Carter, T. (1955), *Collective Bargaining in the Motion Picture Industry*, Berkeley, CA: University of California Institute of Industrial Relations.

Marti, G. (2008), *Hollywood Faith: Holiness, Prosperity, and Ambition in a Los Angeles Church*, New Brunswick, NJ: Rutgers University Press.

McGuigan, J. (1996), *Culture and the Public Sphere*, London: Routledge.

Miller, D. W. (2000), 'The New Urban Studies', *Chronicle of Higher Education*, 18 August, http://chronicle.com/article/The-New-Urban-Studies/3868 [accessed 23 December 2009].

Miller, T. (2005), *Global Hollywood*, London: British Film Institute.

Neale, S. and Smith, M. (eds) (1998), *Contemporary Hollywood Cinema*, London: Routledge.

Nielsen, M. (1983), 'Towards a Workers' History of the U.S. Film Industry', in V. Mosco and J. Wasko (eds), *The Critical Communications Review, Volume I: Labor, the Working Class and the Media*, Norwood, NJ: Ablex Publishing.

Paul, A. and Kleingartner, A. (1994), 'Flexible Production and the Transformation of Industrial Relations in the Motion Picture and Television Industry', *Industrial and Labor Relations Review*, 47 (July): 663–78.

Piore, M. J. and Sabel, C. F. (1984), *The Second Industrial Divide: Possibilities for Prosperity*, New York: Basic Books.

Pollert, A. (ed.) (1991), *Farewell to Flexibility?* Oxford: Blackwell.

Powdermaker, H. (1950), *Hollywood, the Dream Factory*, Boston, MA: Little, Brown.

Ross, M. (1941), *Stars and Strikes*, New York: Columbia University Press.

Sabel, C. F. and Zeitlin, J. (eds) (1997), *World of Possibilities: Flexibility and Mass Production in Western Industrialization*, New York: Cambridge University Press.

Scott, A. J. (1990), 'The Technopoles of Southern California', *Environment and Planning A*, 22: 1575–1605.

Scott, A. J. (1993), *Technopolis: High-Technology Industry and Regional Development in Southern California*, Berkeley, CA: University of California Press.

Scott, A. J. (1999), 'Los Angeles and the LA School: A Response to Curry and Kenney', *Antipode*, 31 (1): 29–36.

Scott, A. J. (2005), *On Hollywood: The Place, the Industry*, Princeton, NJ: Princeton University Press.

Scott, A. J. and Rigby, D. L. (1996), *The Craft Industries of Los Angeles: Prospects for Economic Growth and Development*, California Policy Seminar Brief No. 5, Berkeley, CA.

Scott, A. J. and Soja, E. (1986), 'Los Angeles: Capital of the Late Twentieth Century', *Environment and Planning D: Society and Space*, 4: 249–54.

Scott, A. J. and Soja, E. (eds) (1996), *The City: Los Angeles and Urban Theory at the End of the Twentieth Century*, Berkeley, CA: University of California Press.

Soja, E. W. (1989), *Postmodern Geographies: The Reassertion of Space in Critical Social Theory*, New York: Verso.

Storper, M. (1989), 'The Transition to Flexible Specialization in the US Film Industry: External Economies, the Division of Labor, and the Crossing of Industrial Divides', *Cambridge Journal of Economics*, 13 (2): 273–305.

Storper, M. (2001), 'The Poverty of Radical Theory Today: From False Promises of Marxism to the Mirage of the Cultural Turn', *International Journal of Urban and Regional Research*, 25 (March): 155–79.

Storper, M. and Christopherson, S. (1987), 'Flexible Specialization and Regional Industrial Agglomerations: The Case of the U.S. Motion Picture Industry', *Annals of the Association of American Geographers*, 77 (1): 104–17.

US Commission on Civil Rights, California Advisory Committee (1978), *Behind the Scenes: Equal Employment Opportunity in the Motion Picture Industry*, Washington: GPO.

Wasko, J. (1994), *Hollywood in the Information Age: Beyond the Silver Screen*, Cambridge: Polity Press.

Wasko, J. (2003), *How Hollywood Works*, London: Sage.

Wayne, M. (2003), 'Post-Fordism, Monopoly Capitalism, and Hollywood's Media Industrial Complex', *International Journal of Cultural Studies*, 6 (1): 82–103.

# Soviet film-making under the 'producership' of the party state (1955–85)

GALINA GORNOSTAEVA

## Introduction

Soviet film-making is an example of a creative industry financed and regulated exclusively by the state. Film production, distribution and exhibition were nationalized in 1919 (Taylor 1979: 64–5). Lenin valued the cinema as an important tool of education and propaganda that the Union of Soviet Socialist Republics (USSR) could use to present itself to the world (Dzieciolowski 2006). Therefore, ideological control was necessary (Zhirkov 2001). This chapter describes the shortcomings and unexpected advantages of an industry organized outside of market conditions. It will focus on the period between 1955, just after the death of Stalin in 1953, and 1985, just before the start of 'perestroika' and the subsequent shift to a market economy. These thirty years can be divided into the short period of the Khrushchev 'thaw' (1955–65) followed by two decades of economic and democratic 'stagnation' under Brezhnev (1965–85). The liberalizing tendencies at work in the Soviet Union under Khrushchev in the late 1950s and early 1960s created a set of political and cultural conditions that were favourable to the development of film-making. However, the stabilization policies of the Brezhnev era crushed the reformist impulse in the Soviet Union and tightened government control over the culture industries (Fomin and Kosinova 2011).

The end of political repressions, the introduction of moderate economic reforms and the relaxation of censorship after 1954 created a small window of opportunity for creativity and experimentation in the arts in general and in cinema in particular. However, the continuing political and economic power of the *nomenklatura* – the Communist Party functionaries who occupied key positions in the Soviet bureaucracy – and the gradual strengthening of 'party clientelism' and neo-traditionalism in the Soviet Union (Jowitt 1983; Walder 1984; Afanasiev 1997) gave that creativity a specific twist. The most important characteristic of life in the Soviet Union continued to be uncertainty, something that was intensified by the vagaries of the agents of social power. According to Mikhail Voslensky (1991), the *nomenklatura* effectively usurped political and economic power, evolving into a new ruling class that exploited the rest of society since the bureaucracies they controlled were, in effect, the owners of the aggregated public property. The inefficiencies of the planned economy along with the economic and ideological isolation of the Soviet Union led to material scarcity and restrictions on foreign travel.

Soviet clientelism developed as a result of the end of repressions and the de-mythologization of power after the 20th Congress of the Communist Party in 1956, at which 'the cult of the individual' was condemned. This had the effect of stimulating the 'shadow economy' and led to the spread of so-called *blat* – complex reciprocal relationships between those involved in institutional, business and personal networks (Ledeneva 1998; Michailova and Worm 2003; Butler and Purchase 2004). In the absence of both repressions and market relations, the only way to secure productive work from labourers was to exchange it for social privileges (Afanasiev 1997). In order to secure loyalty, Party leadership had to cultivate stable networks of 'activists' in all social settings. The result was a highly institutionalized network of patron-client relations with asymmetrical reciprocity, in which loyalty to the Party and its ideology combined with personal loyalties between Party officials and their clients (Walder 1984; Lomnitz 1988).

For the film industry, this meant that the ideological loyalty of the salaried film-making elite was maintained by a system of incentives and privileges, which included employment itself, career opportunities, special distributions, business trips abroad and other favours that Party officials were uniquely able to dispense. Private social networks, of which the political and cultural elite were a part, started to play a significant role in the production of films: their financing, decisions about their release or 'shelving', the volume produced for distribution and so on. Disloyalty or an unwillingness to stick to the Communist Party line was punished by a finely tuned mechanism of exclusion from creative, economic and social opportunities. Among creative workers themselves there was a social and ideological divide, which led to mistrust and the atmosphere of a 'witch-hunt' and the isolation of dissenters.

The first part of this chapter gives an overview of the structure and organization of the film industry in the USSR informed by the political and economic situation in which film-making existed at that time. It pays particular attention to the relations between the *nomenklatura*, studio administrators, creative units and talent, all of which were indelibly marked by the Soviet systems of financing and censorship. The second part looks at two specific manifestations of the system of film production in the USSR, both of which demonstrate the complexity and ambiguity of the patron-client relationships which underpinned the operation of the Soviet film industry. The first is the Experimental Creative Studio (ECS), a unique production unit that specialized in entertainment cinema (and the genre of the 'Eastern' in particular) and which was conceived as a means of decentralizing the economic power of the state by creating a 'free-market-like' model of enterprise within the Soviet system of production. The second is the production unit run by film director Andrei Tarkovsky, the foremost example of a Soviet director working in the 'auteur' tradition. The chapter draws on both Russian and Western sources and uses both memoirs and published interviews to describe how films were produced under the conditions of a socialist economy and ideology.

## Organization of the film industry in the USSR

Throughout the 1960s, the demand for film was high in the USSR. Each year 4.5 billion movie tickets were sold, more than double the number in the United States. The average Russian went to the movies more than twenty times a year, whilst the average American went just 6.5 times. In Moscow, in a typical week, moviegoers could choose from 58 different Soviet movies and 87 foreign movies, the latter mainly from the countries of the Eastern bloc and from France, Italy or India (Kessel and Young 1967: 65, 81). The boom was, in part, a reflection of the lack of competition from television, which provided dull programmes subjected to careful editing and censorship. The real driving force behind it, however, was the Khrushchev 'thaw', which brought considerable benefit to the arts in the USSR by reducing censorship and promoting relative freedom in terms of creativity and self-expression. With the ideological leash loosened, film-makers were free to entertain as well as to preach. In the early 1950s, the USSR was producing about fifteen films a year, the majority of which glorified the regime. In the 1960s, film-makers were freer to criticize Soviet society, providing that they attacked not the system or its ideological underpinnings but the people who kept it from functioning properly. The average annual output of the Soviet film industry reached 150 films (Iordanova 2003: 23). Several films transcended the Cold War barrier and were released abroad to considerable critical acclaim. Older directors, suppressed during the Stalin era, re-entered the industry and a wave of new directors emerged. Even so, film-makers at the creative end of the business faced severe controls.

The industry remained one that was financed and governed by the state and its institutions, and any material that was found to be politically offensive was removed, edited or reshot. The state was the producer and distributor responsible for the approval of scripts and budgets. It took decisions on whether to continue produc-tion on a problematic project or to terminate it, whether to release or to shelve a finished movie, and whether to show it countrywide or in selected cinemas. The state remained the sole 'patron' of the arts, distributing its financial and social favours in exchange for ideological loyalty. Film-making in the USSR was part of a highly institutionalized network of patron-client relationships that was maintained by the Communist Party through its Central Committee and the politburo.

State 'producership', monopolistic and powerful as it was, was realized via a hier-archy of agencies (sub-patrons or brokers). The clientelist pyramid had four levels. At the top of the pyramid was Goskino (the Soviet State Film Committee), which operated under the aegis of central government and functioned as patron, producer, financier, distributor and exhibitor. Beneath Goskino were the studios, which as clients of the state, oversaw film production and provided patronage to production crews. The studios were the main sites for the accumulation of the material means of film production – the resources upon which individual film-makers depended both economically and socially. The production process itself was the responsibility of film units, each of which was headed by a leading director and made up of assistant directors, scriptwriters, cameramen, actors, scenic artists, costume makers, builders and post-production specialists.

## Goskino

Goskino was established in 1963 to oversee the Soviet film industry. In effect, it was a gigantic corporation that exercised a monopoly over film production in the USSR. It was responsible for considering and approving scenarios and thematic plans for film production, for determining how many copies of a film were required and for deciding where those copies would be produced. It operated seven plants for producing copies of films, 158 distribution centres and 155,000 projection cameras (Arkus 2010). After 1974, it also had under its jurisdiction the enterprises producing film cameras, film stock and sound systems.

As well as coordinating production and distribution, Goskino also established the rules for exhibition. Together with the Ministry of Finance, it set ticket prices and the wholesale price of film copies. In addition to its core activities, Goskino published film magazines such as Iskusstvo Kino (The Art of Film) and Sovetsky Ekran (Soviet Screen) and oversaw film export, the organization of film festivals and the operation of film archives.

Under the conditions imposed by the Soviet state, the system of governance for film-making generally struggled to strike a balance between the requirements of ideology and the needs of the economy. The economic model worked as follows. The film-goer paid for the ticket and the theatre paid 55 per cent of the ticket price as a local tax, which was used to fund the salaries of trade union officials, teachers, doctors and so on. The rest of the income from ticket sales was used to support a network of movie theatres and to maintain and improve production facilities in the studios. How precisely the money was spent was determined annually by Goskino. When a film was to be made the studio took out a loan from the state bank. As soon as the film had been completed and approved by Goskino, the distributor repaid the loan (Butovsky et al. 2004). None of the organizations involved in this process held any financial risk, and there was no direct monetary incentive either for the director or the production team. If a film generated a profit, it was returned to the film industry and used to support film-making in the Soviet republics, which was generally unprofitable, and the production of 'auteur' films, which usually had low box-office returns.

Goskino was headed by a chairman with a governing board made up of the heads of its various departments (e.g. the Main Administration for the Production of Feature Films), the editor of Iskusstvo Kino, the head of the script editorial board, a deputy chair representing the KGB, and prominent directors, actors and scriptwriters (Shlapentokh and Shlapentokh 1993: 28; Johnson and Petrie 1994: 8). In a sense, it was the most visible manifestation of the network of patronage and clientelism that underpinned the Soviet film industry, a place where senior representatives of the state regularly mingled with their clients in the creative elite. Aleksey Romanov, who chaired it from 1964 to 1972, came from the Propaganda Department and Philipp Yermash (1972–86) from the Department of Culture. Both departments were involved in checking the ideological content of films and operated in such a way as to stifle artistic creativity. The official political connections between the heads of *Goskino* and other members of the *nomenklatura* were supplemented by personal ones. Yermash, for example, was a relative of a member of the politburo, Andrei Kirilenko, a close associate of Leonid Brezhnev (Lawton 1992: 9).

The workings of the Soviet film industry were shaped by horizontal as well as vertical patterns of authority. The Department of Culture, for example, operated not simply at the national level but also at the level of individual republics, districts and cities. Its agents at any one of these levels could play a role in a film's life by holding up its release or even banning it. The head of *Goskino* himself complained that any local party secretary could create trouble for a film if his mother-in-law didn't happen to like it (Johnson and Petrie 1994: 11). The involvement of a huge number of people at different levels of power and authority and with different ideological allegiances, views, tastes and educational backgrounds sometimes created a sense of chaos and unpredictability in the decision-making process. Ideological judgement was distorted by the process of filtration through the network of combined ideological and personal loyalties.

*Goskino* exercised total financial control over film-making and film-makers and established the rules under which studios, creative units and directors worked to produce a movie. The alienation of the production team and the director from the economics of film-making allowed them to concentrate on creative issues more freely than would have been the case in the West, whilst rendering them incompetent in the financial aspects of film production. As the industry's chief patron, *Goskino* used both the carrot and the stick to motivate film-makers. Cuts in film budgets and reductions in fees and bonuses were frequently used to bring recalcitrant film-makers into line, whilst privileges such as employment opportunities, awards, access to film festivals, freedom to travel and to cultivate contacts abroad and even reviews in the press were often offered as incentives. A distinctive feature of Soviet clientelism was the way in which the networks of the *nomenklatura* and the creative elite overlapped and intertwined. A layer of creative Party 'activists' existed, which had close connections with the *nomenklatura*: fellow students and colleagues, former 'equals', could become members of committees and boards. The 'activists' had powers to support or punish those film-makers who were not that close to the Communist Party establishment.

## Studios

The Soviet studio system mirrored the American one, though the monopoly was not of capital but of the state. While Hollywood reorganized itself in the 1980s from the Fordist 'plant' into a conglomerate of distributors, production and post-production companies, however, Soviet studios continued to be integrated and hierarchical. The biggest studio was Mosfilm, established in Moscow in 1923. Other well-known studios include Lenfilm, established in Leningrad in 1918, and Sverdlovsk Studio, established in Yekaterinburg in 1943. Individual Soviet republics also had their own film studios. During the 1970s and 1980s, there were forty studios operating in the Soviet Union with a combined annual output of more than 130 theatrical movies, almost 100 films for television and approximately 1,400 documentaries, popular science and educational films. A third of all films were produced by Mosfilm, which had expanded rapidly during the Khrushchev thaw and, according to some estimates, was bigger than any studio in the West.

For film-makers, the studio was the main unit of ideological, economic and social dependency and a focal point for work as well as the delivery of public goods, services and social advantages. Film-makers were not able to work outside the studio system. The studio controlled access to cameras, editing equipment, sound studios, post-production facilities and costume collections. This put it in a position to impose its ideological authority over the creative product and to claim ownership of it (Tarkovsky 2008). The individual film-makers' dependence on the studio partly reflects the nature of film as a product of 'many signatures', which cannot be produced without finance, equipment and the contributions of many people. However, in the Soviet context, it was also a consequence of the state's ownership of the means of production and distribution.

In the studio, production was concentrated under one roof. Filming took place either at the studio or at the various filming locations across the country. Even the army assisted (for free) on some films. The poor quality of film stock – a consequence of the Soviet Union's inability to access international markets – meant that a scene might have to be shot eight to ten times to ensure a satisfactory result. A film used twenty to thirty reels, all of them of varying quality, so lighting had to be changed accordingly. The film could also be damaged. All of this imposed special requirements on cameramen and post-production technicians. Foreign film stock (Kodak) only started to be imported in 1974 but only in limited quantities, so it was distributed to the select few responsible for the most prestigious productions (Vasilyeva 2004).

## Creative units

A significant increase in the output of feature films from the major film studios in the wake of the Khrushchev thaw made it necessary to decentralize control over the creative process to some degree. To this end, Soviet film studios formed creative units to prepare scripts and shoot movies. The creative unit functioned as the basic production entity and had relative creative autonomy. The directorate of the studio, however, continued to exercise ultimate authority over the approval of scripts and completed movies, as well as to fulfil the functions of planning, finance and technical provision. The functional integrity and bureaucratic hierarchy of the studio and the principle of a unified production cycle remained unchallenged (Goriunova and Chernov 1975; Konoplev 1975). The first creative unit was set up in Poland in 1955 and was followed in the Soviet Union by Mosfilm four years later. Other production facilities across Eastern Europe quickly followed suit (Iordanova 2003: 23).

There were two ways in which units could start to work on a movie: a proposal 'from the top' and an application 'from the bottom'. The former was more prestigious as it was a 'state order' (*goszakaz*): the theme or a script, tested *a priori* for its ideological conformity, was sent out; a trusted director was selected; and, if he agreed to the project, everything went to the studio. It was guaranteed that the completed film would be distributed widely, sent to the international festivals, and would receive positive reviews in the central press. This was the 'normal' functioning of the system. The second way was more complicated. The director, or often the director and the scriptwriter, put forward a proposal to the art board of the studio, which had the power either to approve or to reject it. If approved, the application then went to *Goskino* for ratification. If *Goskino* endorsed the project, a scenario would be written and submitted to the art board at the studio for discussion. Though the members of the board were the author's colleagues, these film-makers and film professionals – for example, the chief editor of the studio whose job required Communist Party membership – were also the censors. After inevitable corrections a script would be sent back to *Goskino* for its final approval. Only when this had been received could film production start. From the Stalin era onwards, there was an un-discussable rule in Soviet film-making: strict censorship started at the stage of writing the script. All proposals were carefully censored long before shooting started, thereby reducing the possibility of the intrusion of anti-Soviet ideas into the finished product. After the script was demonstrated to be ideologically sound, the only task left for the censors was to monitor the director to see whether the shooting strictly followed the lines of the script, without any deviations (Fomin and Kosinova 2011).

Production in both cases consisted of several stages: pre-production, filming, cutting and editing, and re-shooting of some material (whether necessitated by technical problems, the demands of the censor or the whims of the director). Each step took place under the supervision of both the chief editor of the studio and the editor appointed by *Goskino* to oversee the operation of the studio. The final stage in the process was the approval of the completed film by *Goskino* and its allocation to a category. Its category determined how many copies of a film would be produced for distribution and the fees that the scriptwriter, director and other 'above-the-line' workers would receive. It is worth remembering that all workers in the units were salaried employees who only received bonuses upon the completion and release of a new film.

If a film was placed in the 'third category' (known to film-makers as the 'leprosy category'), the creative team that had worked on it would not receive bonuses, and it would only be distributed to third-class cinemas and workers' clubs. Few prints would be made and the film-makers would receive no returns. Involvement in the production of 'third-category' films placed film-makers in danger of being accused of wasting public funds and led to studios having to pay a fee for the supposed misuse of film stock and production facilities. It also had an impact upon the potential future productivity of a studio, since *Goskino* would exercise more caution in granting approval to subsequent proposals if it had delivered a film that was not deemed to be of sufficiently high quality (Marshall 1976: 93). If a film was allocated to 'second category', modest rewards accrued both to the creative team and to the studio. However, the biggest bonuses, the widest distribution and the highest honours in the form of awards and favours from the Communist Party elite were attached to films that made it into the prestigious 'first category' (Fomin and Kosinova 2011).

Creative workers were central to film production in the Soviet Union. However, their roles differed significantly from those of their counterparts in the West. Creative units did not have a producer because this position was too closely associated with the capitalist system of production. The state was the real producer. However, for every individual movie there was a 'managing director' who performed some of the functions of the producer, such as overseeing shooting of the film, allocating the already agreed-upon budget, and ensuring the safety of the cast and crew. He or she acted as an intermediary between the director and the studio, which was where major decisions were taken, such as the elimination, for financial or logistical reasons, of scenes from the original script. The power of the managing director was limited, however, in that he or she did not have the authority to stop the director from reviewing the script or to order delays in shooting while props or costumes were altered (Johnson and Petrie 1994: 58).

Actors in the Soviet film industry worked without ballyhoo in a system without stars. For the 300 actors who worked at Mosfilm in the 1960s, a movie career did not hold out the promise of Western-style stardom – but it did provide a sort of social security. Like other groups of workers in the film studios, they drew a yearly salary, no matter how few films they made, but they also received a bonus for each film in which they appeared. Salaries, high by Soviet standards, were based on talent and experience as much as on popularity with audiences. As well as acting in movies, they were also on call for work on the legitimate stage. A majority of Soviet film actors had a background in the theatre, and they brought theatrical work practices with them into the studios, spending far more time in rehearsal than was usually allowed for in the film budgets in other countries. When a studio needed special talent, it could call on other state organizations – the Bolshoi theatre for ballroom extras and the circus or the army for stuntmen, for example.

## Directors

Though all members of the creative unit played important roles in the production process, it was the director who was the key figure. At the pre-production stage, directors worked closely with scriptwriters and described the films they hoped to make at unit meetings in order to win the unit's approval. The director was not only responsible for the film's content and the delivery of the whole project, including supervision of filming and post-production. He or she was also central to the negotiations that were conducted both internally, within the unit, and externally with the administration of the studio, *Goskino*, and the political authorities over the film's content and its ideological outlook and, to a lesser extent, its financing and the conditions attached to its release. Despite the ideological constraints under which directors operated, the films that they produced were often artistically very good and a tribute to their efforts to put their own stamp on their films. But many of them dreaded the battle. 'If it weren't for bureaucratic channels', observed one, 'we could make twice as many films – twice as good' (Kessel and Young 1967: 67). Many Western film-makers, however, responded to their complaints about censorship by pointing to the pressures they were placed under by financiers, distributors and producers. It is also worth mentioning that all serious decisions about the financing and ideological content of a film were made before and after shooting, so shooting itself was not strictly supervised and, for the director, it was a time of relative freedom, creativity and improvisation.

One of the methods that Soviet directors used to avoid censorship was the so-called 'dog's method'. Like Hollywood directors in the 1930s looking for a way around the Production Code, they would deliberately insert irrelevant scenes that they knew would be cut, in the hope of diverting attention from others, of more central importance to the movie. In effect, they would 'throw a bone' to the censors in the form of an obviously ridiculous scene or scenes of excessive lengths. Such tricks not only increased the coordination costs but also the direct costs of production in the shooting (Savitskaya and Lepeshkova 2003).

Film directors as well as the majority of other staff involved in film production above and below the line were highly educated and very well trained; the majority were graduates of the prestigious VGIK (All-Russian State University of Cinematography). Established in 1919, this was the first higher education institution for film-makers in the world. Courses ran for five years and were taught by established film directors and specialists in literature and script writing. However, practical work with established professionals in the studio, where graduates worked as assistants, was also important.

In spite of their political exposure and apparent vulnerability, directors were deeply embedded in social and political networks that even extended beyond film-making. They were positioned within the cultural elite and were important in the Soviet occupational hierarchy; their career was a most desirable and prestigious one. They were paid by the state and their salaries were high by Soviet standards. However, in the absence of a market, money did not play the main role in creating material and social stratification. It was the system of privileges that was most important: access to better departmental residencies in central city locations, to the departmental health service, to cars with a driver and to restaurants and shops containing goods that were not available in the stores accessible to the general public. Other Mosfilm workers enjoyed some profession-related privileges as well. For example, the staff at Mosfilm often gathered for the screenings of Western films not approved for public exhibition. Another great privilege was the possibility of foreign travel, closed to the majority of Soviet citizens at that time. Travelling abroad (mainly to attend international film festivals) allowed Soviet film-makers to build up networks of foreign colleagues who could provide support and exert political pressure if necessary. The Soviet creative and intellectual elite, to which film directors belonged, was exposed both to the Soviet state and to international observers: more vulnerable and more protected at the same time.

According to Shlapentokh and Shlapentokh (1993: 149), the majority of film directors were 'dissident in thought but conformist in behaviour'. Therefore creativity was directed not only towards the delivery of an idea but also towards avoiding ideological obstacles. In the struggle against bureaucracy, various things would work: the occasional support of influential people in the industry, interest from foreign distributors, a CV that listed foreign awards. Directors were also able to activate their networks of colleagues, friends and like-minded people for support and to engage in direct lobbying over the heads of the chiefs of the studio and *Goskino* to influential members of the government and the Communist Party (Johnson and Petrie 1994: 13). Personal connections were extremely important, especially connections with those in the bureaucracy and party apparatus and their wives and other family members. For example, in 1983 one director, after his movie had been shelved, managed to invite the daughter of Yuri Andropov, first secretary of the Central Committee of the Communist Party. She worked as an editor for the magazine *Muzicalnaya Zhizn* (*Music's Life*) so, when the news of this event spread, it was enough to get the movie distributed through the regular channels.

The positive side of operating outside market relations was that the majority of Soviet directors were more concerned with the artistic rather than the economic success of their product. The absence of economic concerns and the relative creative freedom led to the creation of a large number of philosophical and poetical films – peculiarly Soviet manifestations of 'auteur' cinema. However, as with 'art house' movies in the West, these films had limited audiences. Their cultural value was sometimes underestimated by the general public, and they were rarely profitable. At the other end of the spectrum were the movies that were intended primarily as entertainment, such as the 'Easterns' – the Soviet equivalent of Hollywood Westerns – which played to the tastes of the general public, generated impressive box-office returns and had a more conformist ideological outlook (Dzieciolowski 2006).

## Two examples of creative units in the Soviet Union

### The Experimental Creative Studio (ECS)

The ECS was established in 1964 and was very different from the other creative units operating at that time. The main guiding forces behind it were Vladimir Pozner and Grigori Chukhrai. The biography of Pozner is contradictory and emblematic of his time. Pozner emigrated from Russia to France in 1922, later moving to the United States where he worked for MGM-International. During the post-war Red Scare, he was dismissed as a Soviet spy and was subsequently invited by the Soviet government to assist in the rebuilding of the East German film industry. In 1952, he returned to the USSR, where, despite all of his experience, he found employment as a low-level technician at Mosfilm. In the early 1960s, he was responsible for the organization of film festivals in Moscow. Pozner wanted to create a studio which would work on the kind of economic principles he knew well from the American film industry (Medvedev 1998; Batashov 1999a). Chukhrai was a representative of a new wave of directors producing films during the Khrushchev thaw. He was best known for the film *Ballada o Soldate* (*Ballad of a Soldier*, 1959) which, made without the usual element of Soviet propaganda, received great acclaim both at home and abroad.

The ECS came into existence thanks to the liberal economic reforms introduced by Alexei Kosygin, the First Deputy Chairman of the Council of Ministers, who served both Khrushchev and Brezhnev. The ECS was allowed more creative independence than other units: it could choose its script, select the director and the crew, and choose deadlines for production without negotiation with *Goskino*. The story of the appointment of the director for the film *Beloye Solntse Pustyni* (*White Sun of the Desert*, 1969) was well known in industry circles. The first version of the script had been a failure and none of the directors at Mosfilm (including Tarkovsky) wanted to develop it. Chukhrai took a risk and found Vladimir Motyl, a director who had been banned from film-making for making movies that were viewed by government officials as ideologically unsound. Thanks to the status of the ECS, the authorities failed to notice this appointment. The script was rewritten and the film was shot. The fact that the everyday activities of the ECS were relatively free from surveillance compared to other creative units operating in the Soviet film industry made it unique.

What really set the ECS apart, however, was its relative economic independence. The relationship between the ECS and exhibitors was direct, without the administration acting as an intermediary. Moreover, employees of the ECS, like their counterparts in the West, were on contracts rather than salaries. Their remuneration was directly related to box-office returns and so depended on the commercial success of the movie (Batashov 1999b; Nuzov 2000). Unlike many other parts of the Soviet film industry, the ECS was profitable and the workers it employed received much higher fees than those working on other units. However, its success constituted a challenge to the existing system, which tended to level individual contributions and talent and, with the end of the Khrushchev thaw, the Soviet bureaucracy moved swiftly to curtail its economic and creative independence. In 1968, *Goskino* placed the ECS under the jurisdiction of Mosfilm, where it was informally called 'Chukhrai's studio'. In 1976, it was finally closed, once again for ideological reasons. The government decided that the independence of the unit 'provoked the creation of spectacles rather than films devoted to historical, revolutionary and contemporary issues'. Its legacy was apparent in 1978, however, when the Council of Ministers introduced fixed payments for movies in certain categories based on the profitability of the film and established a system for funding studios that provided additional fees for above-the-line workers.

For all of that, though, it is easy to overstate the creative and economic independence of the ECS. Like every other creative unit, it had to use studio facilities for its work. Even more significantly, it had to submit films to *Goskino*, which still had the final word on whether they would be distributed or shelved. Indeed, the most famous ECS production, *Beloye Solntse Pustyni* (*White Sun of the Desert*, 1969), was not approved by *Goskino* straight away and was shelved for some time. In spite of its apparent freedom to choose the content of its films, several scripts were 'sent down' to it from *Goskino*, following the 'normal' bureaucratic formula. *Goskino*, moreover, continued to exercise its customary control over the ECS's international sales, and the considerable income that these sales generated did not reach the members of the ECS, even in part.

Just as significantly, the ECS's productions were popular but rather conformist in their ideological outlook, and the ECS itself was very much a part of the system. The economic reforms that the ECS pioneered were not of a radical nature and were only possible as an experiment within this single unit. The ECS in its operations relied completely on the unchanged existing production and exhibition systems with only one financier providing both credit and guarantees – namely the state (Arkus 2002: 12). It was also the state – or, more precisely, a particular ideological fraction of the state – that introduced the reforms that made the ECS possible, looking for ways to alter and revive the socialist economy without making it capitalistic. Therefore, the ECS, like other creative units, was a politically, economically and socially dependant client of the Party state. The fate of *Beloye Solntse Pustyni* (*White Sun of the Desert*, 1969) after it was shelved by *Goskino* illustrates just how dependent upon official patronage the ECS was. One day in 1969, Leonid Brezhnev ordered a movie to watch at his country villa and the clerk of the *Goskino* film archive, entirely at his own risk, sent him this particular movie. Brezhnev liked it and, as a consequence, the film was given its theatrical release the following year (IC 2010).

## Andrei Tarkovsky: the film-maker as 'auteur'

Andrei Tarkovsky was the foremost example of a director working in the 'auteur' tradition in Soviet cinema, and his films sit at the opposite end of the scale to the commercially oriented 'Easterns'. By birth and education, he belonged to the cultural elite. His parents were members of the Soviet intelligentsia. He himself was a product of the golden era of Soviet arts education, having received rigorous training at the VGIK where he was heavily influenced by both Grigori Chukhrai and Aleksandr Romm. The Khrushchev thaw and the reduced censorship of foreign films allowed Tarkovsky to familiarize himself with Italian Neorealism, the French New Wave and the work of directors such as Kurosawa, Buñuel, Bergman, Bresson, Mizoguchi and Wajda. From these works, Tarkovsky absorbed the idea that the freedom to function as an 'auteur' was a necessary condition for creativity. After graduation (1960) he was invited to work at Mosfilm, where from the very beginning he was a notable director. His first film at the studio, *Ivanovo Detstvo* (*My Name Is Ivan*), was produced in 1962 at the behest of senior bureaucrats within the Soviet film industry. The film received the Golden Lion at the Venice Film Festival. Tarkovsky started to work on a series of projects supported by his colleagues in the creative unit.

Tarkovsky's subsequent career, however, was not that smooth. By some accounts, he was a martyred artist who put up with great adversity in order to maintain his artistic integrity. He became notorious for his disagreements with senior figures in Mosfilm and *Goskino*. For example, he spent five years crafting the film *Andrei Rublev* (1966) and refused to compromise his vision and make the changes suggested by the authorities. As a result of his stubbornness, the censors cut the budget and delayed the film's release. When it was finally released, it was on a small, unnoticed scale. In 1984, after defecting to Italy, Tarkovsky described the ideological and financial pressures under which he worked in the USSR in an interview with Radio Freedom:

> It was very difficult to work in the sense that I made just a few movies, only six ... That is too few and unsatisfactory for me. I spent a huge amount of time trying to convince the leaders, governing bodies of the importance of making the films that I was proposing. Then it took a lot of time for the finished film to be accepted. Then there were always grievances against my films: there were attempts to change some wording, the length, and some scenes. Time was spent trying to organise the relationship with Goskino so as to save the movie. *Rublev*, for instance, was shelved for five and a half years after its acceptance by Goskino. And during all that time I did nothing, I didn't work, because it was presumed that if I made an 'ideologically unseasoned' picture, then I would have no further right to work until that conflict was settled ... I continuously submitted proposals, ideas to the Goskino, in order to start a new film, but they were always refused ... It was difficult, I had a big family. (Corti 1984)

Another of Tarkovsky's films, *Zerkalo* (*Mirror*, 1975), was also badly received by the authorities due to its 'content and its perceived elitist nature'. It was nicknamed 'a masterpiece of the third category', which reflected its evaluation by Tarkovsky's colleagues, on the one hand, and by *Goskino*, on the other. Tarkovsky later complained,

> I am not satisfied with the organisation of distribution and exhibition (only 73 copies were produced). The film could have attracted more viewers than it was allowed. 'Mirror' was shown only in three cinemas in Moscow and only during two months. People were queuing for a long time to buy a ticket even in advance for tomorrow. Despite all of that the film was quickly taken off from the cinemas. (Korkala 1981)

Both *Andrei Rublev* and *Zerkalo* contained controversial material relating to Russian history and reflected on the nature of and relationship between power and creativity. But for all their ideological failings, they were, at least, given a cinematic release. Many of Tarkovsky's other projects did not make it to the screen at all. However, Tarkovsky's position was ambiguous: whilst some commentators saw him only as a 'martyred artist', others categorized him as 'an allowed dissident', who had the privilege of rebelliousness, or even as a '*Goskino* darling' (Johnson and Petrie 1994: 13). In spite of all his troubles with the authorities, Tarkovsky was still given permission to make many more films than would have been commercially viable in the West. He was also able to present his films at international festivals and make co-productions with colleagues abroad.

These varied evaluations of the extent of Tarkovsky's creative freedoms reflect the contradictions of Soviet party-state clientelism. Tarkovsky and his creative unit operated in conditions of severe economic dependency on the authorities. Reflecting on his relationship with the state, Tarkovsky argued,

> If I was a writer, I could return to Moscow to work ... If I was an artist, too, I could, somehow [manage] ... But because I am a film director and each second of my cinematographic time requires a lot of money, I cannot work independently. I depend in my work on money, on the state, on Goskino. (Corti 1984)

This dependency curtailed his and his unit's financial awareness but at the same time allowed them to concentrate on the creative side of film-making. Later on in his career when working abroad, Tarkovsky found how limited were the financial resources available in the West for the kind of films he produced. In the context of a market economy, ideological censorship was replaced by 'economic censorship' (Johnson and Petrie 1994). In an interview for the Swedish press, Tarkovsky said,

> It is difficult to make films everywhere, but the difficulties are different. The biggest problem here in the West is the shortage of money ... Here money plays the role of the autocrat. At home [in Russia] I never thought of how much everything costs. (Bachmann 1984)

Tarkovsky was firmly embedded in the patron-client system and started to receive the privileges of the distinguished director as soon as he had completed his first movie. He had a team of colleagues working under his lead to help him realize his creative plans. He was regularly offered work from 'the top', some of which he refused because of his creative interests. He had chosen from the very beginning to work on his own ideas and had his own plan for making films. His role in the game was to address the issue of ideological conformity and to maintain a position of respectful subordination in relation to the patron-state. That became a problem with *Rublev* and *Zerkalo*. Tarkovsky did not consider himself a dissident, though he knew and was in touch with members of the dissident community such as Aleksandr Solzhenitsyn and Sergei Paradjanov. In early interviews, he described himself as 'a Marxist' (Gibu 1967). Later on, he emphasized that in his movies he had never tried to criticize Soviet power and that it was not his task as an artist to do so (Corti 1984). In his diary on 1 September 1977 he wrote,

> Isn't the *Zerkalo* a patriotic and highly moral film? Is it inhumane or, perish the thought, anti-Soviet? I am tired of suspicions, sidelong glances, insults behind my back, inspired by kino-bosses. I demand the rehabilitation of my title of the Soviet film director. (Tarkovsky 1994: 140; 2008)

During the early stages of Tarkovsky's career the pressures from *Goskino* were not that severe. The discussions of his movies at Mosfilm and *Goskino* produced mild criticism mainly of a professional nature (see Fomin and Kosinova 2011). Opinions within Mosfilm's creative committee were divided: some members valued his films highly whilst others, especially those from the *nomenklatura*, simply could not understand them. The situation changed from film to film as the ideological factions competing for ascendancy at the top sent out different messages. The decision-making process was clearly influenced by the Soviet system of patronage and clientelism. The opinions of people who had little to do with art, creativity and film-making were sometimes crucial for the release of a film. As a note that Tarkovsky made in his diary on 31 March 1972 reveals, this did not always work to his disadvantage:

> Solaris [1972] was accepted without a single correction. Nobody can believe it. They say that our film was the only one for which the documentation of acceptance was signed personally by Romanov. It looks like someone has scared him very much. I heard that Sizov demonstrated the picture to the unknown three, who lead our science and technology ... And they have too much weight to be ignored. So, miracles can happen. (Tarkovsky 1994: 55; 2008)

As Tarkovsky's career progressed, his relationship with Goskino and the studio deteriorated. The production history of Zerkalo demonstrates how difficult it was for Tarkovsky to negotiate the system of patronage and clientelism that underpinned the Soviet film industry. As Fomin and Kosinova (2011) explain,

> A meeting took place at the directorate of Mosfilm with representatives from Goskino to discuss the corrected version of Zerkalo. Unexpectedly the director of Mosfilm at that time, Sizov, changed his previously benevolent attitude to the film. It may be that this was because Tarkovsky without permission from the studio had shown a version of the movie to the [foreign official] responsible for the selection of films for the Cannes festival. However, the deeper reason for this change was different – something had happened in the 'empyrean office' [Goskino] and it was Sizov's turn to be in disfavour for allowing the film to materialize in such a form.

Tarkovsky was not completely defenceless, however. He could and did approach Mosfilm and Goskino officials as a part of his director's responsibilities. He also felt confident to approach high-level political organizations and leaders to lobby for his films. He had a wide network of friends and supporters among the creative elite – writers, poets, film-makers, composers and actors, some of whom were well positioned in the hierarchy. He had acquaintances at the level of the Party-state nomenklatura as well – for example, Georgiy Kunitsyn, who worked under Pyotr Demichev, chief of ideology in the Central Party Committee, and was instrumental in obtaining permission for the release of Andrei Rublev; and Nikolay Shishlin, who worked in the cultural section of the Central Party Committee with responsibility for socialist countries. In moments of crisis, he activated his networks by organizing private viewings for those who could influence the acceptance of the film (Tarkovsky 2008). On occasion, he even used direct appeal to the highest Communist Party forums to get the 'green light' for his movies:

> After Yermash became the director of Goskino [in 1972] it became even more difficult to make films. The last two pictures Mirror and Stalker, I got permission to make them not from Goskino but it came after my petition to the Presidium of the XXIV and XXV forums of the Communist Party and this is nonsense, laughable, it made me ferocious. (Corti 1984)

From early on in his career, Tarkovsky enjoyed the privilege of attending international film festivals. He privatized and transformed this privilege into his own social capital, building and maintaining a strong international reputation and using it to enhance his position of relative power. He was able to use his network of foreign colleagues and friends as a defence against the system.

Tarkovsky's continued rebelliousness eventually led to the closing of the financial gate, which meant the withdrawal of fees paid for movie production. Tarkovsky's work and lifestyle suffered considerably. As he subsequently explained to an Italian interviewer,

> I expected some additional money as I almost always participated in script writing as well. But I never received any additional money. So, I was damaged, not only morally but materially as well. And, by the way, Goskino always had been selling my pictures to the West, and not cheaply. (Corti 1984)

Goskino also had non-material weapons in its armoury. Tarkovsky was well known and respected abroad, but kept under close surveillance in the USSR. Information about expressions of interest in his work from abroad were withheld from him, and his applications for visas and funding for foreign travel were rejected (Corti 1984). On 30 July 1976, Tarkovsky made the following entry in his diary:

> I'm going to a meeting now, at 9.30, with Sizov and Yermash, about Italy. They are going to ask me to refuse ... I was at Goskino. [I was told that if this producer] wants me to direct a film in Italy, he must first fulfil the necessary formalities with Goskino. And that's it. And if I insisted I'd be acting against 'the interests of the country' ... And they've got me there. (Tarkovsky 1994: 126; 2008)

In 1982, tired of the restrictions that the system of production in the Soviet film industry placed upon him, he moved to Italy to film Nostalgia, a project that was originally conceived as a Soviet-Italian co-production. He never returned to the USSR.

## Conclusions

Despite their apparent differences, the experiences of Andrei Tarkovsky and of his counterparts in the ECS both reveal a great deal about the system of patronage and clientelism that characterized Soviet film-making and demonstrate the degree to which workers in creative units depended – economically, socially and politically – on the Party state and its primary agents, Goskino and the studios. Incentives in the form of monetary 'awards' and, even more importantly, 'favours of access' to scarce resources, meaningful connections and luxury goods were central to the operation of the industry. Both the ECS and the creative unit headed by Tarkovsky came into existence as a consequence of the Khrushchev thaw, and both found their economic and creative freedom sharply circumscribed during the Brezhnev era when support for their activities from the nomenklatura was withdrawn. Personal networks, which overlapped with the professional hierarchy, were also central to the operation of the system.

Goskino and the studios sought to appoint unit heads they could rely on both artistically and ideologically, whilst directors set out to cultivate relationships with officials they could trust in their search for favours. At all times, though, film-makers were required to demonstrate their obedience to their patrons in the state apparatus. When the film-makers associated with the ECS started to gain an international reputation and to earn much more than others in the industry, the state moved quickly to limit their independence. When Tarkovsky started to establish himself in the international film community using the resources provided to him by the patron-state and to ignore its advice and ideological directives, he soon found himself ostracized. In neither case was there the option of a creative existence outside the patron-client pyramid.

## Bibliography

Afanasiev, M. N. (1997), *Klientelism I Rossiskaia Gosudarstvennost*, Moscow: Center of Constitutional Studies.

Arkus, L. (ed.) (2002), *Kino i Kinotext: 1986–1988. The Latest History of National Film, 1986–2000*, Sankt-Peterburg: Seance.

Arkus, L. (2010), 'The History of the State Governance of the Cinematograph in the USSR', *Encyclopaedia of the National Cinematograph*, http://russiancinema.ru/template.php?dept_id=15&e_dept_id=6&text_element_id=55 [accessed 15 July 2011].

Bachmann, G. (1984), 'About the Nature of Nostalgia: Interview with Andrei Tarkovsky', in J. Gianvito (ed.) (2006), *Andrei Tarkovsky: Interviews*, Jackson, MS: University Press of Mississippi, http://tarkovskiy.su/texty/Tarkovskiy/Bachmann.html [accessed 15 June 2011].

Batashov, A. (1999a), 'Born on the 1st of April: Vladimir Pozner: I Shall Tell You about My Father', *Ogonyok (Light)*, 29 March, http://www.whoiswho.ru/old_site/russian/Password/papers/15r/pozdner/stf2.htm [accessed 16 August 2011].

Batashov, A. (1999b), 'I Have Learnt the Nickname of My Father – Kallistrat', *Ogonyok (Light)*, 5 April, http://www.whoiswho.ru/old_site/russian/Password/papers/15r/pozdner/stf2.htm [accessed 16 August 2011].

Bugelsky, Y. and Shipilov, N. (1981), 'Andrei Tarkovsky: We Make Films', *Kino*, Vilnus 10, http://tarkovskiy.su/texty/Tarkovskiy/baum.html [accessed 10 August 2011].

Butler, B. and Purchase, S. (2004), 'Personal Networking in Russian Post-Soviet Life', *Research and Practice in Human Resource Management*, 12 (1): 34–60.

Butovsky, Y., Lisina, S., Listov, V., Matizen, V. and Shkalikov, M. (2004), 'History of the State Governance of the Cinematography in the USSR', in L. Arkus (ed.), *The Contemporary History of National Cinematograph: 1986–2000. Film and Context. V.VI*, Sankt-Peterburg: Seance, http://russiancinema.ru/template.php?dept_id=15&e_dept_id=6&text_element_id=55 [accessed 25 August 2011].

Corti, M. (1984), 'Interview with Andrei Tarkovsky and His Wife Larisa. Milan, Italy, Radio Liberty, 13/14 July 1984', http://www.mario-corti.com/press/#984a [accessed 15 June 2011].

Dondureyi, D. and Venger, N. (2006), *Russian Film Industry: 2001–2006*. Moscow, CTC Media. Open Russian Film Festival 'Kinotavr'.

Dzieciolowski, Z. (2006), 'Kinoeye: Russia's Reviving Film Industry', http://www.opendemocracy.net/globalization-Film/russian_film_3726.jsp [accessed 15 June 2011].

Fomin, V. and Kosinova, M. (2011), 'Masterpiece of the Second Category: Film *Mirror* by A. Tarkovsky', http://tarkovskiy.su/texty/vospominania/Fomin01.html [accessed 13 May 2011].

Gibu, N. (1967), 'Life Is Produced from Disharmony', Interview with Andrei Tarkovsky, http://tarkovskiy.su/texty/Tarkovskiy/Giby1967.html [accessed 13 May 2011].

Goriunova, G. N. and Chernov, V. G. (1975), *Ekonomika Kinematografii*, Moscow: Iskusstvo.

IC (2010), 'White Sun of the Desert (Beloye Solntse Pustini)', http://rufact.org/wiki [accessed May 15 2011].

Iordanova, D. (2003), Cinema of the Other Europe: The Industry and Artistry of East Central Europe, London: Wallflower Press.

Johnson, V. T. and Petrie, G. (1994), The Films of Andrei Tarkovsky: A Visual Fugue, Bloomington, IN: Indiana University Press.

Jowitt, K. (1983), 'Soviet Neotraditionalism: The Political Corruption of a Leninist Regime', Soviet Studies, 35 (3): 275–97.

Kessel, D. and Young, P. (1967), 'USSR's Super Movie Studio', Life, 62 (14): 64–81.

Konoplev, B. N. (1975), Osnovy fil'moproizvodstva, Moscow: Iskusstvo.

Korkala, V. (1981), 'Andrei Tarkovsky: Crucial Time', http://tarkovskiy.su/texty/Tarkovskiy/Sweden.html [accessed 11 July 2011].

Lawton, A. M. (1992), Kinoglasnost: Soviet Cinema in Our Time, Cambridge: Cambridge University Press.

Ledeneva, A. (1998), Russia's Economy of Favours: Blat, Networking and Informal Exchange, Cambridge: Cambridge University Press.

Lomnitz, L. A. (1988), 'Informal Exchange Networks in Formal Systems: A Theoretical Model', American Anthropologist, 90 (1): 42–55.

Marshall, H. V. (1976), 'Andrei Tarkovsky's The Mirror', Sight and Sound, 45 (2): 92–5.

Medvedev, F. (1998), 'Vladimir Pozner. Vicont de Monte Cristo. The Queer Fate of the Former Soviet Propagandist', Who Is Who, 5, http://www.whoiswho.ru/old_site/russian/Password/papers/15r/pozdner/stf2.htm [accessed 15 July 2011].

Michailova, S. and Worm, V. (2003), 'Personal Networking in Russia and China: Blat and Guanxi', European Management Journal, 21 (4): 509–19.

Nekrich, A. M. (1995), 'Renounce the Fear', Neva, 6: 139–60.

Nuzov, V. (2000), Interview with Vladimir Motyl, http://www.peoples.ru/art/cinema/producer/motyl/interview.html [accessed 22 August 2011].

Savitskaya, N. and Lepeshkova, S. (2003), 'Nuclear Explosion in "The Diamond Arm"', Independent Newspaper, http://www.ng.ru/saturday/2003-01-31/13_gayday.html [accessed 3 July 2011].

Shkolnik, L. (2007), 'Intellectual Film of Sergey Azenshtein', Jewish Magazine, http://jjew.ru/index.php?cnt=5419 [accessed 21 August 2010].

Shlapentokh, V. and Shlapentokh, D. (1993), Soviet Cinematography, 1918–1991: Ideological Conflict and Social Reality, New York: Walter de Cruyter.

Suvorov, A. (1999), Short Review of the Censorship Policy of the Soviet State, http://www.bulletin.memo.ru/b20/19.htm [accessed 3 July 2011].

Tarkovsky, A. (1994), Time within Time: The Diaries 1970–1986, London and Boston: Faber and Faber.

Tarkovsky, A. (2008), 'Martyrolog'. Diaries. [International Institute named after Andrei Tarkovsky, Tibergraph, Italy.] Parts of the text were retrieved from http://tarkovskiy.su/texty/martirolog/martirolog.html; http://tarkovskiy.su/texty/martirolog/martirolog-solaris.html; http://people.ucalgary.ca/~tstronds/nostalghia.com/TheDiaries/tempo.html.

Taylor, R. (1979), The Politics of the Soviet Cinema, Cambridge: Cambridge University Press.

Vasilyeva, I. (2004), History of the State Governance of the Cinematography in the USSR, Sankt-Peterburg: Seance, http://www.russiancinema.ru/template.php?dept_id=3&e_dept_id=5&e_chr_id=282&e_chrdept_id=2&chr_year=1990 [accessed 16 July 2011].

Voslensky, M. (1991), Nomenklatura. The Ruling Class in the Soviet Union, Moscow: MP 'October'.

Walder, A. G. (1984), Communist Neo-Traditionalism: Work and Authority in Chinese Industry, Berkeley, CA: University of California Press.

Zhirkov, G. V. (2001), Censorship and Socialist Ideals, Moscow: Aspect Press.

# Making films in Scandinavia

## Work and production infrastructure in the contemporary regional sector

OLOF HEDLING

This article is concerned with the prospects for work and employment and the conditions of such work in an environment that is in some ways representative of recent European film production. However, since the circumstances discussed are quite specific to a situation which has developed in a single European country, Sweden, during the past decade and a half or so, a bit of explanatory background information is needed. An examination of the context in which regional production centres in Sweden have developed and a description of the infrastructures that underpin them will provide useful insights into some of the forces propelling European film at present.

The example of regional film production outlined below is characteristic of a specific national environment. However, this does not mean that there are no implications and conclusions that are significant or hold true in other national contexts or at a transnational level. As of 2004, in the more than thirty countries linked to the Council of Europe's European Audiovisual Observatory, there were 118 bodies – besides the national ones – that were based in a community, in a region or on the local level and that provided forms of funding, support and/or co-production services for film and television production (Lange and Westcott 2004: 46). According to one study conducted in 2005, there are at least 250 'jurisdictions' worldwide that vie for 'runaways' and, in short, to be hubs of film production (Miller et al. 2005: 138). Since these figures were compiled, additional candidates have in all probability joined the list.[1]

Furthermore, a growing number of countries such as Germany, Iceland, the United Kingdom, the Czech Republic and Hungary are offering tax incentives – and not necessarily just to foreign productions – to film companies. More often than not, this practice means that particular geographical sites, regional centres in a way, are established as production hubs. Consequently, regional film production in different forms is a growing enterprise. Moreover, it is both a global phenomenon and one that is particularly important on the European continent. Among the factors at stake are local and regional investment, regional rejuvenation, promoting national and regional production, the strengthening of service infrastructures, the creation of spin-off jobs and more generally, putting a specific place on the map so that people from outside come to spend money in the community.

## Wallander

In January 2010 it was widely reported in Swedish news media that the small Swedish town of Ystad (population 17,000) had scored a financial coup through its chance connection with the character of Kurt Wallander (Olofson 2010). Wallander, a fictional veteran police investigator in Ystad, is the central character in some ten crime novels by Swedish author Henning Mankell, published between 1991 and 2009. Somewhat unexpectedly, these books became national and international bestsellers, with almost 40 million printed copies globally as of the summer of 2008 (Høier 2008).

Since 2004, the Wallander brand has emerged as the focal point of the film and television industry in Ystad. To date, Ystad has turned out some thirty-two Wallander films at a combined cost of approximately €65 million. It has also produced quite a number of non-Wallander-related products. In total, since the beginning of 2000 and up to the end of 2009, thirty-seven theatrical features, sixteen theatrically shown documentaries, seven TV series, 122 shorts and 155 documentaries of various length have been made with support from the regional film fund (Film i Skåne 2010: 3). At the centre of this enterprise are the thirty-two Wallander films, four of which have had a theatrical release, the rest being distributed on DVD and all being broadcast in a number of territories. Evidently this means that Ystad has become a site for more or less continuous film work as well as a place with which both domestic and foreign film workers have become evermore familiar.

The Wallander films have all been set and photographed in and around the town. Studio work has also largely been located here, at the three currently operating sound stages.[2] The films have been produced in blocks, with production schedules consisting of approximately twenty to thirty days per film and with work on at least two instalments being done simultaneously. A total of thirteen Swedish-language films were made in one go during 2004 and 2005, and an additional thirteen were made during 2008 and 2009. A further six English-language films, produced in blocks of three, were made in 2008 and 2009.

A few of these titles have received theatrical release in Sweden. However, the main distribution outlet, domestically and internationally (chiefly meaning Scandinavia and elsewhere in Europe), has been TV. This is a consequence of the fact that most of the funding for the Swedish-language films has come from Scandinavian national broadcasters and film companies and, perhaps more importantly, German TV, in the form of broadcasters and large television corporations such as ARD (Arbeitsgemeinschaft der öffentlich-rechtlichen Rundfunkanstalten der Bundesrepublik Deutschland) and ARD/Degeto Film GmbH. The set-up behind the Anglophone films is similar but with the BBC providing most of the funding to the British production company Left Bank Pictures.

# Proceeds from local and regional film production

The financial coup referred to in the news items mentioned earlier was, of course, the enhanced revenues, general economic activity and the supposed employment opportunities the Wallander boom generated in both Ystad itself as well as in the southern Swedish region of Skåne (Scania) where the town is located. These revenues stem from two main sources: tourism and film and television production.

Almost as soon as the first novels were published and Wallander became a household name, literary tourists began arriving in the town (Sjöholm 2008: 206). Since film production began in 2004, however, the tourist trade has boomed due to the sudden and broad audio-visual exposure of Ystad and the region of Skåne. In short, the diminutive Scanian town has become a site for 'movie-induced' or 'film-induced' tourism, a global phenomenon fuelled by 'the growth of the entertainment industry and the increase in international travel' (Hudson and Richie 2006: 387). More specifically, the particular brand of tourism represented by Ystad can be termed 'on-location film-induced tourism' (Beeton 2005: 185). Increasing numbers of visitors, chiefly from Sweden but also from abroad (initially mainly Denmark and Germany, but later on the United Kingdom), have meant that spending in Ystad on a wide range of goods and services, from food and fuel to restaurants and accommodation, has risen significantly. Film and television production has also benefited the businesses that provide these goods and services as well as generating a demand for film workers of various kinds, some of whom can be supplied locally. Taken together, these developments have raised hope for the long-term economic regeneration of the area. Ystad and the surrounding region have become a place where the expansion of different forms of both qualified and unqualified service production, as well as creative production, all connected to film, appears to be encouraged.

According to a consultant working for a public and media relations company, interviewed and repeatedly cited in the aforementioned news items, the 'marketing value' of the films could be expected to run to several hundred million euros, with income to be divided between the town of Ystad itself and the surrounding region of Skåne. It has also been reported that revenues from tourism in Ystad grew from €45 million a year before the filming started to some €70 million in 2009, representing an annual growth rate of just over 10 per cent a year. Hence, the local tourism industry was undisputedly established as an engine of economic growth.

A further confirmation of these developments may have been the recurring news items themselves. Rather than the result of any new information suddenly being made available, it appears that the series of stories was the result of a local journalist having picked up an article published in *Newsweek* magazine and thus becoming aware of Ystad and of Wallander's mounting international renown. Having then investigated the phenomenon, the local reporter presented his findings in a large piece which was deemed noteworthy enough to be dispensed nationally by the largest national news agency (Unsigned 2010).

The *Newsweek* piece reported that 'vacationers are drawn to the places they first get to know through films' (Werth 2009). It grouped Ystad together with other prominent sites, such as London (*Notting Hill*, 1999), New Zealand (*The Lord of the Rings*, 2001–3) and Salzburg (*The Sound of Music*, 1965), that had gained considerable recognition since appearing as settings for particularly well-liked movies. Ystad was described in the following terms:

> The sleepy Swedish town of Ystad has been happily inundated with dev-otees of the wildly popular Wallander series of crime novels, which have been made into films. The town of 17,000 even opened a film museum that runs regular walking tours of the murder scenes investigated by one of Sweden's best-loved detectives.

Although the article identified film tourism rather than the local film industry as the new local trade, it put Ystad on the international map and linked it with a list of famous luminaries so that its broad connection to film could no longer be denied on the national level. A development that had begun more than a decade earlier had finally brought its rewards.

## The background and the set-up

For most of the twentieth century, media production in Sweden was concentrated in Stockholm. In the case of the film and television industry, this changed in the late 1990s as production, and especially feature film production, migrated to a number of newly founded regional production centres in different parts of the country (Hedling 2008: 8–17, 2010a: 263–90, 2010b: 334–45, 2010c: 70–8). The ensuing change was profound. As a point of reference, according to data from the Swedish Film Institute (SFI), twenty-nine of the forty-five features made in 2005 (64.4 per cent of the annual output) were co-produced by one of the regional production centres and shot in their studios and/or on location in the area (SFI 2006: 48, 56, 58).

The process leading to the present situation started during the late 1980s when ideas about regional centres for film production first began to gain currency, both in Sweden and elsewhere in Europe (Lange and Westcott: 2004: 17). In the early stages of their development, the activities of Sweden's regional centres were directed toward children and adolescents. After Sweden joined the European Union (EU) in 1995, however, the situation changed. Acting entirely independently of each other, the two regions around Trollhättan and Luleå submitted applications to the EU's European Regional Development Fund (ERDF). In both cases, the goal was to stimulate professional film and media production as a way to revitalize a regional economy that was suffering the effects of post-industrial decline.

The two funding applications were approved in 1996. With the help of additional funding from the regional authorities as well as from a dutiful but somewhat unpre-pared SFI, film production in the areas around Trollhättan and Luleå took off and began to attract investment and production capital from other sources. Though the regional film network was nationally planned at the beginning, the later, full impact of it was not. The regional development mapped out here reflects the some-what diluted role of the traditional nation state in stimulating film and television production compared to what was taking place both at the supranational EU level and at the regional and local levels.

The funding system operates on the principle that the regional centre should function as a co-producer, financing between 5 per cent and 30 per cent of a particular project's cost. In return, the production has to be located in the area; the producer must have an office there; half of the employees on a given production must be locals; and more than 150 per cent of the region's investment should be spent in the vicinities by the production company. The rules are enforced through the use of a sometimes contested legal mechanism known as a 'territorialisation clause' (Lange and Westcott 2004: 82). This type of arrangement appears to be common elsewhere in Europe. Other regional funding bodies such as Filmstiftung Nordrhein-Westfalen in Germany and Filmfonds Wien in Austria (Bizern and Autissier 1999: 11) impose very similar conditions.

The application of territorialisation clauses by regional production centres in Sweden appears to have been quite firm at the beginning. Later on, however, enforcement appears to have become somewhat less strict. In effect, the regional production centres have started to act more like traditional film financiers, although with their own peculiar agendas. Film i Väst, for example, contributed as a co-producer to Lars von Trier's Cologne-shot *Antichrist* (2009) as well as to the Stockholm-based production of crime writer Stieg Larsson's globally successful *Millennium Trilogy* (2008–9), even though the main producers had other funds from their main regional partners. It seems this was done not as a result of a belief that the investment would generate revenues but rather because it was important that the organization be visible in connection with these kinds of prestigious projects. It is also symptomatic of a growing tendency towards funding co-productions taking place at the interregional level, a development that has fostered artistic, technical and creative exchange in Europe. Nevertheless, these centres have come to fulfil a crucial role on the margins of the industry, as suppliers of 'the last million' (Dahlström and Hermelin 2007: 114). By contributing modest amounts to production budgets, they are able to get producers from outside to spend money in the local economy.

In economic terms, one may perhaps compare the system to a sort of Keynesian interventionism applied at the local or regional level with film and media production functioning as an engine of economic growth and an important source of jobs. In 2004, not long after the centre at Ystad had commenced its activities in earnest, a regional politician expressed the hope that 500 jobs would be the outcome of the efforts of the regional authorities to stimulate regional film-making (Krona 2006: 88).

## Conditions for the development of film production in a small Swedish town

In some respects, Ystad was a special case. First, it was not added to the small group of locations where regional feature film production was supported by the SFI until 2000, a couple of years after the establishment of the centres at Trollhättan and Luleå. Thus, the town became part of a fundamental change in film production somewhat later than its national competitors. Second, because the town, or rather the region in which it is located, did not, as the other two had, receive support from the European structural funds for its film and television industry, it took years of local and regional mustering of financial strength before something resembling continuous production was possible. In terms of the funding it received from regional, national and supranational sources, Ystad simply did not compare with Trollhättan and Luleå.

However, the town had something else: the brand of Wallander was intimately connected to Ystad. Moreover, the owner of the rights to the brand, the author Henning Mankell, together with a Danish film producer, had set up a company, Yellow Bird, in 2003, the primary initial aim of which appears to have been the exploitation of the Wallander rights with regard to audio-visual media. Mankell, it seems, was also in favour of situating the production of film and television adaptations of Wallander in Ystad, a place he appears to have been both keen on privately – he lives or has lived there at times – and ready to promote. He played a vital role in securing funding for the beginning of the shoot of the first series of thirteen Wallander films in 2004, an occasion that marked the real emergence of Ystad as the third full-blown Swedish regional production centre for feature films.

Equally important was the systematic approach that local representatives took to increasing Ystad's attractiveness and competitiveness both as a tourist destination and as a site for film and television production. In the old garrison area of the town, where the present film studio is located, a visitor's centre, called Cineteket, was built early on in the development process. As well as describing and illustrating the general process of film-making, Cineteket offers visitors the chance to try their hands at common cinematic practices such as blue screen filming. The local authorities have also attempted to coordinate events around film-related activities. Since 2007, an annual gala show has been arranged, celebrating and presenting awards to extras of different categories who have worked on regionally produced films. The event takes place in autumn and has been labelled 'The Silver Fish Gala' (Silverfiskgalan). In October 2009, a local annual film festival, with the crime genre as its focal point, was inaugurated. Other infrastructure projects were also initiated with a view to supporting future activity in the region. Lund University, for example, received funding for research on regional film production as well as for starting master's programmes in film and media production and film music composition, the aim being to augment the future workforce. In another important initiative, the local council provided financial support for the development of housing specifically aimed at people working on various audio-visual projects.

Ystad's decision to use the fame it has achieved through its association with the character of Wallander – as well as the various attempts to reinforce its identity as a 'film town' – can, therefore, be seen as both successful and ambitious in many respects. The development has been important for place promotion, rebranding and as a catalyst for a partial restructuring of the town's economic life. The town can now be described as a new hub for film production. It has also successfully tapped into one important consequence of the audio-visual exposure, cultural tourism (OECD

2009). As of now, Ystad is almost certainly the only Swedish and Scandinavian town that has been able to make the fact that a series of books and films were set and shot there into a vital business.

## Conceptual maps

The phenomenon of using regional film centres to rejuvenate the identity of a particular region is one that can be explored from a variety of theoretical perspectives. By looking at Ystad's development in relation to the work of key scholars in the fields of urban and economic development – and especially that which deals with the complex cross-pollinations that characterize the production and consumption of popular culture – we can begin to place it in a global and comparative context.

The process behind the increasing number of visitors coming from abroad to Ystad, following in the footsteps of Wallander, may be described as simply film or literary tourism. If we bear in mind that these visitors have been motivated to travel to the town by a rather multifaceted and wayward chain of events, however, the picture starts to look more complicated. First there are the Swedish books, permeated by a strong local flavour and intriguing bits of detail, partly written in Africa, and gradually translated into more and more languages, German and English chief among them.[3] The books have given local and regional interests, the author among them, the idea to team up with national film and TV companies which, in turn, have collaborated with Scandinavian and German TV executives to supply the funds for films to be produced on location in Ystad. German investors, besides noting the books' success on the German charts, probably also consider the project's 'Swedishness' an attraction, well aware of the long-lasting fascination with all things Swedish and Scandinavian in Germany (Vonderau 2010: 148).

After the films have been shown, some fans of the books and the films will take the decision to travel to the town. They will either make arrangements on their own or perhaps be enticed by a website or a poster in a travel agency. Once they arrive in Ystad, visitors engage in a peculiar kind of cultural worship, exploring the city with the help of location maps, visiting the Cinetek and buying tickets for murder walks. When they get hungry, they can treat themselves to a special pastry named the Wallander sold by one of the local cafés.[4]

The emergence of Ystad as both a centre for film production and a tourist destination is an example of what Henry Jenkins, in an influential turn of phrase, has termed 'convergence culture' – that is, 'the flow of content across multiple media platforms, the cooperation between multiple media industries, and the migratory behaviour of media audiences who will go almost anywhere in search of the kinds of entertainment experiences they want' (Jenkins 2006: 2–3). What has happened in Ystad is the outcome of a complex negotiation between different national popular cultures; between different media platforms and products; between a Swedish writer and German, Swedish and Scandinavian corporate televisual interests; between migratory consumers of popular culture; and between books, films, websites, travel agents and even pastry shops. In the sense that Ystad has become a representative part of contemporary convergence culture, it may be concluded that recent efforts to restructure the local economy and, in a way, to assume a post-industrial identity have been enormously successful in some respects. To borrow another phrase from Jenkins, the southern Swedish town has become an entry point through which consumers can immerse themselves in the story world of Kurt Wallander.

As mentioned earlier, however, the decision to try and change the town's character was necessitated, at least in part, by regional and local economic factors that do not necessarily fit the convergence culture model. The Ystad phenomenon might be better described in terms of Ystad, the town, and Skåne, the region, adapting themselves to the demands of a contemporary 'experience economy', a process that Jeremy Rifkin, in his book *Global Access*, has argued is a defining feature of 'hypercapitalism':

> More and more cutting-edge commerce in the future will involve the marketing of a vast array of cultural experiences rather than just traditional industrial-based goods and services. Global travel and tourism, theme cities and parks, destination entertainment centers, wellness, fashion and cuisine, professional sports and games, gambling, music, film, television, the virtual worlds of cyberspace, and electronically mediated entertainment of every kind are fast becoming the center of a new hypercapitalism that trades in access to cultural experiences. (Rifkin 2000: 7)

In adapting itself to the needs of an 'experience economy' and placing itself in the landscape of 'hypercapitalism', moreover, Ystad is engaging in what is known as 'franchise capitalism', a concept described by Patrick Vonderau in the following terms (Vonderau's formulation is in turn inspired by Keane and Moran 2008: 155–69):

> Franchising is about licensing; it is based on an arrangement where the owner of a concept enters into a contract with an independent actor, or franchisee. The latter uses a specific model to sell goods or services under the former's trademark. Franchise capitalism, in turn, ostensibly is all about the recognition of sameness, as it globally reproduces and replicates Starbucks or Disney World as much as American Idol, Survivor, Big Brother or Dancing with the Stars. (Vonderau 2010: 143)

Ystad's efforts to tie key parts of the local economy to the Wallander brand appear in many ways typical of the strategy Vonderau outlines. The local agents could be said to play the role of a franchisee of sorts. That the tourist office, the 'local' film industry, the Cineteket and the film festival as well as various cafés and pastry shops increasingly connect their activities to the brand further indicates its quality as an attraction and its growing importance in marketing and selling Ystad as a place of visitors' longing and belonging or, in other words, as a place to please their demand for experiences. The brand is thus vital for the town's bid to be part of what Rifkin (2000: 13) refers to as 'the global cultural sphere', the area in which he predicts future economic power will be increasingly situated.

A third conceptual map to which Ystad – and, to some extent, the other Swedish regional film production sites – may be linked is that encompassed in urban studies theorist Richard Florida's twin notions of 'the creative class' and 'creative cities'. Although controversial and contested, Florida's ideas appear to have found a wide audience, not least among groups well outside of the borders of traditional academia.[5] Florida's central thesis is that 'place is the key economic and social organizing unit of our time' (Florida 2004: xix). He argues that the economic future and the best potential for urban regeneration belong to those places, regions and nations that are attractive to the creative class, a group that, in the United States and the 'advanced' European countries, consists of those roughly 30 per cent among the employed involved in 'science and engineering, architecture and design, education, arts, music and entertainment, whose economic function is to create new ideas, new technology and/or new creative content' (Florida 2004: xiv, 8). Prime examples of such sites in the United States are the San Francisco Bay Area and Austin, Texas, both of which are characterized by a high density of universities, research institutes and the like; tolerance and openness towards varying lifestyles, gays and immigrants; socio-economic and racial integration; and high scores on the aptly titled 'Bohemian Index'. Although Florida's (2004: 11) main focus is on large metropolitan areas in the United States, he also looks at smaller towns and communities that have attracted significant concentrations of the creative class, such as Boulder, Colorado, Gainesville, Florida and Huntsville, Alabama.

Another of Florida's concerns is whether the United States can maintain its lead in what he terms 'the new global competition for talent' (Florida 2005: 3). He argues that countries such as Sweden, Denmark, Japan, the Netherlands, New Zealand and Norway have begun to challenge the primacy of the United States in 'creative matters'. He uses the example of the flourishing film and effects industry that developed in Wellington, New Zealand during and after the production of Peter Jackson's three-part *The Lord of the Rings* (2001–3) to demonstrate how spaces far away from those historically associated with a particular industry have begun to attract the creative class globally.

Turning back to Ystad and Skåne, one may once again note how developments in the town and the region can be contextualized in terms of larger global trends, both real and perceived. Small as the town is, one can regard it as being almost on the barricades in terms of developing strategies to secure a future of economic growth. The decision to settle on film and television production and the town's location in a country scoring high on Florida's (2005: 275) Global Creativity Index suggest a promising future. In fact, Ystad fits the analytical model set out by Florida so closely that it appears almost as if the authorities are following a textbook approach to regional development, ticking off particular prerequisites and essential attractions along the way, as they attempt to carve out a path towards new economic pastures in a post-industrial society. Attracting film production, tempting film workers and others within the arts sector to relocate to the region, luring higher education to the town, setting up annual film festivals and supporting initiatives to stimulate tourism can all be seen as cognizant stratagems intended to transform Ystad into something resembling a creative city, thereby securing growth and an increased preparedness for what the future may bring.

## Some outcomes, some work

Ystad's recent tourist boom has attracted positive attention both in other regions of Sweden and at the national level. In 2009, the town was selected as the recipient of the annual High Award for Tourism by the Swedish Agency for Economic and Regional Growth. The 'Regional Turn' in Swedish film production has also been praised by critics and commentators, representatives of the business community and politicians representing areas where centres of regional production are located. A pride, unmistakably associated with the new local industry, could be detected early on in the speeches and statements of civic leaders, most of whom stressed the economic benefits of an improved image and expanding tourist industry (Johansson 2004).[6]

This positive outlook is still very much in evidence. The Film Policy Report of 2005, for example, predicted that film production would 'evolve into a dynamic new growth industry' (Roger 2005: 4). This may sound like nothing but a cliché, but it marked a decisive break with earlier Film Policy Reports and reflected an optimism regarding prospects for the film and television sector that had not existed for decades. In short, the regional set-up developed within the Swedish film and television industry during the past decade has had a very significant impact.

However, one factor that has rarely come into focus is how the development of regional hubs like Ystad has affected the people who work in film and television production (Dahlström and Hermelin 2007). Questions relating to their prospects for employment, earnings and standard of living have rarely been asked, and little or no effort has been made to elicit their views on these sites of regional production. In what follows, I would like to explore the implications of the 'Regional Turn' for film work.

Without question, the 'Regional Turn' has meant a boost to film production in Sweden. Additional funding has become available and production has expanded. Yet this expansion appears to have brought few economic benefits to film workers. In 2006–7, two Swedish social and economic geographers conducted a survey among film workers employed in the present regionalized set-up. Their respondents ranged from highly skilled A-functions to semi-skilled C-functions. The overall results were somewhat downbeat, rarely indicating an especially glamorous existence for those earning their living in the film and television industry. Only 25 per cent of the film workers in the survey received 75 per cent or more of their income from film work (Dahlström and Hermelin 2007: 120). Most of them worked as freelancers. It is noteworthy that in the three regional production centres, an average of more than 25 per cent were recipients of unemployment benefits (which are notoriously difficult for freelance workers in Sweden to obtain) during the year of observation. As a result, many longed for more opportunities to do film-related work. Given the problems that film workers experience in finding regular employment, it may be asked whether places like Ystad provide the best environment in which to develop their professional skills.

Most film workers had to display a high degree of functional and task flexibility, working in several capacities and at various levels of the industry hierarchy. Many also worked simultaneously outside the film sector to support themselves. One of the key findings of the study was that 'the project form of film production means that film work is temporary and that workers have limited terms of employment, frequently as freelancers'. It was also observed that the actual work was not rewarded by high levels of remuneration. This led the investigators to conclude that the film sector is 'a tight and difficult sector for regular incomes' (Dahlström and Hermelin 2007: 117).

A subsequent survey undertaken on behalf of the Swedish Arts Grants Committee supported Dahlström and Hermelin's conclusions whilst, at the same time, revealing additional details about what it was like to work in Sweden's regional production centres. It found, for example, that people working in film had to put in the most hours within the aggregated arts sector – on average some forty-nine hours per week – and confirmed that there was a trend towards freelancing rather than permanent employment. It also demonstrated that earnings remained low and that people working in film often relied on financial assistance from family members in order to get by (Flisbäck 2011: 13). What we can conclude from this is that not everyone involved in the new economy surrounding these sites has been able to reap the rewards that some theorists predicted would be the outcome of the era of 'hypercapitalism' and creative cities.

The term 'business cluster' is frequently heard and used in connection with the regional film centres. Hence, a regional politician might casually talk about 'the film cluster in Skåne', as if such a thing unquestionably existed. As early as 2004, however, another Swedish social and economic geographer, Per Assmo, expressed strong reservations regarding the use of the term in connection with Swedish regional film centres. Inspired by American scholar Michael Porter's work on business clusters, Assmo defined a cluster as a conglomerate or an accumulation of independent and competing companies and businesses whose collective behaviour generates a larger accumulated value than would have been the case if they had not been part of the informal collective that constitutes the cluster (Assmo 2004: 17). Assmo claimed that the centre at Trollhättan (Film i Väst), the largest of such entities in Scandinavia and already bigger and more comprehensive than the one at Ystad is presently, simply did not meet these criteria (Arpi 2004: 9). His argument was that the companies surrounding the centrally positioned, publicly funded Film i Väst simply did not qualify as independent businesses precisely because their respective fortunes were far too intertwined with that of Film i Väst. If the public funding was withdrawn, he predicted, almost all of these businesses would stop functioning almost overnight. To sum up, very few businesses have been set up that can act independently, be responsible employers, provide good regular income to their employees and be comparatively secure in terms of their worth and proficiencies without the support of a single, publicly funded agent.

Even though the regional film production set-up has now been in place for more than a decade, skilled film workers remain reluctant to actually relocate to Trollhättan, Luleå or Ystad. Producers, actors, directors, cinematographers and so on appear in the regional centres for location scouting, principal photography and certain parts of post-production but tend to leave immediately afterwards, preferring to live in Stockholm, the regions around other large cities such as Gothenburg and Malmö or even abroad. The same goes for many of the skilled professions less publicly profiled. According to Dahlström and Hermelin, 'the net flow of film workers between regions in Sweden means that film workers from Stockholm dominate film production in Norrbotten [around Luleå] and make up a substantial proportion of those in Västra Götaland [around Trollhättan]' (Dahlström and Hermelin 2007: 117). 'Territorialisation clauses', regulating where parts of the people working on a given production have to come from, have not always been effectively enforced. This is a situation that has been much lamented, not least by spokespeople for the regional centres themselves who have tended to explain it in terms of the lack of talent and expertise in the region (Stern, Svensson and Toll 2003: 27). If the plan is for these sites to develop into the sorts of creative cities described by Richard Florida, the lack of a resident creative class may prove to be a major obstacle.

The factors that have given rise to this state of affairs are most likely manifold. In the case of Ystad, it may be that film workers are reluctant to move there permanently because they recognize that the centre's heavy dependence on the Wallander brand makes it vulnerable and are worried about what will happen to film-making in the region as the brand passes its prime. Another reason for not relocating may be that it is simply not economically feasible. In a recent interview, one producer who is based in the region (although not in Ystad itself) and has extensive knowledge of Ystad as a production environment told the author that he was very reluctant to move his operation into town. Explaining himself, he simply stated that there are only two reasons for shooting in Ystad: you have a story set there, as in the case of the Wallander series, or you get some kind of financial incentive for doing so – for example, substantial production support to which a 'territorialisation clause' is attached or the use of the studios at a cut-price rate as part of a co-production deal (Hedling 2010c: 76). To this particular industry professional, the nascent audio-visual environment in Ystad was simply not attractive enough. It is also worth noting in this context that one of the main obstacles to setting up a master's programme in film and media production in Ystad has been the difficulty of persuading lecturers, academics and film professionals to go there and teach.[7]

As regional film-making began to have an impact upon film-making in the capital, tension and competition between various regions, as well as between the diverse groups of film workers associated with them, became increasingly apparent. In a 2004 report, financed by the regional authorities in Stockholm, the situation was scrutinized and presented as 'against the natural order of things' (Andersson-Greek 2004: 16). The findings even became an item on the prime-time news. Interviewed on television, some film workers in the capital, angry at the lack of opportunities to practise their trade 'at home', attacked the regional centres for employing 'non-professionals' simply because they lived near the centres. Others described manipulating their national registration records in order to be able to work in the regional centres. Still others insisted that more travelling and more pollution were the most notable outcomes of regional film-making (Rapport 2004). More recently, territorialisation clauses have been less strictly enforced so it may be that the anger and the tension that they created has subsided.

Even though some film-makers have embraced the current film production regimen, many others view it as a limiting contrivance. The requirement to do principal photography at the geographical sites has been widely denigrated as a very tangible restriction in terms of what kind of scripts can be written and what types of stories can be told. Since the three major regional centres – the new fund in Stockholm aside – are located in rather small, nondescript towns (Ystad may be an exception here), certain types of film, like a big city thriller, for instance, are unlikely to be produced. The required environment and cityscape are simply impossible to replicate. Amongst film critics, there was, for a while, considerable concern as to how the production set-up might influence the kind of films that got made, a concern that was heightened by the inordinate number of 'country bumpkins' who seemed to pop up in film after film (Eriksson 2005; Wallengren 2006).

Even when film workers are finally in place at the regional centres in question, production does not always progress smoothly. In autumn 2010, widespread labour discontent on one production, eventually completed as both a feature and the third season of a television series, was widely reported in the domestic news media (Cato and Helmerson 2010). According to disgruntled workers, rules regarding scheduling, the acceptable amount of overtime and how much nightly and weekly rest the crew was due had been breached. The union representing Swedish film workers was called in to intervene, but it took quite some time for the conflict to be resolved. Shortly thereafter, the production company publicly threatened to move the production of a fourth season to another location and thereby to take away future work and employment opportunities (Engström 2011). The reason it gave was that the level of support it received from the regional centre was far too meagre and that production would be more financially viable if it was located elsewhere. What we have here is an example of what production studies scholars Ben Goldsmith and Tom O'Regan have termed the 'unstable and unequal partnership between a footloose international production economy and situated local actors and intermediaries'. The incident demonstrates the vulnerability of initiatives like regional film funding in a highly competitive global environment (Goldsmith and O'Regan 2005: xii). If nothing else, these quarrels also make it clear that this supposedly new economy is by no means free of traditional labour conflicts, with greed, friction and dissatisfaction being displayed on both sides and in various ways.

This examination of how the emergence of regional centres of production in Sweden has affected the lives of workers in the film and television industry is by no means exhaustive. Nevertheless, it demonstrates that the radical transformation of production conditions has given rise to a whole slew of outcomes for those working in film, some positive, some unforeseen and some even negative. Working in the film and television industry, it appears, is still difficult in more than one respect.

# Conclusions

The current Swedish regional production set-up has, without question, produced at least some of the sought-after regional economic effects that were on the agenda when the experiment was initiated. More films have been made while previously unseen parts of Sweden have been systematically exposed to audiences. This has undeniably put places like Ystad on the map and shaped how they are experienced and perceived. It has also attracted tourists who want to visit, to see and to experience these places for themselves. This has generated handsome financial rewards, particularly for Ystad.

What is striking, however, is that the people working in the audio-visual production sector do not appear to have gained a great deal from the new set-up except insofar as there is somewhat more work on offer than there was in the past. Rather, their role in the process has been as providers of very specialized services that have worked primarily to the benefit of hotels, restaurants, tour guides, gas station attendants and, above all, the collectors of local and regional taxes. Top-down directed projects like this one, aiming for local and regional economic rejuvenation as well as image-related gains, have met with unforeseen resistance at lower levels. This is perhaps most clearly exemplified by the reluctance of film workers to move to the regional production sites.

In setting out, on the one hand, to establish self-supporting, thriving audio-visual clusters and, on the other, to stimulate various service providers, as a replacement for former industries and the public sector, regional production initiatives have, in a sense, created a workforce on the sidelines that is often scantily rewarded but which is still indispensible to the set-up. Its members have had to deal with high levels of unemployment, the replacement of permanent positions with short-term contracts and low wages. The rewards that they receive compare poorly in many ways with what was available to workers in an earlier economic order before traditional industries drifted into terminal decline. What is clear is that recent attempts in Sweden to create a new economic infrastructure at the regional and local level with audio-visual production at its very centre – like many paradigmatically interrelated instances presently taking place in Europe and Scandinavia – have proved problematic, not only in relation to working conditions in the film and television industry but also in relation to the wider quest for sustainable economic and structural renewal.

## Notes

1  See Hedling (2010c: 70–2) regarding some of the difficulties involved in compiling reliable data as regards sites that support endeavours of audio-visual production in Europe.
2  In fact, low-budget, small-scale TV productions and feature films adapted from the Wallander books were made frequently from the mid-1990s on. None of these, however, used Ystad as a production base.
3  Since the mid-1980s, Mankell has spent at least half of the year living in Maputo, Mozambique.
4  Early on, a local café started to sell Wallander pastries, 'Wallanderbakelser'. The producers as well as Mankell himself intervened and the business stopped. However, shortly thereafter

a family, named Wallander, from another part of Sweden called the café and gave it permission to use the name freely after all (Sjöholm 2008: 209).

5   Speaking to, for instance, local councillors, administrators and executives, both public and private – as I have, doing the kind of investigation the present piece is an example of – one gets the impression that Florida's ideas have had a tremendous impact although his name seems to be unfamiliar to most. Had it not been the case that 'the regional turn' in Swedish film production started well before Florida's book was published, one may almost have ascribed the phenomenon solely to him.

6   In one of the few attempts at evaluating the effects of regional film-making, an economist at Luleå Technical University in northern Sweden came to the conclusion that regional film-making in the north of Sweden represented a cost rather than a revenue for the region. He readily admitted, though, that the difficulty of separating different costs, effects and results was almost insurmountable (Johansson 2004).

7   Personal knowledge of the author who has coordinated the programme since its inception in 2008. Furthermore an old friend, working as a director of photography and for several years based in Stockholm but now in Los Angeles, mentioned that the regionalization of Swedish film production, and all the travelling it involved, was one of the reasons he had left Sweden.

## Bibliography

Andersson-Greek, U. (2004), 'Varför görs det så lite film i Stockholm-Mälardalen?' [Why Are So Few Films Made in the Stockholm Region?], unpublished report written on behalf of Länstyrelsen i Stockholms län [The Regional Authority], och Mälardalsrådet 2004.

Arpi, T. (2004), 'Filmindustrin i Trollhättan sårbar' [The Film Industry in Trollhättan Is Vulnerable. The article is an interview with Per Assmo], HTU Nu: Aktuellt magasin från Högskolan i Trollhättan/Uddevalla: 8–10.

Assmo, P. (2004), Creative Industry Cluster Growth in a Global Economy: The Example of Film i Väst, Uddevalla: Högskolan i Trollhättan/Uddevalla.

Beeton, S. (2005), Film-Induced Tourism, Clevedon: Channel View Publications.

Bizern, C. and Autissier, A.-M. (1999), Public Aid Mechanisms for the Film and Audiovisual Industry in Europe, Vol. I, Strasbourg: European Audiovisual Observatory.

Cato, C. and Helmerson, E. (2010), 'Facket granskar "Maria Wern"-inspelningen' [The Union takes a Look at the 'Maria Wern' Production], Gotlands Allehanda, 17 November, http://www.helagotland.se/noje/default.aspx?articleid=6420309 [accessed 3 July 2011].

Dahlström, M. and Hermelin, B. (2007), 'Creative Industries, Spatiality and Flexibility: The Example of Film Production', Norwegian Journal of Geography, 61 (3): 111–21.

Engström, V. (2011), 'Överväger överge ön då filmfonden backat' [Production Company Considers Leaving as Film Fund Hesitates], Gotlands Allehanda, 17 January, http://www.helagotland.se/nyheter/artikel.aspx?articleid=6587913 [accessed 3 July 2011].

Eriksson, T. (2005), 'Filmbranschen överger storstan' [The Film Business Leaves the Big Cities Behind], Dagens Nyheter, 27 January, http://www.dn.se/kultur-noje/filmbranschen-overger-storstan [accessed 1 July 2011].

Film i Skåne (2010), Verksamhetsberättelse 2009 [Annual Report 2009], Ystad: Film i Skåne.

Flisbäck, M. (2011), Konstnärernas inkomster, arbetsmarknad och försörjningsmönster [Employment, Labour Market, and Income: Time Allocation and Earning Patterns of Swedish Artists], Stockholm: Konstnärsnämnden.

Florida, R. (2004), The Rise of the Creative Class, New York: Basic Books (originally published in 2002).

Florida, R. (2005), The Flight of the Creative Class, New York: HarperCollins.

Goldsmith, B. and O'Regan, T. (2005), The Film Studio: Film Production in the Global Economy (6th edition), Lanham, MD: Rowman & Littlefield.

Hedling, O. (2008), 'A New Deal in European Film? Notes on the Swedish Regional Production Turn', Film International, 6 (5): 8–17.

Hedling, O. (2010a), 'Murder, Mystery and Megabucks? – Films and Filmmaking as Regional and Local Place Promotion in Southern Sweden', in E. Hedling, O. Hedling and M. Jönsson (eds), *Regional Aesthetics: Mapping Swedish Media*, Stockholm: Kungliga Biblioteket.

Hedling, O. (2010b), 'The Regional Turn: On Recent Developments within Scandinavian Film Production', in M. Larsson and A. Marklund (eds), *Swedish Film: An Introduction and a Reader*, Lund: Nordic Academic Press.

Hedling, O. (2010c), 'A Film-Friendly Town? Assessing a Decade at a Small Swedish Production Centre', *Film International*, 8 (6): 70–8.

Høier, A. (2008), 'Marked for skandinavisk krimilitteratur?' [The Market for Scandinavian Crime Fiction?], talk given by Mankell's international agent at the symposium *Skandinavisk krimiindustri* [Scandinavian Crime Industries], in Ystad, 2–3 June 2008.

Hudson, S. and Ritchie, J. R. B. (2006), 'Promoting Destinations via Film Tourism: An Empirical Identification of Supporting Marketing Initiatives', *Journal of Travel Research*, 44 (4): 387–96.

Jenkins, H. (2006), *Convergence Culture: Where Old and New Media Collide*, New York and London: New York University Press.

Johansson, S. (2004), *Filmindustrin i Norrbotten: Framväxt, nuläge och ekonomisk betydelse* [The Film Industry in Northern Sweden: Rise, Current Status and Economic Significance], Luleå: Luleå tekniska universitet.

Keane, M. and Moran, A. (2008), 'Television's New Engines', *Television & New Media*, 9 (2): 155–69.

Krona, M. (2006), 'Filmfinansiering och regionalism. Wallanderprojektet på Österlen', in E. Hedling and A.-K. Wallengren (eds), *Solskenslandet – Svensk film på 2000-talet*, Stockholm: Atlantis.

Lange, A. and Westcott, T. (2004), *Public Funding for Film and Audiovisual Works in Europe: A Comparative Approach*, Strasbourg: European Audiovisual Laboratory.

Miller, T., Govil, N., McMurria, J., Maxwell, R. and Wang, T. (2005), *Global Hollywood 2*, London: British Film Institute.

OECD (2009), *The Impact of Culture on Tourism*, Paris: OECD Publishing.

Olofson, S. (2010), 'Wallander värd tre miljarder för Skåne' [Wallander's Worth for Skåne Is Three Billion], *Skånska Dagbladet*, 30 January, http://www.skanskan.se/article/20100130/YSTAD/701299811 [accessed 1 July 2011].

Rapport (2004), Seven O' Clock News, 24 November.

Rifkin, J. (2000), *The Age of Access: How the Shift from Ownership to Access Is Transforming Modern Life*, London: Penguin.

Roger, S. (2005), 'Filmavtalet 2006–2010' [The Film Agreement 2006–2010], *Teknik & Människa*, 5: 4–6.

SFI (2006), Svenska Filminstitutets verksamhetsberättelse 2005 [Annual Report 2005], Stockholm: Svenska Filminstitutet.

Sjöholm, C. (2008), 'Mördarjakt i Ystad' [Man Hunt in Ystad], *RIG Kulturhistorisk tidskrift*, 4: 205–20.

Stern, P., Svensson, M. and Toll, B. (2003), *Film, TV och moderna medier i Västra Götaland* [Film, TV and Contemporary Media in the Region of Västra Götaland], Göteborg: Film i Väst.

Unsigned (2010), 'Wallander värd miljarder för Ystad' [Wallander Is Worth Billions for Skåne], *Dagens Industri*, 30 January, http://di.se/Default.aspx?pid=199757_ArticlePageProvider&epslanguage=sv [accessed 1 July 2011].

Vonderau, P. (2010), 'Just Television: Inga Lindström and the Franchising of Culture', in E. Hedling, O. Hedling and M. Jönsson (eds), *Regional Aesthetics: Mapping Swedish Media*, Stockholm: Kungliga Biblioteket.

Wallengren, A.-K. (2006), 'Kultur och okultur – bilden av landsbygdens folk' [Culture and Wilderness – Picturing the People of Rural Sweden], in E. Hedling and A.-K. Wallengren (eds), *Solskenslandet – Svensk film på 2000-talet*, Stockholm: Atlantis.

Werth, C. (2009), 'The Places I've Seen', *Newsweek*, 3 December, http://www.newsweek.com/2009/12/02/the-places-i-ve-seen.html [accessed 1 July 2011].

# Manoeuvrable spaces

# No room for manoeuvre

## Star images and the regulation of actors' labour in silent-era Hollywood

chapter

# 5

SEAN P. HOLMES

For the relatively small number of performers who won a place in the cinematic firmament in the 1920s, conditions of employment were, on the face of it, far from onerous. Signed up to long-term contracts, they were extraordinarily well rewarded for their labour and, for the most part, they enjoyed a very cosseted professional existence. Even so, the silent era in Hollywood was punctuated by bitter and sometimes very public power struggles that arose out of the efforts of star performers to challenge producers and studio managers for control over the terms of their commodification. Film theorist Barry King has argued that stardom allows individual screen performers to carve out what he terms a 'manoeuvrable space' in their dealings with their employers that is not available to actors and actresses further down the occupational hierarchy (King 1984: 167–8). His point is an important one in that it highlights the relationship between status and power in the screen acting community. But what he loses sight of is that 'manoeuvrable space' is not a property that is inherent in stardom as a cultural institution. Rather, it is something that is historically contingent and, as such, it has to be staked out and defended by individual performers, often at great personal cost. Outside the field of entertainment law, the 1928 case of *Goudal v. Cecil B. De Mille Pictures Corporation* has received little scholarly attention. In exploring the contractual relationships between screen actors and their employers, film historians have tended to focus on more high-profile cases such as Warner Brothers' legal battles during the 1930s and 1940s with Bette Davis, James Cagney and Olivia de Havilland.[1] In terms of the precedents it set for employment practices in Hollywood, however, the Goudal case was at least as important as these later cases in that it established the right of screen stars to exercise a degree of control over how their star images were constructed.

In the early years of the studio era, the vast majority of stars had only limited room for manoeuvre. As Danae Clark has observed, studio managers and motion picture producers wielded a discursive power that was simply not available to the actors they employed (Clark 1990: 6). With unlimited access to the national media, industry leaders could construct screen luminaries in such a way as to strip them of their identity as workers and to obscure the realities of the conditions under which they laboured. By the late teens, a discourse of screen acting had emerged in the United States that detached stars from the world of work and defined stardom almost exclusively in terms of the rewards that accrued to it. 'You simply do not know the diamond-studded truth about Hollywood', began one 1929 article in the fanzine *Motion Picture*. 'You haven't any conception of how money pours, free green rain through golden sieves. You have heard of reveling Rome. You ain't heard nothing yet!' (Hall 1929: 34). Performers who complained about the terms of their employment or who sought a role in the construction of their screen images found themselves characterized as temperamental egotists whose professional idiosyncrasies posed a threat to the smooth operation of the Hollywood 'dream factory'. As the experience of actress Jetta Goudal demonstrates, when they tried to fight back against their employers they found that the odds were heavily stacked against them.

Goudal first emerged as an actress of note in 1921 when she appeared on Broadway in the role of Mme Cecile Florent in William Devereux' *The Elton Case*, a melodrama based on a recent unsolved murder that had been something of a *cause célèbre* in metropolitan social circles. Alexander Woollcott, the notoriously caustic drama critic for *The New York Times*, rubbished the play. 'As literature and as entertainment,' he wrote, 'it is about on a par with one of those inexpensive detective stories you buy at the Grand Central, read avidly as far as Albany, and forget at Utica' (Woollcott 1921: 20). But Woollcott was sufficiently impressed by Goudal to pick her out for special mention and, though the play ran for less than three weeks, her performance was noteworthy enough to win her a contract with Inspiration Pictures, a small film production company based on the East Coast. Her screen debut opposite matinee idol Richard Barthelmess in *The Bright Shawl* (1923) garnered considerable critical acclaim and established her screen persona as a woman who, as one reviewer put it, 'is beguiling and treacherous, one who can smile while she stabs her victims' (Benham 1999).

Like many other transplanted stage players, Goudal struggled to come to terms with the demands of a technology and a set of production practices that stripped her of much of her accustomed autonomy as a performer.[2] When she first watched *The Bright Shawl*, she was appalled at how her performance had been butchered in the editing process. 'So many scenes were missing', she recalled many years later in an interview with film historian Charles C. Benham. 'I still do not understand. There was so little of me' (Benham 1999). Her misgivings about the medium were not enough, however, to deter her from signing a new contract with another East Coast studio, the Distinctive Pictures Corporation. Her performance in a supporting role in *The Green Goddess* (1923), a star vehicle for George Arliss and Alice Joyce, opened the way for her to complete the transition from stage to screen by relocating to Los Angeles, already the undisputed centre of motion picture production in the United States. 'If this picture marks a new era in anything, it is in Jetta Goudal's career', wrote one reviewer. 'When she lands in Hollywood, it will be time for many of our present stars to fold up their tents and make-up kits.' Shortly after *The Green Goddess* hit the theatres, she signed a three-picture deal with the Paramount Pictures Corporation and headed for California, drawn there, so she told one would-be biographer, as much by the climate as by the career opportunities that it might afford her (Bodeen 1974: 450).

By her own admission, Goudal was an intensely private woman who, in an era in which the extra-filmic narratives that motion picture studios constructed around leading performers had already become central to stardom as a cultural institution, was determined to protect her personal life from public scrutiny. 'I never discussed my private life in any interview', she told film historian and sometime screenwriter DeWitt Bodeen in the early 1970s.

> It has always been against my principles. Remembering a luncheon at the Ambassador Hotel where I lived when I first came to Hollywood, I can quote verbatim my answers to some personal questions. I was born on the moon two thousand years ago. I said it smilingly and politely but it registered. My age is still two thousand. (Bodeen 1974: 452)

Recent research suggests that Goudal's real name was Julie Henriette Gouderet and that she was born in Amsterdam in 1891 to an orthodox Jewish family engaged in the diamond trade. But what few biographical details she disclosed to interviewers during the 1920s (that she was born in Versailles in 1898, for example) were deliberately misleading – evidence perhaps of a desire to distance herself from her Dutch-Jewish roots (Donaldson 1985: 319). Goudal's need for privacy invested her with an air of mystery that appealed to moviegoers because it gave them the opportunity to colour in the blank spaces that surrounded her. '[S]ome said she was the daughter of Mata Hari,' claims DeWitt Bodeen in his 1973 profile of the actress, 'others that she came from the Hague, born of a French father and a Javanese mother, a few maintained that she was actually born on New York's Lower East Side and that her accent was phony' (Bodeen 1974: 449). But it also had the less desirable effect of creating a void which her employers moved quickly to fill.

To contextualize her screen appearances as an exotic *femme fatale*, publicists at Paramount represented Goudal as a highly strung and volatile performer who was prone to fits of irrational rage. 'They warned me', read one 1924 profile that captured the essence of what quickly became the Jetta Goudal persona. 'They said that the lady was quite electrical and that if I displeased her she was quite liable to plunge a fork into my heart across the dinner table' (Untitled clipping-a 1924). Goudal had serious reservations about the extra-filmic identity that the studio was creating for her. She quickly discovered, however, that her opinions carried little weight. 'I saw the first story of that type that was ever written', she recalled in an interview in the early 1930s. 'It was while I was at Paramount, and when I objected, horrified, they assured me that it was a swell stunt and would be continued, no matter what my feelings on the subject might be' ('Long Arm of Coincidence' 1931). In the context of the system of production that prevailed in Hollywood in the 1920s, Paramount's reluctance to give ground on this issue was entirely understandable. As Goudal was to discover to her cost, her persona was more than simply a marketable commodity. It was also an instrument of control, a weapon that managers and producers at Paramount and elsewhere could use against her to reinforce their authority at the point of production and beyond.

Right from the outset, Goudal's relationship with Paramount was a troubled one. The first role in which she was cast was that of Dona Florencia in *A Sainted Devil* (1924), a star vehicle for Rudolph Valentino. Though Joseph Henabery, the actor who played Abraham Lincoln in D. W. Griffith's *Birth of a Nation* (1915), was nominally the director of the film, Natacha Rambova, Valentino's wife and a costume designer of some note, took control over the production process and immediately clashed with Goudal. According to Charles C. Benham, Goudal, who had clearly identified the right to select her own wardrobe as one of the keys to seizing back control over her star persona, disliked the costumes she was required to wear. When she made her feelings known to the producer, she was accused of causing major production delays and dismissed from the picture. In the press, however, what was essentially a struggle between a performer and the studio that employed her over the terms of her commodification was recast as a spat between two temperamental women competing for the attention of the movie's star and thereby stripped of its wider significance (Benham 1999). Nor was Goudal's experience on the set of her next picture, *The Spaniard* (1925), any more positive. According to contemporary reports, Goudal threw the shooting schedule into disarray by temporarily withdrawing her labour after shooting a rain scene on the Lasky Ranch in what is now Universal City. 'When drenched to the skin and no-one brought her a wrap,' reported the fanzine *Motion Picture Classic*, 'she left for home. Retakes were necessary and some fifty technical workers had to be taken back to accomplish what should have been accomplished the first night' (Benham 1999). To most moviegoers, Goudal's behaviour presumably looked like yet another manifestation of her alleged temperament. But placed in the context of an industry in which workplace safety often took second place to the need to keep production costs to a minimum and even major stars sometimes found themselves in life-threatening situations, her actions might be read as entirely rational.[3]

Working on her final film with Paramount, *Salome of the Tenements* (1925), was an altogether happier experience for Goudal and one that she looked back on with some fondness in later life, not least because the opening scenes allowed her to play against type as a young child. It was not so happy as to convince her to extend her stay at the studio, however. As her reputation as an actress had grown, so too had her perceived exchange value. In the wake of her departure from Paramount, she was courted by a number of studios, most notably Metro-Goldwyn-Mayer (MGM). In the end, she chose to cast her lot with director Cecil B. De Mille, who had recently formed his own production company, the Cecil B. De Mille Pictures Corporation, and engineered a distribution deal through the Producers Distributing Company, a subsidiary of Paramount (Slide 1980: 130).

For Goudal, the move was an opportunity to exert a greater degree of control over the production of her image. Unwilling to allow the studios to continue to dictate the parameters of the debate over her professional conduct, she tried to put her case to the press. 'Miss Goudal is frank in admitting her disagreements and is willing to talk of them', reported one Oklahoma City newspaper in 1925.

> She maintains that she knows something about pictures and is entitled to some say in the direction of her own. She bases her right upon the fact that a poor picture hurts her standing more than it hurts anyone else connected with it. Therefore, she states, she refuses to do anything in any scene which she feels is not good. (Untitled clipping-b 1925)

Her efforts to reinvent herself as a dedicated cultural worker with legitimate concerns about how she was represented on the screen were in vain, however. In the eyes of most commentators, she was simply a pampered prima donna who had run into problems with her employers because, in the words of one article, 'her highly Latin soul refused to bend before either directors or producers' (Untitled clipping-c 1927). Nor was Goudal's new employer willing to grant her the freedom to remake her star persona. Her first project after signing with De Mille was The Coming of Amos (1925), a film that was completed under the supervision of a secondary production unit that the director had set up to keep his leading players employed when they were not working under his direct supervision. A close reading of it demonstrates how Goudal's screen roles increasingly converged with the extra-filmic narratives that the studios created around her to reinforce the popular perception of her as a woman of temperament and to further reduce her room for manoeuvre.

Directed by Paul H. Sloane, a cinematic practitioner whose reputation in Hollywood rested less upon his artistic vision than upon his efficiency and his productivity, The Coming of Amos is a loose adaptation of a William J. Locke novel that had been serialized in Good Housekeeping in 1924. A melodrama that for all its pretensions is not afraid to poke fun at the excesses of the genre, it features Goudal in the role of Nadia, a Russian princess living in exile on the French Riviera who, according to the decidedly tongue-in-cheek caption that introduces her, 'has played havoc with many European hearts, including the Scandinavian'. When first we encounter her, she is posing for a portrait at the home of one David Fontenay, a middle-aged member of the local fast set whom a caption describes as 'six times a husband and never a correspondent'. Resplendent in a bejewelled robe and an elaborately decorated kokoshnik (a type of headdress), she exudes an air of haughty allure and an exoticism that marks her out from the wealthy socialites who surround her. We are left in no doubt whatsoever that we are in the presence of a powerful woman who is used to getting her way.

The sitting is brought to an abrupt halt by the arrival of Fontenay's nephew, Amos Burden (played by rising matinee idol Rod La Rocque), a guileless young Australian lately arrived from the outback at his late mother's instruction to learn how to conduct himself in polite society. Intrigued by Amos's untutored ways, Princess Nadia steps down from her pedestal and offers him a cup of tea and a cigarette. When his uncle takes Amos to task for his lack of social graces, she leaps to his defence. 'Do not spik cross to him,' she chides, 'he is so or-riginal.' A quick demonstration of his skill with a boomerang sends his uncle into paroxysms of rage but serves only to pique her interest further. 'Tell me about thees Australia', she begs him. 'Are all the men beeg and r-rough and beautiful as you?'[4] As well as being powerful, she is also unabashedly sexual in her dealings with male admirers. But the incipient romance between Nadia and Amos is rudely interrupted by the arrival of Ramon Garcia (played by perennial screen villain Noah Beery), a menacing figure who we soon discover engineered the escape of the princess from revolutionary Russia in the hope of making her his own and subsequently dispatched three of her suitors. 'Making love to the Princess,' observes one of the guests at Fontenay's house party, 'is like flirting with an undertaker.'

What follows is a narrative of female subjugation in which Princess Nadia, caught between the two men whose actions drive the plot, is gradually stripped of the power that she is accustomed to exercising. We next encounter Amos two months after his arrival on the Riviera, and he is utterly transformed. Having been expertly coached in the art of elegant deportment by one of his uncle's wealthy associates, he is, as a caption puts it, 'shaved, shined and shampooed – and dedicated to the proposition that all gentlemen are created in Bond Street'. A chance encounter with Princess Nadia, now dressed in a shepherdess's costume that would not have looked out of place at Marie Antoinette's Petit Hameau, at a local tea shop (located, rather bizarrely, in a beached galleon) affords him the opportunity to renew his acquaintance with her. But just as the two of them are about to profess their love for one another, Amos is handed an envelope full of newspaper cuttings detailing the violent deaths of Nadia's previous admirers. Quick to realize that the package was dispatched to him by the murderous Ramon Garcia, Nadia moves to protect her would-be lover by affecting an air of imperious detachment and taking him to task for addressing her by her first name. 'I mus' remind you that I am a Princess of Imperial Russia, my young shepherd boy', she warns him. 'It would be dangerous to forget.' That all this is for show is demonstrated both to Amos and to the audience when she surreptitiously hands him a bracelet inscribed in Russian with the words 'Never forsake me.' All her feminine wiles are not enough to protect Amos from the wrath of Ramon Garcia, however. Amos's training in how to be a gentleman has not extended as far as duelling, and when he confronts his nemesis over his dastardly treatment of the princess, Garcia symbolically emasculates him by cutting his cravat from his neck with a sword.

Having humiliated Amos, Garcia moves swiftly to consolidate his victory. In the next scene, his henchmen kidnap Princess Nadia and carry her away to his clifftop castle. When she resists his advances, he locks her in an underground dungeon and, in a scene that even for contemporary audiences must have verged upon parody, opens up the sluices to let in the sea, proclaiming triumphantly, 'My last wife changed her mind down here.' All is not lost, however. Determined to rescue the woman he loves, Amos takes out Garcia's guards with boomerangs that he has cunningly contrived from a pair of boathooks and breaks into the castle. In a final confrontation, Garcia is stripped of his cravat with a pair of scissors – the emasculator has become the emasculated – and dispatched to his death in the now-flooded dungeon. With the final obstacle to their love removed, the hero and heroine are reunited. But Jetta Goudal's Nadia is no longer able to play an active role in determining her destiny. Shorn of the trappings of royalty, she is left prostrate and helpless in the arms of Amos – a woman tamed.

Off-screen, the perennially strong-willed Goudal remained determined to retain a degree of control over the direction in which her career was heading. For her next film, De Mille cast her as a gypsy in *The Volga Boatman* (1926), a high-profile project on which he would be the director. As far as Goudal was concerned, it was an entirely inappropriate role for her, and she had no qualms about making her feelings known to her employer. 'Upon [De Mille] asking my opinion,' she told film historian DeWitt Bodeen, 'I stated that I did not consider myself right for the part which, as he told us, was full of slapstick' (Bodeen 1974: 456). Unwilling to force Goudal to play a role with which she was clearly not comfortable, De Mille released her from her obligation to play in the film, replacing her with his one-time mistress, Julia Faye. In the press, however, it was reported that Goudal had marched off the set in a fit of high dudgeon, an accusation that incensed the actress not least because it reinforced the perception that she was a disruptive presence in the Hollywood dream factory. 'I never, never walked off the set of *The Volga Boatman* or of any other film in which I was cast', she insisted in her interview with Bodeen (1974: 456).

Reluctant to leave Goudal idle whilst he was shooting *The Volga Boatman*, De Mille decided to loan her out to a film unit operated by Frances Marion, one of the leading screenwriters of the 1920s, for a picture entitled *Paris at Midnight* (1926). Marion had misgivings about taking Goudal on. 'Everybody warned me that Jetta Goudal was hell on wheels and I must handle her with kid gloves', she told an interviewer shortly before her death in 1973. 'We were making the picture on a very limited budget and I could not bear the expense any delays a temperamental explosion might cause' (Bodeen 1974: 456). Rather than seeking to impose her will upon Goudal, however, Marion opted for an alternative strategy – one that highlights the gendered character of the relationship between studios and the performers they employed in Hollywood during the 1920s. Shortly before production began, she invited Goudal to her office and proposed a mutually beneficial compact that would enable them to confound the expectations of industry insiders who could not conceive of a relationship between two strong-willed and talented women in anything other than adversarial terms. 'I told her she probably knew how they were laying bets around the lot as to how soon she and I would clash', she remembered. '"They don't think that two women like you and me can work together," I told her. Shall we fool them?' (Bodeen 1974: 456).

Conscious of the need to keep production costs down, Marion turned Goudal's hitherto frustrated desire for greater control over how she looked on screen to her advantage by suggesting that she might want to design her own costumes, an arrangement to which Goudal readily assented. 'I told her we couldn't afford a top designer but I had seen her wearing some stunning clothes which I understood she herself had designed', she recalled.

> She was very pleased and the upshot of the whole thing was that she agreed to use some gowns from her own wardrobe to fit the period and to design the balance to suit the film as well as her personality. This she did successfully and at a minimum cost. (Bodeen 1974: 456)

Viewed from the perspective of a manager who saw collaboration rather than coercion as the key to getting the best out of performers, Goudal's assertiveness in the workplace begins to look less like a manifestation of temperament than a carefully considered response to the power imbalances that underpinned employment practices in the motion picture industry. Freed from the constraints imposed upon her by autocratic producers and directors, she proved to be a far more tractable employee than her detractors might have predicted, and Frances Marion's experience of working with her was an entirely positive one. 'I must say, I really enjoyed working with her', she told DeWitt Bodeen. 'She was entirely cooperative and an expert actress' (Bodeen 1974: 456).

Returning to the De Mille fold, Goudal was cast in the lead role in *Three Faces East* (1926), a spy drama set in London during the Great War. So great was the film's success at the box office that De Mille felt compelled to release a press statement announcing that Goudal had finally been ordained as a major star. 'The public, not I, promoted Miss Goudal', he insisted. 'Her sweeping success in *Three Faces East* has brought a veritable deluge of telegrams from the public and exhibitors' (Benham 1999). As Goudal's perceived exchange value grew, so too did the interest of other studios. When Warner Brothers made a bid for her services to play opposite John Barrymore in a historical drama entitled *When a Man Loves* (1927), De Mille agreed to allow Goudal to decide whether she was ready to move on, a concession that was doubtless symptomatic of the underlying tensions in their relationship. But Goudal was not yet so disgruntled with her employer that she wanted to leave him to work elsewhere. 'On Mr. De Mille's request,' she remembered, 'I went to see the great Barrymore and reported back to him that I found him greasy and smelly (alcohol) and I preferred to remain [with the Cecil B. De Mille Pictures Corporation] which pleased him no end' (Bodeen 1974: 458).

This period of relative amity between De Mille and Goudal proved short-lived, though. According to DeWitt Bodeen, Goudal was De Mille's first choice for the role of Mary Magdalene in *King of Kings* (1927) (Bodeen 1974: 458), a prestige production with a budget of over US$1,250,000 (as compared with about US$477,000 for *The Road to Yesterday* (1925), Goudal's second picture with De Mille) and a shooting schedule that ran to months rather than weeks (Pierce 1991: 316). But after his accountants pointed out to him that he was contracted to the Producers Distributing Company to supply an annual number of Goudal's pictures and that he would not be able to do so if he employed her on a major project, De Mille rescinded his offer of the part. Over the next year or so, Goudal went on to make four more movies for De Mille – *Her Man O'War* (1926), *White Gold* (1927), *Fighting Love* (1927) and *The Forbidden Woman* (1927) – all of them shot on modest budgets by De Mille's secondary unit. For a performer who was looking to cement her position in the cinematic firmament, it was not a desirable situation. What finally brought things to a head between Goudal and her employer, however, was not her growing frustration at the lack of opportunities available to her but a salary dispute. De Mille had signed Goudal to a five-year contract with options at six-monthly intervals, which required an incremental rise in her weekly salary. At the end of the second year, he refused to pay the increase of US$1,000 per week to which Goudal was entitled (Bodeen 1974: 458–9). When Goudal protested, he responded by terminating her contract even though it still had three years left to run upon the grounds of persistent insubordination, asserting that he could not work with an actress whom he described as 'a little cocktail of temperament' (Unsourced clipping-a 1927). With her professional reputation on the line, Goudal hit back with a lawsuit against the Cecil B. De Mille Pictures Corporation, demanding US$85,607.14 in damages from her erstwhile employer on the grounds of breach of contract. According to DeWitt Bodeen's account, a week before the case was due to come to court, De Mille offered to settle in full but Goudal insisted on pressing her suit, seeing it as her best opportunity of casting off the star persona that had been imposed upon her in the early 1920s by Paramount (Bodeen 1974: 458–9).

Almost from the moment that Hollywood had emerged as the capital of the burgeoning movie industry in the second decade of the twentieth century, the courts in California had operated upon the assumption that the labour of creative workers in the motion picture studios was qualitatively different from that of other occupational groups. In 1919, the Californian state legislature had enacted a law that allowed judges to issue injunctions to prevent breach of contract in cases where 'the promised service is of special, unique, unusual, extraordinary, or intellectual character which gives it peculiar value, the loss of which cannot be reasonably or adequately compensated in damages in an action at law' (Yankwich 1956: 126). An implicit acknowledgement of the increasingly important role that actors (and, to a lesser extent, other above-the-line workers) played in the process of product differentiation in the film industry, its purpose was to protect the studios against the arbitrary loss of employees whose labour could not be replaced. The principle that studios could fire workers upon the grounds of insubordination had also been firmly enshrined in California state law. In 1920, for example, the courts had ruled that the New York Motion Picture Corporation was justified in discharging a female performer upon the grounds that she had persistently failed to report for work at the time set by the studio (*May v. New York Motion Picture Corp.* 1920; Youngman 1954: 5; Yankwich 1956: 127). What had yet to be established, however, was whether disobedience as manifested in disagreements between individual screen performers and their employers over how they went about their work amounted to grounds for dismissal.

In his autobiography, De Mille claimed that the case – which the judge, Leon R. Yankwich of the Los Angeles County Superior Court, agreed to hear in the evenings in De Mille's office on the MGM lot – was conducted on a very amicable basis.

> [Yankwich] first questioned Miss Goudal. Was Mr. De Mille a bad director, had he ever been violent or abusive toward the plaintiff? Oh, not at all.

He was an excellent director and a perfect gentleman. The judge then turned to me. Miss Goudal now, was she in my opinion a competent actress? Oh, yes, one of the best. Did I just dislike her then? No, I did not dislike her at all. She was a fine person, and a particular friend of my daughter's. This was just a difference of opinion about some money due or not due. (De Mille 1959: 269)

Thirty years on, however, De Mille still had a vested interest in playing down the importance of *Goudal v. Cecil B. De Mille Pictures Corporation*, not least because of its long-term implications for employment practices in the Hollywood film industry. Reproduced in the daily press for the consumption of a moviegoing public that was as interested in the off-screen lives of the stars as it was in their appearances on screen, court transcripts revealed a quite different picture.[5] Testifying in support of De Mille, three directors, among them Paul L. Stein, claimed that Goudal's 'artistic temperament' together with her 'insubordination and willfulness' made her impossible to work with and that her behaviour had cost the studio somewhere between US$80,000 and US$100,000 (Unsourced clipping-b 1929). Even in the witness stand, Goudal struggled to divorce herself from her star persona. Her efforts to justify her position to the court were represented in the newspapers as the emotional outpourings of 'a temperamental and artistic actress caught between picture directors and producers who had their own ideas about how she should do her work' (Unsourced clipping-c 1929). But what she was able to do was to demonstrate to the satisfaction of the judge that De Mille's central contention – that he had terminated her contract because her temperament was costing his company money – was false. 'Having a clear conscience, I demanded to see the books', she told DeWitt Bodeen in the early 1970s.

Much to the disgust of my lawyer and the surprise of the judge, De Mille stalled. The judge then insisted and, believe it or not, the following day when De Mille had to bring in the books, to the amazement of and surprise of everyone, including myself, the books showed that not only had we not exceeded the budget on any one picture, we had always remained below the budget. The figures belied Mr. De Mille's statements and exonerated me. Of course my lawyer advised me to sue for defamation of character but I considered this beneath my dignity. I was not after money as such. With me it was a question of honor and principle. (Bodeen 1974: 459)

In a decision that set an important precedent in the field of employment law, Yankwich ruled that 'refusal or failure to perform the conditions of a contract of employment' required 'a willful act or willful misconduct' and that Goudal was guilty of neither. Locating Goudal's value 'not in her ability to obey slavishly ... but in her ability to inject the force of her personality, experience, and intelligence in acting', he went on to assert that as an artist she was not required to demonstrate the level of obedience that a master might reasonably expect of a servant. '[W]as she not within her rights in objecting to particular scenes which did not give full scope to her artistic abilities or demanding that they be changed so as to show her to her best advantage?' he asked in a final rhetorical flourish. 'We believe that she was' (*Goudal v. Cecil B. De Mille Pictures Corp.* 1931).

Reluctant to lose face by paying Goudal the US$30,000 to which Yankwich deemed she was entitled, De Mille challenged the decision. When his appeal reached the courts two years later, however, it was rejected out of hand. In his ruling, Judge Charles William Fricke took up Yankwich's point about the special nature of creative work and pushed it even further, arguing that Goudal not only had the right to challenge the judgement of directors when she felt they were at fault but also a legal obligation to do so. 'Even in the most menial forms of employment there will exist circumstances justifying the servant in questioning the orders of the master', he opined:

> And when the employment is of 'a special, unique, unusual, extraordinary, and intellectual quality' as agreed by the contract here under considera- tion to be rendered 'conscientiously, artistically, and to the utmost of her ability,' sincere efforts of the artist to secure an artistic interpretation of the play, even though they may involve the suggestion of changes and the presentation of arguments in favor of such changes even though insistently presented, do not amount to willful disobedience or failure to perform services under the contract, but rather a compliance with the contract which basically calls for services in the best interests of the employer. (*Goudal v. Cecil B. De Mille Pictures Corp.* 1931)

The case of *Goudal v. Cecil B. De Mille Pictures Corporation* constitutes a key moment in the history of labour-management relations in the motion picture industry. As well as vindicating Goudal's position in her dispute with De Mille, it also established the wider principle that leading screen performers were entitled to a say in how they were presented on screen. But for Goudal herself, it was a hollow victory. 'After my break with the studio, I was crushed and ill', she told DeWitt Bodeen. 'I had trusted Mr. De Mille like a father and that lawsuit nearly killed me' (Bodeen 1974: 461). According to press reports, job offers dried up entirely in the wake of the case, even though it was only a year or so earlier that she had been courted by several of the major studios, among them the Fox Film Corporation and MGM. 'Producers may not have a blacklist,' observed *Photoplay*, a fanzine that had featured Goudal on its cover as recently as November 1927, 'but they do not look with favor on temperamental stars' (Benham 1999). Surveying her career from the vantage point of old age, Goudal claimed not to have been unduly concerned by her *de facto* blacklisting. 'It didn't bother me at all', she insisted at a symposium organized by the Academy of Motion Picture Arts and Sciences (AMPAS) in 1980. 'I never wanted to be in films and I was perfectly happy not to work 'til calls came' (Slide 1980: 132). However, her response to D. W. Griffith's offer of an audition for a starring role in a movie entitled *Lady of the Pavements* (1929) suggests that her dispute with De Mille followed by several months without any prospect of work had left her chastened and bereft of confidence.

Mistakenly assuming that Griffith (another one-time Hollywood luminary whose star was no longer in the ascendancy) would be looking for a leading lady in the mould of Lillian Gish or Carol Dempster, performers whose star images were firmly rooted in Victorian notions of femininity, she decided to remake herself accordingly. 'I went dressed for the part – low-heeled shoes, a little flat', she recalled.

And I happened to have a little suit that Lillian or Carol might have worn. I slouched down as low as I could and the secretary announced 'Mr. Griffith, Miss Goudal is calling.' So I walked in as small as I could. D. W. Griffith looked at me and said 'Are you Miss Goudal? You always look tall and stately in your films and here you are now. ... This is not what I want at all. I want you to be sophisticated and tall and daring.' (Slide 1980: 133)

To Goudal's delight, Griffith asked her to 'dress tall' for her screen test, explaining that she would need to tower over her co-star, Mexican actress Lupe Velez. Having offered her the part, moreover, he asked her if she would be willing to design her own costumes, a request to which she readily assented. 'I said I would be delighted', she told her fellow participants in the AMPAS symposium. 'It was a lot of extra work but who cares. Work was not what I cared about. Success, yes. Doing the work to the best of my ability, yes. But otherwise, work was nothing. That was part of the game' (Slide 1980: 133).

As well as draining her of self-confidence, Goudal's experiences at the hands of her employers also had a radicalizing effect upon her and encouraged her to seek out collective solutions to the problems that she had encountered as an individual. In June 1929, the Actors' Equity Association (AEA) instructed its members in Hollywood to refuse to sign contracts until the studios agreed to the implementation of the so-called 'Equity Shop', an arrangement under which they would be required to ensure that all the performers they employed were AEA members.[6] With ample reason for resenting the power differential that structured relations between screen actors and their employers, Goudal cast her lot with the AEA and spoke regularly at the weekly rallies that the union staged at the American Legion Stadium in Hollywood. 'When I was asked to be on the dais for the Equity meetings I acquiesced, having no idea that I would be required to speak', she recalled in an interview in the early 1970s.

Do not forget, my English then was forty years worse. I had been listening to others when suddenly I heard 'And now we will have a few words from Miss Goudal.' I still think it is partly the cause of my present heart condition. Of course, there was no alternative but to get up. What I said I will never know but I was supposed to have been the success of the evening. They laughed and applauded and carried on. I can assure you that from then on I came prepared. (Bodeen 1974: 460)

But if Goudal had invested her hopes for the future in trade unionism, she was to be sorely disappointed. In the wake of the strike call, the Hollywood acting community split along lines that were determined, in part at least, by the workings of the star system. Hollywood's lesser players, drawn by the promise of protection against unfair labour practices, flocked to the Equity banner. Higher up the occupational hierarchy, by contrast, there was little sympathy for the Equity cause. A few of Goudal's fellow stars, on the basis of their commitment to the principle of collective action or their harsh experiences at the hands of studio bosses, welcomed the efforts of the AEA to organize the movie industry. But an overwhelming majority, including many who had made their names on the stage, reacted with hostility to the AEA's attempts to 'Broadwayize' Hollywood, seeing it as a threat to their autonomy and a denial of the specificity of their work. In August 1929, the 'Equity Shop' campaign collapsed and the AEA withdrew from Hollywood, leaving Goudal even more exposed than she had been as a consequence of her court victory over Cecil B. De Mille (Holmes 2005a: 44–5).

What dissuaded employers in Hollywood from permanently blacklisting Goudal was her fluency in French. In the wake of the sound revolution, the major Hollywood studios, sensing that their hegemony was under threat, had begun shooting foreign-language versions of their top releases in a bid to bolster their market share in Europe. Less than a year after the AEA's abortive attempt to organize the film industry, MGM offered Goudal a featured part in *Le Spectre Vert* (1930), a French-language remake of *The Unholy Night* (1929), at the much-reduced salary of US$1,000 a week. Eager to relaunch her career, Goudal accepted the offer but refused to cash her salary cheques. 'I was willing to do it for nothing but could not jeopardize my position and career by doing it for the salary offered', she explained later. 'I did not want anyone to say "She did it for MGM for $1,000 so she can do it for us"' (Statement of Jetta Goudal 1930). Her experience of working on *Le Spectre Vert* was not a happy one, however, and her comeback came to a premature end when studio bosses allegedly reneged on a promise to give her star billing when the film was exhibited at MGM's Madeleine Theatre in Paris (Decision of Actors' Branch Executive Committee 1930). Exhausted by her ordeal at the hands of her various employers, Goudal suffered a nervous breakdown (evidence, for those who sought it, that her alleged temperament was a symptom of psychological instability) and was committed to a sanatorium (Unsourced clipping-e 1930; Unsourced clipping-f 1930). She returned to the screen in 1932 in *Business and Pleasure* (1932), a Will Rogers vehicle, playing a role that parodied her earlier screen incarnation as a *femme fatale*, but her acting career was effectively over. Unable to escape the constraints of the identity that the studios had imposed upon her, she set up an interior design company with her husband, one-time Hollywood art director Harold Grieve, and disappeared into relative obscurity ('Long Arm of Coincidence' 1931).

'I don't like being called a silent star', Jetta Goudal observed in an interview in 1985. 'I was never silent.' What her experiences in silent-era Hollywood demonstrate, however, is how difficult it was for the stars of the silver screen to make their voices heard either individually or collectively. Both the roles in which she was cast and the extra-filmic narratives that were created around her worked to identify her as a woman of temperament and thus to deny her a space in which to articulate her concerns as a worker. In challenging Cecil B. De Mille in the courts, she helped to ensure that subsequent generations of screen stars would have greater room for manoeuvre in their dealings with their employers. But she did so at the cost of her career, and it was only when she was rediscovered by silent film enthusiasts in the early 1970s, some of whom went to great lengths to hear what she had to say, that her rehabilitation began. In the early 1980s, she was awarded a Rosemary Award, an honour created to give screen performers of the silent era belated recognition of their achievements, at a small ceremony in Los Angeles. Articles reporting on the event foregrounded not her alleged temperament but her commitment to making the films in which she appeared as good as they possibly could be, something for which she had received scant credit at the height of her fame. 'She always improved any film on which she worked', observed the *Hollywood Studio Magazine*. 'For Jetta Goudal was that curiosity in silent cinema, an actress who was intelligent, artistic, creative, and – despite her French accent – articulate' ('Jetta Goudal Receives Rosemary Award', n.d.).

## Notes

1  See, for example, Gaines (1991); McDonald (2000: 59–66).
2  On the difficulties that transplanted stage actors experienced in the motion picture studios, see Holmes (2005b).
3  On the dangerous situations in which stars were sometimes placed, see Holmes (2000: 105–6).
4  The quotes are transcribed from the original title cards.
5  On the reproduction of power struggles between screen actors and their employers as 'gripping narratives', see Gaines (1991: 146).
6  On the AEA in Hollywood, see Holmes (2005a).

## Bibliography

Benham, C. C. (1999), 'Jetta Goudal: The Exotic', *Classic Images*, 291 (September), http://www.classicimages.com/past_issues/view/?x=1999/september99/goudal.htm [accessed 10 January 2010].

*Birth of a Nation* (1915). Film. Directed by D. W. Griffith.

Bodeen, D. (1974), 'Jetta Goudal Brought Mystery As Well As Beauty to her Acting', *Films in Review*, 25 (October): 448–61.

*The Bright Shawl* (1923). Film. Directed by John S. Robertson.

Clarke, D. (1990), 'Acting in Hollywood's Best Interests: Representations of Labor During the National Recovery Administration', *Journal of Film and Video*, 42 (4) (Winter): 3–19.

*The Coming of Amos* (1925). Film. Directed by Paul H. Sloane [DVD]. US: Televista, Inc.

Decision of Actors' Branch Executive Committee, 8 August 1930, 'Goudal, Jetta vs. MGM Case #58', Academy of Motion Picture Arts and Sciences Collection, Conciliation Committee Files, Margaret Herrick Library, Los Angeles.

De Mille, C. B. (1959), *The Autobiography of Cecil B. De Mille*, edited by Donald Hayne, Englewood Cliffs, NJ: Prentice-Hall.

Donaldson, G. (1985), Letter, *Films in Review*, 36 (May): 319.

Donaldson, G. (1986), Letter, *Films in Review*, 37 (May): 319.

*Fighting Love* (1927). Film. Directed by Nils Olaf Chrisander.

*The Forbidden Woman* (1927). Film. Directed by Paul L. Stein.

Gaines, J. M. (1991), *Contested Culture: The Image, The Voice, and The Law*, Chapel Hill and London: University of North Carolina Press.

*Goudal v. Cecil B. De Mille Pictures Corp.*, 5 P.2d 432, 435 (Cal. Dist. Ct. App. 1931).

*The Green Goddess* (1923). Film. Directed by Sidney Alcott.

Hall, G. (1929), 'Diamond Studded Whims', *Motion Picture* (July): 34.

*Her Man O' War* (1926). Film. Directed by Frank Urson.

Holmes, S. P. (2000), 'The Hollywood Star System and the Regulation of Actors' Labour, 1916–1934', *Film History*, 12 (1): 97–114.

Holmes, S. P. (2005a), 'And the Villain Still Pursued Her: The Actors' Equity Association in Hollywood, 1919–1929', *Historical Journal of Film, Radio, and Television*, 25 (March): 27–50.

Holmes, S. P. (2005b), 'Canned Cooking: Stage Actors, Screen Acting and Cultural Hierarchy in the United States, 1912–1929', *Journal of American Drama and Theatre*, 17 (Winter): 9–15.

'Jetta Goudal Receives Rosemary Award' (n.d.), *Hollywood Studio Magazine*, no page, Goudal, Jetta, Microfiche Collection, British Film Institute Library, London.

King, B. (1984), 'Stardom as an Occupation', in P. Kerr (ed.), *The Hollywood Film Industry*, London and New York: Routledge & Kegan Paul.

*The King of Kings* (1927). Film. Directed by Cecil B. De Mille.

*Lady of the Pavements* (1929). Film. Directed by D. W. Griffith.

*Le Spectre Vert* (1930). Film. Directed by Jacques Feyder.

Locke, W. J. (1924a), 'The Coming of Amos', *Good Housekeeping*, 78 (January): 18–20, 152–64.

Locke, W. J. (1924b), 'The Coming of Amos', *Good Housekeeping*, 78 (February): 36–8, 92–106.

Locke, W. J. (1924c), 'The Coming of Amos', *Good Housekeeping*, 78 (March): 60–3, 251–60.

Locke, W. J. (1924d), 'The Coming of Amos', *Good Housekeeping*, 78 (April): 37–9, 101–35.

Locke, W. J. (1924e), 'The Coming of Amos', *Good Housekeeping*, 78 (May): 70–2, 179–94.

Locke, W. J. (1924f), 'The Coming of Amos', *Good Housekeeping*, 78 (June): 92–4, 247–74.

Locke, W. J. (1924g), 'The Coming of Amos', *Good Housekeeping*, 79 (July): 88–90, 194–204.

'Long Arm of Coincidence Replaces Goudal on High', unsourced clipping, 21 June 1931, in Goudal, Jetta, microfilmed clippings file, Margaret Herrick Library, Los Angeles.

*May v. New York Motion Picture Corp.*, 45 Cal. App. 396, 403, 187 Pac. 785, 788 (1920).

McDonald, P. (2000), *The Star System: Hollywood's Production of Popular Identities*, London: Wallflower Press.

*Paris at Midnight* (1926). Film. Directed by E. Mason Hopper.

Pierce, D. (1991), 'Success with a Dollar Sign: Costs and Grosses for the Early Films of Cecil B. De Mille', in P. C. Usai and L. Codelli (eds), *L'Eritta De Mille*, Pordenone: Edizione Biblioteca dell'imagine: 308–17.

*The Road to Yesterday* (1925). Film. Directed by Cecil B. De Mille.

*A Sainted Devil* (1924). Film. Directed by Joseph Henabery.

*Salome of the Tenements* (1925). Film. Directed by Sidney Alcott.

Slide, A. (1980), 'Silent Stars Speak', *Films in Review*, 31 (March): 129–41.

*The Spaniard* (1925). Film. Directed by Raoul Walsh.

Statement of Jetta Goudal before the Actors Adjustment Committee, 26 June 1930, 'Goudal, Jetta vs. MGM Case #58', Academy of Motion Picture Arts and Sciences Collection, Conciliation Committee Files, Margaret Herrick Library, Los Angeles.

*Three Faces East* (1926). Film. Directed by Rupert Julian.

*The Unholy Night* (1929). Film. Directed by Lionel Barrymore.

Unsourced clipping-a, 7 January 1927, no page, in Goudal, Jetta, microfilmed clippings file, Margaret Herrick Library, Los Angeles.

Unsourced clipping-b, 2 February 1929, no page, in Goudal, Jetta, microfilmed clippings file, Margaret Herrick Library, Los Angeles.

Unsourced clipping-c, 5 February 1929, in Goudal, Jetta, microfilmed clippings file, Margaret Herrick Library, Los Angeles.

Unsourced clipping-d, 18 March 1929, in Goudal, Jetta, microfilmed clippings file, Margaret Herrick Library, Los Angeles.

Unsourced clipping-e, 23 May 1930, in Goudal, Jetta, microfilmed clippings file, Margaret Herrick Library.

Unsourced clipping-f, 21 June 1930, in Goudal, Jetta, microfilmed clippings file, Margaret Herrick Library.

Untitled clipping-a, *Los Angeles Times*, 22 June 1924, no page, in Goudal, Jetta, microfilmed clippings file, Margaret Herrick Library, Los Angeles.

Untitled clipping-b, unidentified Oklahoma City newspaper, September 1925, no page, in Goudal, Jetta, microfilmed clippings file, Margaret Herrick Library, Los Angeles.

Untitled clipping-c, *Brooklyn Standard*, 1 August 1927, no page, in Goudal, Jetta, microfilmed clippings file, Margaret Herrick Library, Los Angeles.

*The Volga Boatman* (1926). Film. Directed by Cecil B. De Mille.

*White Gold* (1927). Film. Directed by William K. Howard.

Woollcott, A. (1921), 'The Play', *The New York Times*, 12 September, Section: Amusements, Hotels, and Restaurants, p. 14.

Yankwich, L. R. (1956), 'The Development of the Law of Intellectual Property and Creative Arts in the Western States', *Hastings Law Journal*, 7 (February): 123–42.

Youngman, G. (1954), 'Negotiation of Personal Service Contracts', *California Law Review*, 42: 2–17.

# Working as a freelancer in UK television*

chapter

# 6

RICHARD PATERSON

## Introduction

Freelance working is now the dominant mode of employment in UK television production. The pressures of regulatory change and increased competition in the emerging market space, with quotas for independent production, shaped the new conditions of employment practice with short-term contracts increasingly normative. Employment became bounded in television production by the emergent and changing organizational forms: a layered situation in which the BBC, ITV and independents (of varied organizational size) increasingly converged in their employment practices despite their differences in structure and history.

Changes in the UK television labour market were similar to those in other industries where self-employment grew in the 1990s. Flexibility of the workforce had become an ever more explicit objective of government economic policy, but the broader consequences of these new non-standard forms of employment were unknown. In the United Kingdom, 15.4 per cent of men and 6.9 per cent of women across all industries were self-employed in 1998 (by 2010 these numbers had grown to 17.8 per cent of men and 8.5 per cent of women), and the majority of these were effectively contract workers (Dex and McCulloch 1997). Television production provides a significant case study of some consequences of radical changes in modes of employment (Davis and Scase 2000).

The available labour force in television showed considerable growth in the 1980s, but there was a constant churn as people joined and left the labour pool. This essay considers a series of factors associated with the increasing use of freelance labour in UK television using data collected between 1994 and 1998 as part of a major research study, the British Film Institute's (BFI) Television Industry Tracking Study. In particular, the essay focuses on the impact of changes in the labour market and how freelance workers responded to the emerging contractual discourse.

## Background

A study of employment in television in the late 1980s (Varlaam *et al.* 1989) identified the increasing problems associated with the growing freelance labour market, particularly for the future training of a skilled workforce. In early 1994 the total television production workforce was estimated to be 29,000 of which about 13,000 were freelance (Woolf and Holly 1994). The rapid transition from an open to a closed labour market in the British television industry introduced different employment processes. The concomitant evolution of market-related issues in television also led to the emergence of a dialogue contesting the prevailing public service-oriented discourse.

Work in programme production in the United Kingdom in the late 1980s became increasingly synonymous with short-term contracts, as had long been the case in the United States (Gray and Seeber 1996). The gradual demise of the sentiments and structures of collective creativity in television, along with the advent of a predominantly freelance labour market, was significant for organizations and communities of practice (see, for example, Ursell 1998). This rebalancing continued after 2000 but following industry consolidation after regulatory changes the proportion of freelancers dropped slightly (cf. Doyle and Paterson 2008; Skillset 2009).

Historically, freelance employment had always been important in the film and television industries in the United Kingdom, particularly for directors, producers and editors. Management theorists have suggested that the emergence of flexible specialization and of portfolio careers are a necessary prerequisite of modern industry (see Christopherson and Storper 1989; Gallie *et al.* 1998), implicitly recognizing the growing use of short-term contracts.

With growth in the freelance sector, job security showed a marked decrease and the career expectations of a job for life were erased. The destabilization of an 'ordered' environment necessitated the development of new principles for contracting employment. Workers in the industry recognized the insufficiency of their existing organizational base and were forced to embrace more market-driven solutions. The development of a different set of interpretations of the employment contract was fundamental: contracts require transactions and how these have subsequently been ordered has played a contributory part in forging the characteristics of the new TV labour market.

Freelance workers in television production are engaged in project-based work (DeFillippi and Arthur 1998) and often work successively on short-term contracts in different firm environments. They encounter different organizational cultures and are seldom 'part of' the organization. Freelancing is synonymous with occupational individualism: individuals can be seen to act as self-motivated agents negotiating their working lives through the structural impediments they negotiate. The careers of freelance workers in television are not boundaryless (Arthur and Rousseau 1996), and indeed, arguably, they negotiate more boundaries than those who work as members of staff within organizations (cf. Jones 1996). They regularly participate in forming new project teams and become embedded in, sustain and nurture networks

(Burt 1992; Uzzi 1997), constantly renegotiating their work values and positioning their creative input inside distinct projects in order to accentuate their reputation and its exchange value so that they become known in the labour market.

All firms function to draw together resources and to varied degrees maintain, nourish and replenish them in order to sustain their businesses (Coase 1937). There is a constant migration of individuals across different projects and firms within the industry, and the rate of movement increased dramatically with the advent of wide-spread independent production. Freelancers both began to shape the organizational cultures of the industry and were shaped by them (Douglas 1987). The values of the production industry became more dependent on these freelance workers whose priority increasingly was to self above any loyalty to the companies employing them. While firms identified with their past productions when seeking new commissions, these commissions became increasingly reliant on the attachment of specific free-lance workers with good reputations. At the same time, the individual's reputation depended mainly on association with particular programmes rather than their relationship with specific firms.

Ideas are an important element of the market power of freelancers and can provide high recompense for a 'talented' individual worker who is in demand (Peiperl et al. 2000). However, the sharing of reward and of knowledge between the individual worker and the company wishing to deploy those ideas is bounded by a strict conditionality, which encourages opportunistic behaviour by both parties. Furthermore, while financial reward is contractually defined, the instantiation and later dissemination of the intangible reputation account is tied to performance on the project and the critical reception for the programme. The passage of production provides leverage for both parties in negotiating further contracts.

## The new labour market in television production

With the establishment of a flexible production sector in the television industry (Storper 1989), interconnected internal and external labour markets emerged with an unplanned and sometimes inadequate articulation of skills needs. Recurrent contracting emerged as a modus operandi for many individual workers, which facili-tated flexible and responsive project arrangements. Short-term contracts enabled monitoring and auditing of performance capabilities for both buyers and sellers in the labour market. This led to a minimization for the employer of fixed overheads and the ability to modulate financial outgoings to the availability of commissions and the demands of the specific production.

Transaction costs became a more visible part of the production process. In televi-sion production of any kind, complex combinations of specialized activity have to be assembled. In the contemporary television labour market, this has led to contracting from project to project in an open market. Where previously staff would be assigned to programmes through an internal mechanism (Anderson 1990), in restructur-ing the producers were put into the controlling position as buyers in a market where there are many alternative sources of supply. Notwithstanding the often contingent factors forcing firms to act opportunistically in the market, there were significant economic advantages to companies in such a market solution offsetting 'the diseconomies of large, once-for-all contracts that are often coupled to sustained role commitments' (cf. Williamson 1975; Faulkner and Anderson 1987). The entailment of freelancers' work is the need effectively to sustain their own employment bureaucracy: they need to negotiate contracts as well as to maintain records of income and expenditure for tax purposes. Some find this part of the freelance way of working to be a positive freedom: the quasi-psychological contract (Rousseau 1995) is with the self rather than the company – contractual individualism matching the industry's altered structuring.

There is a complex and contradictory logic to labour market trends in television. While companies seek to attract and retain certain talent, they remain dependent on the broadcaster to commission their programmes and sustain their projects. Firms as well as individual workers need to be embedded in the broadcasters' circle: hence the constant struggle to maintain links to commissioning editors or to secure preferred supplier status; the felt need to be visibly present at conferences and in trade associations and to develop a firm's reputation. The linkage between nodes within the company (and its penumbra of linked workers) has to be paralleled by links to commissioning editors (cf. McKelvey 1999).

Skilled workers on short-term contracts are attracted by prestigious projects where assessment is further boosted by the reputation of the company and the key personnel and talent attached. Workers with good reputations progress in their careers, while those with only moderate reputations do not, and those with poor reputations experience employment difficulties and often leave the labour market. In short, lack of success leads to lack of employment.

The positive gloss on information about the 'independent' or freelance world in its key formative period was a crucial factor in helping turn the labour market from a closed one to an open one. After the foundation of Channel 4 and the subsequent imposition of quotas for independent productions on BBC and ITV, opportunities seemed to be available to workers for new ventures, which suggested independence of activity and greater rewards. In theory, the creation of an open labour market with jobs freely available should ensure that people are able to find a better job, but the evidence shows that this did not happen. Becker (1993) noted how people spend resources acquiring information to the point where it is not worthwhile to acquire any more, leading to 'rational ignorance'. Many in television employment had just such a rational ignorance, which they willingly or unwittingly played as their career option.

Another way of expressing this is that the serendipitous nature of success in television is partly a result of being in the right place at the right time. As with the film industry, 'what makes single-project organisations particularly intriguing from career and mobility perspectives is that careers are produced by projects (and their controllers) making distinctions among individuals' (Faulkner and Anderson 1987). Where previously a form of pre-selection occurred of who was allowed to enter the television labour market, with a strong Oxbridge influence and advantage, there was now a different set of serendipities which our research indicated were related to family or connections: class connections have endured and emerged in a different form (BFI 1999).

## Finding work – the evidence

The overall supply of labour at any point in time is a crucial factor in the availability of work to individuals. While employers noted that some roles in television production were hard to fill, the oversupply in other areas led to difficulties for some workers in finding work. The downward pressure on budgets for programmes was often passed on to freelance staff, who were sometimes employed at a fixed contract price with no overtime payments. Companies took advantage of the shortage of work and the oversupply of labour to drive down rates but still expected additional hours of, effectively unpaid, work from staff. Furthermore, there was a belief among established workers that wages were undercut by younger and inexperienced workers willing to work for less pay. The difficulty of maintaining the rate for the job, let alone increase it, was a common complaint among freelance staff. Furthermore, there was the constant flow of willing unpaid workers wishing to break into the industry.

In any labour market, the ways in which work is found are critical to the smooth functioning of the services that the sector provides. The labour market seeks to match sellers of labour (workers) with buyers (the employers). Television – as a creative industry offering non-standard products, and one that had been in transition from a closed to an open labour market – developed a distorted set of job-seeking characteristics among workers. The use of 'personal contacts' was consistently the 'most important method' of finding work throughout the survey. A regular pattern emerged with between 46 and 61 per cent of the respondents identifying personal contacts as their most important method of finding work (BFI 1999), confirming the findings in many other industries (cf. Brown et al. 1998). Less than 5 per cent of all respondents indicated 'response to adverts' as their most important method for finding work.

Freelancers were found to be more likely to use personal contacts as a method of finding work than those with staff jobs. In the May 1998 questionnaire, 63 per cent of freelancers indicated personal contacts as their main method of finding work, compared to 33 per cent of independent staff and 36 per cent of broadcaster staff. Staff employed at a broadcaster were most likely to use job adverts and formal applications.

The operation of the labour market is crude but effective. When respondents were asked in November 1997 what their sources of information were when seeking jobs, the informal, contacts network proved to be the primary source of information (68 per cent). In comparison, 21 per cent indicated newspaper advertisements, and 18 per cent the trade press. When seeking information on changes in the media industry, respondents predominantly turned to formal sources with 88 per cent of the sample indicating using the trade papers, newsletters and journals as a main source of information on the industry.

In November 1997 employers who recruited staff were asked about their practices. Two-thirds indicated the use of personal and work contacts to find staff, with

44 per cent relying on personal recommendations as their main recruitment method. Among all other methods mentioned, trade press gained less than 15 per cent of the responses. Furthermore, recruiters in the independent sector, perhaps unsurprisingly given the non-bureaucratic cultures and the lack of formal equal opportunities policies to be adhered to in employment matters, were more likely to use informal methods for seeking staff. In total, 69 per cent of independent employers used these networks, compared to 32 per cent of those in the ITV companies and 33 per cent of recruiters at the BBC.

## The contractual discourse

Freelance workers addressed their uncertain employment prospects with a range of strategies. These were expressed discursively in the Industry Tracking Study in relation to freelance employment in what might be termed a contractual discourse – the predominant determining features of freelance life.

After the changes in labour market conditions in UK television, short-termism was quickly taken to extremes with contract periods in many cases of weeks rather than months (see Paterson 2001a). This was partly due to the project nature of television work but was exacerbated by the precarious economic position of many production companies. The short contract periods became widespread throughout the industry as managers looked to reduce costs, and sufficient numbers of an ever more insecure workforce proved willing to endure hardships to gain or retain a foothold in television production. The work histories of freelance workers are built upon a succession of joined work events and involve recurrent contracting under conditions of bounded rationality and precarious certainty. In fact, there is a high level of variability in the frequency and length of contracts offered to freelancers, including multiple short contracts in the same firm (often as a rolling contract and almost akin to full-time staff employment) or serially across different firms, jobbing from one company to the next on contracts of varying length and with different periods of layoff.

The transformation of labour market practice altered the approaches of those working in television to the idea of a career: moving from the structural approach to careers (basically that we may have agency but are constrained by structure) to one based on psychological self-motivated determination (Peiperl et al. 2000). Freelance work provided individuals with wide-ranging opportunities, but this was counterbalanced by the uncertainties associated with securing ongoing employment. Doubts about the future varied from individual to individual, but people acted rationally trying to find work in different ways in the new environment. For example, many reduced their forward financial commitments to provide a cushion against the new insecurities.

Attrition among the labour force, due to a range of industrial and individual factors, ensures that only a fraction of qualified and talented industry personnel get the chance of success and an even smaller number achieve higher levels (cf. Faulkner 1983). Even the most successful freelance workers sometimes fell foul of the preference and selection system, which operated, often perversely, to deny employment even to those with successful track records. There are various explanations for the lack of success in gaining employment – from ageism and fear of experienced workers on the part of employers to workers simply falling out of the loop of the network of contacts in a particular genre.

Uncertainty is a defining feature of the television freelance labour market (Dex *et al.* 1998). Short-term contracts provide no guarantee of future work and income, and therefore no basis for planning life commitments. On entry to the industry, often as a single person fresh out of higher education or looking for a career in television following an initial period in an adjunct field, future plans are as much an aspiration as an achievable objective. However, the evidence showed that it takes a relatively short time for the excitement and glamour of the job to seem less attractive. The impact of the demands of work in television production (long hours, uncertainty etc.) could be considerable in the domain of personal life and sometimes began to create resentment.

The industry's constant roller-coaster, feast-or-famine modality – the contingencies of restructuring, mergers, commissioning freezes and so on – had a direct impact on the freelance labour force in the period of data collection. Uncertainty provides employers with considerable additional power in the workplace. The counterbalancing force previously offered by the trade unions when there was restricted entry to the workforce – when they could exert some influence on the conditions of work – was absent. Freelance employees found it difficult to register discontent and criticism with an employer who resisted criticism and who had the power to affect future employment prospects. The force of fear in poor labour market conditions was considerable.

The collective organization necessary for television production requires a high level of team working once a programme has been commissioned. Team working, interpreted as good working relationships, was identified by 84.1 per cent of respondents as a critical factor in securing optimum conditions and realizing the most 'creative' outputs (Paterson 2010). The team working environment and the ease of working together have been seen by some analysts (Faulkner and Anderson 1987; Jones 1996) as the elements most at risk in the industry as its labour market practices were transformed. Production work on programmes is team driven but the new and different organizational types and cultures had created a degree of instability and uncertainty in this area. Work was increasingly carried out with a wider set of risk factors. With ever more broken strings in the networks of effective working relationships (Burt 1992; Paterson 2001b), with individuals on short-term contracts and living with uncertainty, some form of compensatory framework was necessary. The team environment created for each programme production – however temporary – offered some element of certainty.

Individuals responded to the variations in the labour market conditions in different ways dependent on their position in the industry at transition points between contracts. For some, serial contracts were a necessity to maintain a living, but there was a common desire for better pay and more senior roles. This was more difficult to achieve when work in companies was only for short periods. A longer period of work – sometimes through successive contracts in the same firm – was needed to facilitate career advance, often achieved after trust and the values of reputation had accrued and the worker's potential had been seen.

As Female 20-2,[1] a researcher, commented (November 1997), 'In my experience the problems of working on short contracts go beyond the worry of just getting work. It is not really sustainable for me to work on short contracts at all. I think it may even be better to stay on benefits – but I want to pursue my career'. Female 20-10, assistant producer, Indie 12, suggested (November 1997),

> My company has a 'convenient' way of employing on short-term con-
> tracts. Because mine has rolled I'm told that I'm lucky to have the security
> and therefore am paid at a lower salary. In fact no security exists – how
> can it on a one-month contract? I have no pension plan [or] health
> scheme and am paid at the same rate as I [was] as a junior researcher
> over a year ago, although I've developed and pitched ideas, worked as
> an assistant producer. I now feel little loyalty to the company and am
> extremely cynical and untrusting of management. I seek to leave as soon
> as possible. There should be very strict parameters for employing an
> ever-increasing, short-term contract workforce.

For Male 20-21, a junior researcher, the situation was really difficult (November 1997): 'I have been out of work for nearly a fortnight now with certainly no prospect of being employed in the immediate future by Granada. This is due to lack of production at the moment, but it's certainly making me feel frustrated and uncertain.'

In short, the career path of freelancers is marked by discontinuities. Traditionally, careers required 'a sort of running adjustment between a man [sic] and the various facts of life and of his professional world' (Hughes 1971). However, freelancers in television production face an unstable environment and career progression can only be haphazard. The transitions in freelance work histories were variable in form and necessarily contingent on a series of factors, including the developing technologies and economics of television, work availability, elements of reputation accrued and degree of embeddedness (cf. Granovetter 1985). Such conventional indications of career development as promotion, and an increase in responsibility, were effected differently for freelance workers. The notion of promotion still operated as a concept within the freelance world but problematically, as it derives from the continuities of an organizationally-based employment regime. There was a desire to move up the hierarchy of creative jobs defined by budget size and scheduling slot, and to be associated with talent both behind and in front of the screen. 'Freelance careers' were built across companies in an uncontrolled pattern. Once a reputation was established, it became possible to act in a more measured way with longer periods of stable employment when trust and a consolidation of reputation could be estab-lished. The target for many in the panel remained securing full-time, long-term employment in the BBC or one of the large companies, and in the course of the data collection for some workers this was achieved.

For freelance staff the development of contacts becomes a central part of their routine working life. The ex-broadcaster staff often had ready-made networks – particularly at the craft and support staff levels inside the duopoly companies – but these needed to be nurtured and sustained in the long term, and extended to the independent sector. Male 30-3, a freelance producer, commented in November 1994 that he found great differences between the philosophy of staffing at independent production companies and those in his previous employment at Thames Television (one of the biggest UK commercial broadcasting organizations in the 1980s holding the London weekday franchise). His experience was that the independents engaged in buying people with specific skills for specific projects.

It is in the interest of a freelance worker to be embedded in the informal networks of many independent production companies and to be considered skilled and trust-worthy. Freelance workers seek a promiscuous or serial embeddedness. It has been argued that multiple weak ties are more advantageous than a few strong ties in gain-ing work, even though the nature of the network ties is just as important (Burt 1992). Female 40-3, a freelance director, commented (May 1996) that 'we sporadically-employed freelance drongos feel that no one is sympathetic or concerned about the workers at the coalface. After all, we're so easily replaced'.

Achieving an embedded status is a consequence of the continual testing of a worker's reputational value in day-to-day production. As Uzzi (1997) has noted, freelance workers have to 'follow heuristic and qualitative decision rules rather than intensely calculative ones'. It is in their interest to cultivate long-term cooperative ties rather than narrowly pursue self-interest. This in turn encourages a network dynamics, leading to cooperative behaviour because it is in all actors' best interests, and to some extent counteracts the opportunistic behaviour predicted by transac-tion cost economics (Ghoshal and Moran 1996).

The use value of networks and the need for an exchange value of reputation to ensure their smooth functioning confirmed Faulkner's (1983) analysis of Hollywood. He identified three major areas of analysis: the clustering of links themselves into blocks of networks, the pattern of dominance and success within these networks, and the pattern of ties that any freelancer has.

In television production, the freelancer is reliant on the support of networks to sustain, connect and communicate about employment opportunities, and this facility is based to some extent on his or her reputation. If television production is considered as a set of communities of practice, then the networks are the building blocks enabling the intersecting communities. There is a need actively to negotiate the presentation of self, and to ensure potential employers are aware of skills that can be deployed by the individual, as well as a sense that he or she is compatible with the organization's culture. Freelancers seek to widen network contacts and accrue credits to gain leverage in the contractual system of this labour market. The resulting reputation is a constructed narrative, both heterogeneous and acting through network nodes to confirm both individual attributes and the shared community ideologies.

Reputation is a product, and while it has been noted that 'the power of the nor-mative contract lies in members who trust that others will play by the same rules' (Rousseau 2001), that is, its contemporaneousness, the central lesson of bounded rationality in the study of economic organization is that 'all complex contracts are unavoidably incomplete' (Rosen 1991). They are part of a developing reputational narrative for the individual worker, which, as noted above, accrues a value and is deployed in recruitment decisions (Paterson 2010).

## Differentiated work histories

The work histories of freelance workers are built upon a succession of joined work events, and involve recurrent contracting under conditions of bounded rationality and precarious certainty (Faulkner 1983; Paterson 2001a).

Inevitably there was a range of responses to the entailments of a freelance life. Male 50-34, freelance TV news journalist wrote (November 1997), 'This is the good thing about freelancing, which I enjoy enormously – the freedom firstly, and then the variety of the days and the sheer sense of delight of not having to get somewhere by 9 every morning like clockwork.' A large number of freelancers expressed a strong preference for staff employment, and Female 30-18, a former staff director, recounted (March 1994), 'In the present climate I prefer the freedom of being freelance. Staff directors in drama now seem devalued.'

Expressing a management perspective, Male 40-26, a senior executive in ITV noted (March 1994), 'When working with freelance contract staff, there is no continuity and no real loyalty from them to company aims. Often aims of company different from freelance staff.'

Individual experiences of employment were inevitably very varied, with age a key variable. Female 50-1, a former BBC producer, noted in November 1996,

> Due to a large number of redundancies within Children's Department, I was not offered a freelance contract for the second year. During this time therefore I have been making contacts, developing ideas and attempting to get various projects off the ground ... I feel slightly disheartened that with all my experience I have found it so difficult ever to get to see people, and am staggered that so many executives – who know me either personally or by my previous work – have on many occasions not even acknowledged my letter.

The freelance director, Female 40-3 (May 1996), described how there had been a need for constant readjustment in 1996 and had found being out of work qualitatively worse than before – and a sense of being treated as a non-person – leading to deep anxieties about work; the main problem of not being 'in' (embedded) with some companies was that she had no one to take ideas to. This contrasts with Male 50-24, an ex-ITV production supervisor who, in May 1996 after being made redundant, wrote 'I am now involved as camera supervisor on the ITV morning worship programme each Sunday and sending out my CV and waiting for the phone to ring during the rest of the week', but a year later noted that 'due to lack of trained staff at Anglia Television, my main employer, I find I am being used more and more'. However, in contrast, Male 50-8, series producer, Indie 68, recounted, 'After nearly four years on the freelance stump I have finally left that faceless army of souls who flit from regional outpost to regional outpost with CV in one hand and suitcase in the other.'

Younger workers reflected more on the demands of the industry: Female 20-3, an assistant producer, commented in May 1994 that 'either way I will have to maintain flexible attitude and skills for life, not job for life, and broaden contacts outside of Central', while Male 20-16, a props buyer, wrote (May 1997), 'I dislike the uncertainty of short-term contracts', and looked to the establishment of a network and regular team situations. Female 20-25, associate producer at an ITV network company, noted (May 1996), 'Whilst I had a contract I had to constantly prove myself, so I worked very hard.' Female 20-16, a freelance producer, focused on the entertainment and youth genre and attached herself to talent, constantly building contacts and establishing a successful career niche: 'just keep working, keep making contracts' (May 1997). This approach applied in particular to on-screen talent – and where in the past this had been a battle between broadcasters (e.g. over Morecambe and Wise or Bruce Forsyth), with the growth of independent production the situation had transformed so that companies predicated on the talent of a key star had emerged. These changes in some of the fundamentals of the production business had also been the basis for the emergence of more writer-led or producer-led independent production companies.

There was some variation in the views of freelance working across different job types. In 1997, 73 per cent of those in post-production and technical roles were satisfied with working freelance, compared to 40 per cent of producers and directors. Some in technical roles such as editing or camerawork were able to command a higher rate and achieve regular work in the freelance sector where their expertise was in demand. Where skills were in short supply, work was readily available for freelance workers and they were better rewarded.

Availability could be determined by location. On securing a long-term contract, Male 30-2, an executive producer at a small independent, wrote (November 1997), 'It's an example of the free-market working in my [a freelance's] favour, since the company has wanted to guarantee my availability to them when there is a shortage of experienced freelance producers in Manchester and the company is anticipating a period of expansion in 1998.' It could also be determined by skill. Female 40-15, freelance production manager, reported (November 1997), 'I have generally speaking never had to worry about/look for work. I continually turn it down because I'd be working forty-eight hours a day and that wasn't the idea of going freelance.'

As noted above, there was a key difference among workers, which was defined by age and experience (Paterson 2010). Older freelance workers tended to have similar work histories within the duopoly: most of the career boundaries they experienced while developing their careers had usually been crossed before they assumed freelance status. They had been employed in their formative years in the corporate world of large organizations, achieving promotions and constructing their reputations. The younger age cohorts, particularly those who had joined in the post-1980s period, seldom had any corporate experience, but their work histories had settled into recognizable patterns of movement between firms, even if only a limited number of firms, reflecting their network reach.

Those who had known staff status and benefited from security and regular training, and from relatively open opportunities for career progression (especially through attachment schemes in the BBC), had, in the freelance world, been forced to adjust to a different labour market with separate contractual norms. Contracts, payments and bookings now had to be negotiated, and opportunistic behaviour was necessary.

Male 40-8, head cameraman at an ITV network company, wrote (November 1997) about a former cameraman colleague who had decided to go freelance:

> He has worked almost constantly since he left, which is excellent for him, but I think [it] also shows how respected the operators from TLS are when available in the outside world. My two senior cameramen colleagues have also been extremely busy doing freelance work since taking 'early retirement' – there isn't enough space on this page to put down all my views on this ridiculous system of paying people to get them off the permanent wage bill only to have to bring them back to work because we are so short staffed.

Seeking security, Female 40-24, a PA at an ITV company wrote (November 1997), 'I have tried to work on programmes that have a certain amount of permanence, such as Coronation Street, but even this is no longer a secure area as the new administration would prefer to use people on short-term contracts and are redefining the job descriptions.'

For experienced workers who had been made redundant there was a second level of problem: the challenge to self-esteem caused by restructuring. Some former staff members had seized the opportunity of freelance work when it arose, seeking a new freedom. Others were structural 'casualties', and for some this mode of working was accepted but not welcomed. Individuals sometimes discovered that their lifetime investments in knowledge and skills and the intra-firm relationships were now redundant (cf. DeFillippi and Arthur 1998). The changed attitudes were sometimes attributed to ageism, which was a regular source of complaint by older freelance workers, and there was a perception of an emerging generational gap in television (Paterson 2010).

There were further heterogeneities in the freelance workforce in television, with clear differences between men and women in terms of job continuity. While this was to the detriment of women, in most cases women were found to fare better within the more structured environment of broadcasting than in independent companies (Willis and Dex 2003). Gender differences in experience and expectation were distinctive so that, for example, maternity pay was a great concern to many younger freelancers, and some women turned down work because of the desire not to work away from home and their children.

For the most talented, work was usually available. For the ambitious there was the magnet of future achievement. The market power of some talented individuals was unquestionable. Their reputations were based on achievements, which might include industry awards, information spread informally by word of mouth about skills and knowledge or their reported ability to work within budget and to schedule. The elite core of the industry is small and there is both a periphery and a wider aspirant group in all areas. For many others there was an in-between state, which became increasingly vexatious as people got older and failed to achieve success.

The lack of stability and purpose in the freelance world and the high level of alienation sometimes undermined the creative environment.

## Contracts and their discontents

The discursive entries collected in the Industry Tracking Study revealed issues highlighting numerous discontents of freelancers with their contracts. Comments from three female workers in their thirties illustrated the issues. A writer, Female 30-1, commented (May 1997), '[W]hen at the BBC contracts were restricted to short periods only – that is, six months instead of one year – this meant less job security and the need for more flexibility.' A year later she was under greater pressure, noting 'the need to be multi-skilled and [finding it] hard to achieve this with so few training opportunities. Contract work very sporadic. Insecure when you work in editorial/development when you are independent and don't have the subsidy of a large department behind you.' An assistant producer (Female 30-7) who had been forced into ever shorter contracts wrote (May 1995),

> I have found myself chasing work of shorter contracts. Sometimes I have worked for only one or two weeks. I have therefore had to spread my net of contacts much wider. My salary has varied considerably depending on the type of work from £500 per week to £650, and I have found it initially impossible to negotiate a rate. There always seems to be plenty of people willing to take the work for the salary being offered. I have tried to specialize in music and arts but the last year has been very sparse in that area.

By May 1996 the vagaries of the industry's uncertainties had had a major impact, as she commented, 'Have held on to possibility of long-term project and not pursued other companies as a result. What was to have been a one-year contract has now shrunk to seven weeks but may be renewed each seven weeks or so.' Finally, a director/producer (Female 30-15) was highly critical of the industry situation in November 1994, explaining,

> [T]he hours and the unpredictability of when these hours are going to be – coupled with working as a freelancer for independents, or broadcasters who have no interest in developing you, or looking after you – means that the work conditions have become Dickensian. From 19 September to 21 October I worked without a single day off, and the last two weeks of that period were both ninety-hour weeks ... We desperately need some kind of regulation brought back in.

At the same time, many freelance workers disliked long contracts. They were seen as holding back career development, or more often as removing the participant from contact with the networks, which provide employment opportunities and opportunities for career progression. The elements of reputation were not being accrued and becoming known in the industry networks. A female production manager (Female 20-21) commented (November 1996), 'I think the twelve-month contract as a production manager was a mistake – it held me at the same level for too long. Only now am I able to plan moves as producer/director in future.' And an editor (Male 40-5) noted in November 1995,

> In the back of my mind ... is the thought that by the end of January 1996 I will be looking for work ... The problem with this current job is because it's such a long contract I have lost day-to-day contact with many people. Working from home has its advantages but the essential social side of the job is missing.

Further confirmation came from a director (Male 30-12) in May 1996 who observed that 'offers of work cannot be ignored. I've probably stayed too long with some companies and lost other clients by doing so. I find that work is easier to come by now, but it's still worrying when a contract is coming to an end and there's no work on the horizon'.

However, some freelance workers – those with insufficient accrued reputation capital – would 'never say no' because of the level of competition for jobs, the insecurities and uncertainties, and real or potential financial problems.

The research data showed that having been unemployed in the previous six months was associated with a large reduction in the likelihood of being employed in the next period, although being unemployed in the previous year did not (Dex and Smith 2000). Furthermore, being freelance significantly reduced the probability of being employed and increased the probability of being unemployed in any given month, and the effect was larger for men than for women.

Casualization undermined the collegial approach identified by a number of respondents as most conducive to good programme making. Forging relationships based on trust and entering fully into teamwork could be problematic for the freelance employee working serially on projects in different firms. There was no psychological contract and too little participation in any collective identity because they were not part of the organization. Some firms addressed this problem by establishing a pool of trusted freelance workers as a core virtual team – personnel on whom they could rely and to whom they first turned to offer work. Indeed, many independent owners claimed to try, to the extent possible within fragile business plans, both to keep talent and build trust. They had a consciousness of their dependence on high-quality freelance staff and, as important, needed to minimize transaction costs (in putting project teams together) while maximizing guarantees of quality outputs. However, as noted above, inevitably in the increasingly individualized employment environment, while the need of the independents was to achieve a reputation for their company, the interest of the individual worker was to gain credit for his or her work – to boost his or her reputation as an individual rather than that of the company.

The interests of an individual worker may also differ in other ways from those of the firm he or she is temporarily working for. Although many owners attempted to introduce 'new blood' to their firms for a variety of reasons (training, expanding the pool of contacts), in terms of opportunism, this was not in the interest of the existing pool of workers. Owners and managers talked about embedding freelancers into teams and the difficulty of maintaining continuities in independent production companies.

Notwithstanding these inherent contradictions, it is the nature of television production that distinct networks emerge from persistent patterns of contracting. When commissioned, producers with given resources tended to settle into self-reproducing business transactions and contract from a relatively small and distinct pool of freelance workers (cf. Faulkner and Anderson 1987).

Although companies would often have a preferred group of freelance workers to whom they would initially turn, the uncertainties in time frames inherent in commissioning could make such people unavailable when they were needed – the other side of the opportunism paradox. Problems arose when decisions were made very late by the commissioning editors so that the independent companies sometimes faced major difficulties in hiring staff. While being part of a core of regular contract workers can be reassuring, the desired degree of attachment can be very variable when reputation distinctiveness is so important.

There were further consequences from the vagaries of both serial contracting and late decisions. For instance, according to one producer, freelancers often spend time worrying about their next contract rather than attending to the job in hand in an increasingly insecure industry.

One of the negative consequences of the proliferation of short-term contracts was that the lack of stability and purpose in the freelance world, and the high level of alienation, undermined creative environments (Paterson 2010). Some expressed the view that fewer and fewer employers were willing to take risks with ideas or to innovate, and this inevitably affected the approach of creative workers. In a market where uncertainty is prevalent, it is possible that the most secure career path may mean taking the least risky option or the least innovative direction. For example, when asked, over a third felt that short-term contract work had made them cautious about new ideas, and over half were uncertain about a long-term TV career (BFI 1999). The picture is complex as for some workers – particularly younger ones – short contracts provided an opportunity to gain a wider range of experiences at work. So, for example, of those who had worked on short-term contracts, 73 per cent believed that the experience had given them a taste of other genres.

## Conclusions

Freelance life in television is bounded by the tension between occupational individualism and the collective nature of and necessary teamwork for successful television production. The individualistic approach of workers in the competitive labour market developed after the disappearance of the duopoly control of television by the BBC and the large integrated producer-broadcasters in the United Kingdom. With most job offers secured through personal contacts, reputation – and the networks that transmit information about individual workers – became central to the functioning of the labour market. These reputations are established through the development of a narrative of ability based on fragments establishing social and cultural capital and providing a scoring of the individual's worth. Reputation acts as the informal currency of information exchange between workers and prospective employers.

The complexity of the social market of employment and its transactional variables necessitates a broad analysis of the specificities of freelance life in TV production. As noted, there are a number of key terms that are relevant: idiosyncratic contracting, reputation, networking, embeddedness, psychological contracting, values and purpose, and these relate further to some important defining issues in the maintenance of an industry defined by 'creativity': skills availability and training provision, communities of practice and boundaries.

A range of contractual parameters – legal and psychological – supports the effective functioning of this labour market and underpins the freelance employment relationship in television. Whereas a staff member usually has a contract of employment with a job description and associated terms and conditions – a narrative contract – the freelancer's contemporary contract (whether written or not) defines a relatively short term of employment. This may be at, above or below the going rate and is based on a contract of engagement. These 'idiosyncratic deals' focus on specific short-term deals in which creative people typically see themselves as unique individuals with unique skill sets. The organization's commitments to the worker for the future is expressed formally only through accreditation on the programme produced, but informally by the *post hoc* reputational residue from the role performed, which can then be communicated more widely through different networks.

The different contractual relationships of creative workers in television reflect the different types of firm-subcontractor relationships in project work. There are individuals who work only once for a firm. More frequent are relationships that lead to repeated work for one or more firms, but for no one primary firm. Lastly, there is the traditional exclusive employment relationship.

The lack of stability and purpose in the freelance world and the high level of alienation undermine a creative environment. Insecurity in the industry, and the prevalence of short-term contracts, may have wider consequences for the creative future of TV broadcasting as a whole. Some expressed the view that fewer and fewer employers were willing to take risks with ideas or to innovate, and this inevitably affected the approach of creative workers, leading to extreme caution about new ideas. In a market where uncertainty is prevalent, it is possible that the most secure career path for a worker means taking the least risky option or the least innovative direction when working on programmes. Attention to the contingencies of the creative environment requires equal attention to the intellectual health of the freelance workforce and their conditions of employment.

## Notes

* The research in this chapter has benefited from a research grant from the Economic and Social Research Council (Contract R 000 23 7131) and earlier funding from the Hoso Bunka Foundation and Skillset. An earlier version was delivered at the SASE Conference, University of Minnesota, Minneapolis, June 2005.
1 The designation of the workers has been made anonymous where they are quoted: a worker designated Male 30-17 is the 17th male worker in the 31-40 age cohort. The independent production companies were identified by a number (e.g. Indie 7).

# Bibliography

Anderson, K. (1990), 'The Management and Organisation of BBC's Television Programme-Making Process', in R. Paterson (ed.), *Organising for Change*, London: BFI.

Arthur, M. B. and Rousseau, D. M. (eds) (1996), *The Boundaryless Career*, Oxford: Oxford University Press.

Becker, G. (1993), *Human Capital* (third edition), Chicago: University of Chicago Press.

BFI (1999), *BFI Television Industry Tracking Study: Third Report*, London: British Film Institute.

Brown, W., Deakin, S., Hudson, M., Pratten, C. and Ryan, P. (1998), *The Individualisation of Employment Contracts in Britain*, Employment Relations Research Series 4, London: Department of Trade and Industry.

Burt, R. (1992), *Structural Holes: The Social Structure of Competition*, Cambridge: Harvard University Press.

Christopherson, S. and Storper, M. (1989), 'The Effects of Flexible Specialisation on Industrial Politics and the Labor Market', *Industrial & Labor Relations Review*, 42 (April): 331–47.

Coase, R. H. (1937), 'The Nature of the Firm', reprinted in R. H. Coase (1988), *The Firm, the Market and the Law*, Chicago: University of Chicago Press.

Davis, H. and Scase, R. (2000), *Managing Creativity: The Dynamics of Work and Organisation*, Buckingham: Open University Press.

DeFillippi, R. and Arthur, M. B. (1998), 'Paradox in Project-Based Enterprise: The Case of Film Making', *California Management Review*, 40 (2): 125–38.

Dex, S. and McCulloch, A. (1997), *Flexible Employment: The Future of Britain's Jobs*, London: Equal Opportunities Commission.

Dex, S. and Smith, C. (2000), 'The Employment Experiences of the Self-Employed: The Case of Television Production Workers', *Research Papers in Management Studies*, Cambridge: Judge Institute of Management Studies.

Dex, S., Willis, J., Paterson, R. and Sheppard, E. (1998), 'Freelance Workers and Contract Uncertainty: The Effects of Contractual Changes in the Television Industry', *Work, Employment & Society*, 14 (2): 283–305.

Douglas, M. (1987), *How Institutions Think*, Basingstoke: RKP.

Doyle, G. and Paterson, R. (2008), 'Public Policy and Independent Television Production in the UK', *Journal of Media Business Studies*, 5 (3): 15–31.

Faulkner, R. R. (1983), *Music on Demand: Composers and Careers in the Hollywood Film Industry*, New Brunswick, NJ: Transaction Books.

Faulkner, R. R. and Anderson, A. (1987), 'Short-Term Projects and Emergent Careers: Evidence from Hollywood', *American Journal of Sociology*, 92 (January): 879–909.

Gallie, D., White, M., Cheng, Y. and Tomlinson, M. (1998), *Restructuring the Employment Relationship*, Oxford: Clarendon Press.

Ghoshal, S. and Moran, P. (1996), 'Theories of Economic Organization: The Case for Realism and Balance', *Academy of Management Review*, 21 (1): 58–72.

Granovetter, M. (1985), 'Economic Action and Social Structure: The Problem of Embeddedness', *American Journal of Sociology*, 91 (November): 481–510.

Gray, L. and Seeber, R. L. (1996), *Under the Stars: Essays in Labor Relations in Arts and Management*, Ithaca: ILR Press/Cornell University Press.

Hughes, E. C. (1971), *The Sociological Eye: Selected Papers*, Chicago: Aldine.

Jones, C. (1996), 'Careers in Project Networks: The Case of the Film Industry', in M. B. Arthur and D. M. Rousseau (eds), *The Boundaryless Career*, Oxford: Oxford University Press.

McKelvey, B. (1999), 'Avoiding Complexity Catastrophe in Coevolutionary Pockets: Strategies for Rugged Landscapes', *Organization Science*, 10 (May–June): 294–321.

Paterson, R. (2001a), 'The Television Labour Market in Britain', in J. Tunstall (ed.), *Media Occupations and Professions*, Oxford: Oxford University Press.

Paterson, R. (2001b), 'Working Lives in Television', *Media, Culture & Society*, 23 (4): 495–520.

Paterson, R. (2010) 'The Contingencies of Creative Work in UK Television', *Open Communication Journal*, 4: 2–9.

Peiperl, M., Arthur, M. B., Goffee, R. and Morris, T. (eds) (2000), *Career Frontiers: New Conceptions of Working Lives*, Oxford: Oxford University Press.

Rosen, S. (1991), 'Transaction Costs and Internal Labour Markets', in O. Williamson and S. G. Winter (eds), *The Nature of the Firm: Origins, Evolution and Development*, Oxford: Oxford University Press.

Rousseau, D. M. (1995), *Psychological Contracts in Organizations*, Thousand Oaks, CA: Sage.

Rousseau, D. M. (2001), 'Idiosyncratic Psychological Contracts: Are Flexibility and Consistency Mutually Exclusive?', *Organizational Dynamics*, 29 (4): 260–73.

Skillset (2009), *Employment Census 2009: The Results of the Seventh Census of the Audiovisual Industries*, London: Skillset.

Storper, M. (1989), 'The Transition to Flexible Specialisation in the US Film Industry: External Economies, the Division of Labour, and the Crossing of Industrial Divides', *Cambridge Journal of Economics*, 13 (June): 273–305.

Ursell, G. (1998), 'Labour Flexibility in the UK Commercial Television Sector', *Media, Culture & Society*, 20 (1): 129–53.

Uzzi, B. (1997), 'Social Structure and Competition in Interfirm Networks: The Paradox of Embeddedness', *Administrative Science Quarterly*, 42 (March): 35–67.

Varlaam, C. et al. (1989), *Skill Search: The Key Facts Part 1: Television, Film and Video Industry Employment Patterns and Training Needs (IMS Report)*, Brighton: Institute of Manpower Studies.

Williamson, O. (1975), *Markets and Hierarchies*, New York: Free Press.

Willis, J. and Dex, S. (2003), 'Mothers Returning to Television Production Work in a Changing Environment', in A. Beck (ed.), *Cultural Work: Understanding the Cultural Industries*, London: Routledge.

Woolf, M. and Holly, S. (1994), *Employment Patterns and Training Needs 1993/4: Freelance and Set Crafts Research*, London: Skillset.

# Behind the scenes

## The working conditions of technical workers in the Nigerian film industry

chapter

# 7

IKECHUKWU OBIAYA

Behind-the-scenes workers in the Nigerian video film industry, like their colleagues in other film industries, rarely if ever get into the limelight. It therefore comes as no surprise that most of the attention generated by this industry has been focused on the more visible players such as the actors and the directors. Consequently, not much is known of the workers who operate behind the scenes. The goal of this chapter is to provide some insight into the interior workings of the Nigerian video film industry by focusing on this group of workers, the film crew.

Following the economic downturn of the 1980s, the film industry in Nigeria went into decline thanks to soaring costs and lack of facilities. The subsequent shift to video film production led to its revival. This highly successful approach to film-making has generated a lot of interest and a growing body of scholarly work. However, although a few studies have been carried out on the work of some directors (for instance, Haynes 2007a, 2007b), very little attention has been given to the large group of people that constitute the crew. Apart from the occasional reference to the quality of the work of this group and the absence of adequately trained technical people, they rarely feature in the discussions on the industry. The decision to carry out a study of the working conditions of those of the technical crew was guided precisely by this gap. Also, the successes of the industry and the public lives of its celebrated actors have given rise to an impression of economic buoyancy and glamour, and one of the key questions that this study sets out to answer is whether this view obscures the realities of the working lives of technical crews and ancillary workers.

Data for the study were derived from interviews carried out in 2010 and 2011. The selection of persons for the interviews was done randomly and was highly dependent on the possibility of getting personal introductions, through acquaintances, to the potential interviewees. The importance of the personal introductions lies in the fact that it was a quick means not only of establishing contact but also of overcoming initial distrust. However, arranging meetings with the interviewees was difficult given the unpredictability of their working hours and the fact that they were located in other cities or on set. As a consequence, the interviews were largely carried out on the telephone at times convenient to the workers. Thus, the interviews had to be scheduled for either before or after their working hours and were held either early in the morning, in the late afternoon or at night. A small number of them were carried out during breaks in shooting.

An added difficulty faced during this study was that of obtaining an accurate figure of the population of such workers in the industry. Although it is widely accepted that the growth of the Nigerian film industry has led to an increase in employment possibilities, concrete figures to back up this claim are not available. The FountainHead Research group estimates that 'Nollywood employs over a million people' (FountainHead 2008: 9). However, this figure cannot be verified. There are neither state nor industry regulatory bodies responsible for collecting data on new entrants. Thus, this makes it difficult to be precise as to the number of those employed in the sector. All the behind-the-scenes workers interviewed in the course of this research admitted that the field was heavily populated and that the numbers in the industry kept increasing, but each one, speaking for his or her own trade, professed an inability even to give an estimate in terms of numbers.

## The Nigerian video film industry

Nigeria is credited with being one of the largest producers of films worldwide. A global cinema survey conducted by the UNESCO Institute for Statistics (UIS) placed Nigeria second after Bollywood in terms of the sheer number of productions (UNESCO 2009: 2). The low-budget Nigerian films are largely produced in video format at an average of about 1,000 a year. In spite of its relatively low-budget productions, the industry 'generates significant returns for the Nigerian economy [and] is estimated to contribute an average of about N79.4 billion [US$529 million] to the Gross Domestic Product' (FountainHead 2008: 119). According to Lobato (2010: 341), 'while Nollywood is not the world's largest film industry in terms of revenues or audience, it's likely that it produces more films that significant numbers of people actually watch than anywhere else in the world.' Nigerian films are distributed widely across Africa (Künzler 2006) and stocked by 'African grocery store owners in Germany, and website entrepreneurs in the US and the UK' (Haynes 2007c) and hawked in the Caribbean (Cartelli 2007).

The widespread distribution of the video films has accompanied the striking growth that has taken place in the country's film industry. The year 1992 is generally recognized as when the video film boom began. It was in this year that Kenneth Nnebue's *Living in Bondage* was released. Although *Living in Bondage* is considered the pioneer video film, Nnebue was not, strictly speaking, the first to resort to the video technology. The Yoruba travelling theatre artists had begun to put their work on video as early as 1988. What Nnebue introduced was the commercial reproduction of the tapes and the appeal to a wider audience. From this point, the number of productions steadily increased; it peaked in 2005 with the production of 2,194 video films (National Film and Video Censors Board 2006).

It is widely recognized that the video films have surmounted many of the obstacles that held back celluloid film production in Africa. The video films, which have a 'grassroots character' (Haynes 2007c), have succeeded in establishing new modes of distribution. However, the video film's 'triumph does not necessarily imply the displacement of the celluloid film medium, but rather the transcendence of the limitations imposed by the conventions of celluloid film making' (Ukadike 2000: 243).

The technical workforce has grown with the industry and is composed of 'a cadre of experienced, full-time professional filmmakers' (Haynes 2007d) as well as a large body of persons with no formal training who, as it were, learn on the job. The presence of the latter group is in large part thanks to the uncomplicated equipment, such as the camcorder, which has made it easy for the non-professional to enter into the film producing business. Both groups coexist largely without tension in the industry but, as was obvious in the interviews, the trained workers were rather disdainful of those who, due to their lack of training or experience, were ready to sell themselves cheap. According to them, this is the source of many of the problems faced by the crew. The skilled workers take solace in knowing their worth and their ability to attract higher fees. It should be noted, however, that a good number of those who joined the industry in the beginning were skilled people who had previously worked in television.

## The working conditions of the Nigerian film workers

All those interviewed expressed a desire for an improvement in their working conditions. There was a tendency to lay the blame for inadequate conditions on ignorance or poor training on all sides. The phrase that cropped up frequently in this regard was 'lack of professionalism'. Byron Ene is a cameraman who began working in television in 1992 before moving into the video film industry. He pointed out the problem of low or non-existent entry requirements. According to him, many of those who present themselves as cameramen in the industry do not have the required training or knowledge. This lack of professionalism, he added, was the cause of the poor treatment generally meted out to members of the crew (B. Ene, personal communication, 27 January 2010). This was a view backed up by Leonard Nformi, a cameraman who has worked in the industry virtually since its beginning. According to Nformi, many of the cameramen are not respected because they are not adequately trained (L. Nformi, personal communication, 24 January 2010).

Complaints of poor treatment were a common thread in the various interviews. Such complaints covered issues like insufficient remuneration, delayed payments, discriminatory treatment and poor working conditions in terms of long hours and inadequate housing facilities. Chinwe Elevo, a make-up artist and costumier, for instance, talked about sometimes being kept on set for long hours with no provision for rest or meal breaks (C. Elevo, personal communication, 21 January 2010). One reason for the long hours appears to be the desire to get a lot done in as little time as possible. John Adeloju, a director of photography, points out that 'they want to quickly wrap up what they are doing because they want to save money ... But there's no way to make a proper film without spending money and time' (J. Adeloju, personal communication, 23 June 2011). And according to Elevo, 'Producers don't have enough time: the more time they waste, the more money they spend. So, they are always in a hurry' (C. Elevo, personal communication, 23 June 2011). This is a view corroborated by Joshua-Philip Kalu Kanu Okeafor. Joshua-Philip is a director but, while still in film school, he took on various jobs as a below-the-line worker. With respect to the latter experience, he noted that the hours were fluid.

> When we stopped working, that's when we stopped working. You know we shoot a lot of films here. So, if we had twelve scenes to shoot and it took us up to 3 a.m., we were going to shoot those twelve scenes up to 3 a.m. If it got to 5 a.m., then we would have to shoot till that time. And if we had to wake at 8 or 9 the following morning, then we were going to wake at that time [so there were no fixed hours]. You started when you started, and you finished when you got done. (Joshua-Philip K. K. Okeafor, personal communication, 24 January 2010)

Joshua-Philip was quick to point out that although the situation was still far from ideal, the current situation had improved greatly. Even so, he went on to identify anomalies such as that pertaining to the situation of grips. Grips, according to Joshua-Philip, are referred to in the industry as production assistants and are 'pretty much the engine of the entire production; they do all sorts of things. In fact, in some productions – not ours because we won't allow it – they do even stuff like laundry. Those are some of the things that are still going on right now' (personal communication, 24 January 2010).

Other respondents spoke about a certain disrespect that the crew sometimes faces from members of the cast or the director/producer. Elfrida Ehonwa, a make-up artist, spoke of her experience on sets where no appreciation was shown for the role of the crew. Rather, members of the crew were seen as being inferior to the rest of the cast and treated accordingly. They were, she said, given the 'housemaid treatment' (E. Ehonwa, personal communication, 29 January 2010). For her part, Chinwe Elevo noted the discriminatory attitude of actors who did not respect the professional competence of these workers. She pointed out that make-up artists and costumiers, people in her line of work, often had to put up with the fact that many actors rejected their professional assessments, seeking instead to impose personal preferences.

However, all the respondents were quick to point out that this way of dealing with the crew was not common to everyone. The kind of treatment meted out largely depends on the persons involved at both the giving and the receiving end. Frank Cletus, a cameraman who has spent over ten years working on films, stated that 'the conditions depend largely on the professionalism of the individuals one works with. The more professional ones speak to technical persons as human beings' (Frank Cletus, personal communication, 21 January 2010). Chinwe Elevo also attributed some of the problems encountered to the lack of professionalism, this time, however, on the part of the crew. Speaking with reference to make-up artists and costumiers, she noted that some of the fault for the absence of respect lay with them because they 'fail to do sufficient research for the costumes and make-up, and do not stand up to defend their decisions, if need be, when the director has the wrong ideas' (personal communication). And she noted that with respect to her job the directors often had the wrong ideas: 'They think that [the job of costumier] is just to wear clothes, [and] they don't understand the way blood flows. They just tell you, "pour the thing; pour the thing"' (personal communication).

Don Collins Onuekwusi, who has been working as a continuity person since 1994, expressed the belief that those who are insulted are those who permit it. In his words, 'it has to do with packaging, how you present yourself' (Don Collins Onuekwusi, personal communication, 24 January 2010). Byron Ene supported this view, insisting that it is all 'relative'. 'Sometimes, they don't see us as relevant', he observed.

> They fix dates and shots without the input of the crew. I have worked with a director who [in the face of a suggestion of mine] once told me, 'You shouldn't think!' But some others consider you and treat you well. Nevertheless, to a large extent, we are really insulted. I see [my time on sets] as a period of insults. But all this is our fault sometimes, as crew members, in that we don't walk away; we accept things that way.
> (B. Ene, personal communication, 27 January 2010)

Although Byron Ene agreed, in a subsequent interview some months later, that things were beginning to improve for the cameramen, he still stressed that any improvement 'equally depends on the individual too [the cameraman] because it's the packaging you give to yourself that your client and whoever is coming along will carry on with' (B. Ene, personal communication, 21 June 2011).

With regard to remuneration, there are no established rates for the different jobs of the crew. Prior to a hiring, negotiations are carried out in which factors such as the experience of the worker concerned and the nature of the job play a key role in determining the sum to be paid. The fees are decided based on either a daily rate or a fixed sum covering the entire period of shooting. The government-approved minimum wage when the interviews were conducted was N15,000 (US$99.33) per day, but it does not appear that this or the rates paid in other sectors played any role in determining fees. Frank Cletus noted that personal considerations come into play in determining wages. According to him, some cameramen have their fixed rates and demand 60 to 70 per cent of the payment upfront, but Frank himself, in determining his fees, takes into consideration his assessment of the prospective employer. He tends to give better rates to persons he has worked with in the past and with whom he has a good relationship (personal communication). Emeche Ogiri, a props person, took a similar view, noting that fees are often determined based on the production budget and the individual concerned (E. Ogiri, personal communication, 8 February 2010). Chinwe Elevo noted that each artist signs a contract independently of what others might be asking, adding that 'there's not too much room for haggling because there are always others who would be willing to do it for less if one holds out for more money' (personal communication). But Joshua-Philip Okeafor stressed that 'it's pretty much a question of which producer is handling it. Some producers are known for treating people a bit more fairly than others, and [with] some others you [work] with them with your heart in your mouth because you might not even get your money at all' (personal communication).

Nearly all those interviewed spoke of the need to increase the earnings of crew members. According to Byron Ene, many producers use the fact that they are working on 'low-budget productions' as an excuse for paying low wages. However, he admitted that things are improving, for the cameramen at least, thanks to the influence of reality shows where much higher fees are paid. This leads workers to demand more for film shoots (personal communication). Nevertheless, Sandra Mbanefo Obiago, a producer and the executive director of Communicating for Change, a non-governmental media organization dedicated to changing attitudes on vital social and environmental issues, noted that

> creative talent today is earning good money. People don't fully recognize the amount of money being paid and generated in the film industry. We come up with our production budgets and people say, 'Ah, it's a lot.' But, a good editor today costs about N35,000 [US$231.78] a day. Once studio fees are removed, he will take home at least N20,000 [US$132.45] a day. A good cameraman will take anywhere from N50,000 to N125,000/ N150,000 [US$331.126 to US$827.81/993.37] a day. The make-up artists can earn N15,000/N20,000 [US$99.33/132.45] a day. And if they have to do special effects, then it's a lot more. (S. Mbanefo Obiago, personal communication, 11 January 2010)

Perhaps the emphasis here is on 'good' and, according to Leonard Nformi, 'Generally, you must be extremely good to make two hundred to three hundred thousand per movie – in Nollywood' (personal communication). Thus, while the experienced, well-known worker can demand high fees, the case is not quite the same with the less well established who generally agree to work for much lower fees. Along these lines, it is notable that in a second interview with Chinwe Elevo, about a year and six months after the first one in which she expressed the position stated earlier, she indicated that she was now more selective about the jobs she took on. Having moved on from her earlier position, she now tended to hold out for higher fees, motivated by a desire to provide a higher quality in her work. Like all make-up artists, Elevo provides her own cosmetics and other materials as required (C. Elevo, personal communication, 23 June 2011).

In the face of complaints about delayed payments, overstretched working hours and poor housing conditions, the question was posed as to whether these workers had the protection of signed contracts. All the respondents admitted that the practice of the crew signing contracts prior to a shoot existed in the industry. However, they also generally agreed that these contracts were often breached and offered no protection. Some accused the producers they had worked with of a certain dishonesty in that copies of the contract were withheld from the crew. But Elfrida Ehonwa was quick to point out that if such a thing happened it would be the fault of the crew. This had not been her experience, she said, for she had always made it a point to read through her contract carefully and obtain a copy of it (personal communication). Byron Ene attributes the failure of members of the crew to demand their rights with respect to the contracts to the fear of being labelled 'too big for their britches' (personal communication), a judgement that would affect their future job prospects. Although Leonard Nformi agreed that 'signing a contract here is as good as signing no contract', the problem, for him, arose more from ignorance: 'There's no training and people don't really know their rights on some of these things' (personal communication). He also noted the absence of industry employment lawyers who could guide the individuals in the signing of such contracts. Thus, the respondents generally did not place much trust in contracts as a means of protection or obtaining redress if the need arose.

## The role of the guilds in promoting the cause of workers

The boom in video film production and the corresponding growth in the number of film workers have been accompanied by a proliferation of guilds. The term 'guild' is used here in the simple sense of a group of people who have come together on the basis of common interests and goals. The Nigerian Film Corporation (NFC, 2007a) gives a list of sixteen associations of this nature. Included among them are bodies such as the Nigerian Society of Cinematographers, the Screenwriters Guild and the Creative Designers Guild of Nigeria, which are aimed at the below-the-line workers. These associations have supposedly sprung up with the aim of protecting the interests of the various groups involved. The associations use the word 'guild' to refer to themselves as an expression of the fact that they are a body of craftsmen who share the same trade. The word will be used here also for ease of reference.

The various guilds were established, at different times, by members of the crafts who saw the need to come together as a means of defending their common interests. The defence of these common interests, as understood by the guilds, consists of the establishment of minimum entry levels for prospective members, training and the pursuit of adequate working conditions and salaries. However, all those spoken to expressed the view that the guilds were not promoting their interests, especially in terms of providing support and making job and education opportunities available. Although they had all joined the relevant guild at some point, they had withdrawn or reduced their participation because they felt they were not gaining any benefits. For instance, Byron Ene, who identified himself as one of those who had started the guild of cinematographers, expressed his disappointment that the guild was not living up to what the founders had intended it to be. He had, for that reason, cut back on his involvement in the guild's affairs. His guild, according to him, could not be considered as having achieved anything until it was able to control the entry of cameramen into the industry and to win recognition and respect for its members.

> Apart from that, until my [guild-issued] ID card stands out for me in Nigeria [such that] anywhere I am recording if a policeman says, 'Why, who are you?' and I bring out my ID card as a cinematographer, they will allow me

to film anywhere I want to film in Nigeria, I have not actually [received recognition as a cinematographer]. (B. Ene, personal communication, 23 June 2011)

Another complaint was about the leadership. Muyiwa Adu, a production manager, was quite clear about this: 'How can illiterates be leading learned people? They don't know where they are going' (M. Adu, personal communication, 23 June 2011). A related observation by the FountainHead research group is that 'the guild and union elections have seen the emergence of unqalified individuals going to extra lengths to secure certain seats of authority in the various unions and organisations' (FountainHead 2008: 134). Frank Cletus, on his part, was of the opinion that the officials of his guild were in it merely for personal benefit. According to him, they were motivated by a fear that energetic young people might take all the jobs; the guild was their way of maintaining some form of control by making it a forum for sharing news about jobs (personal communication). Don Collins Onuekwusi was also of the opinion that the purpose of his guild had been defeated, with the result that they were now 'pursuing shadows instead of the main object' (personal communication). Nonetheless, he continues to be a paying member of the guild even though he prefers not to attend meetings.

Chinwe Elevo, who belongs to the Creative Designers Guild, gave a different reason for not being involved in the activities of her guild. She reported that she was the only member of the guild in the town where she lived and, as a result, no activities of the guild were carried out there. Nevertheless, she did not consider that there were any benefits to be gained in being a guild member since the guild played no role in defending the rights of its members or resolving their problems.

One of the reasons for the apparent ineffectiveness of the guilds could be the fact that they are not truly representative of the technical workers. The guilds were established on the initiative of small groups of individuals without any contribution from the larger collection of the workers concerned. Consequently, the majority, who still have no say in the running of the guilds, have no sense of commitment to them. Also, there is no requirement that compels anyone working in the industry to be involved with the guilds. Hence, the guilds are not in a position to establish standards since they cannot control entry into the trade. Furthermore, since the guilds are not representative of all the workers, they lack the authority to establish and enforce standard salary structures. They can neither carry out collective bargaining to determine wages nor sanction either the employers or members who flout their directives.

The task of imposing salary structures or sanctioning employers might perhaps have been better suited to trade unions, but there are no trade unions in the Nigerian film industry. Henry Odugala, Secretary General of the Radio, Television, Theatre and Arts Workers Union of Nigeria (RATTAWU), argues that film industry workers ought to fall under the jurisdiction of his union (Henry Odugala, personal communication, 10 February 2010). RATTAWU was formed in August 1978 following the merger of various unions from the different regions in the country and functions largely in the public sector. It represents all public sector workers who are employed in radio, television, the theatre and the arts, regardless of the kind of jobs they hold – administrative, technical or otherwise – with the exception of those who are in management positions. It is affiliated with the Nigerian Labour Congress (NLC), a national confederation of unions representing about four million Nigerian workers. Trade unions operating under the NLC umbrella have made considerable progress in Nigeria in recent years, especially in the public sector where strikes or the threat of strikes have been instrumental in extracting concessions from the government. But they have yet to establish a foothold in the video film industry, Henry Odugala's claim that RATTAWU is engaged in 'ongoing work to organize media workers' notwithstanding (personal communication).

What may have more impact on the lives of Nigerian film workers are proposals for the creation of a Motion Picture Council of Nigeria (MOPICON), a regulatory body that will monitor the activities of the guilds and the industry at large. The idea of MOPICON was first mooted by film practitioners, mainly producers and directors, and has the support of the government. The council is intended to be the regulator of the industry and will be charged with, among other things, establishing the entry qualifications and production standards that must be met by practitioners in the industry. It will also function as an arbiter in the disputes that might arise among those who work in the industry. To give legal backing to the council, a bill is presently being prepared for passage through the Nigerian House of Assembly. But, this legal backing notwithstanding, it will be the film-makers themselves who will be responsible for the affairs of MOPICON. The establishment of MOPICON is intended to shift the industry away from 'the personality cult that has characterized [it], where individuals rather than structures have held sway' (Ajeluorou 2009). The managing director/chief executive officer of the NFC, Afolabi Adesanya, stressed the regulatory role that MOPICON is expected to play:

> MOPICON is a welcome development ... in the sense that we have had complaints over the years of people saying 'I registered this association or this guild therefore I have absolute control to decide who is in, who is out or who heads'. With MOPICON, there will be none of this because all associations and guilds will be registered through MOPICON. Therefore, no one person can claim ownership. (A. Adesanya, personal communication, 26 January 2010)

In the meantime, the various guilds and associations of the industry have banded together to form the Coalition of Nollywood Guilds and Associations (CONGA) with the goal of promoting their common goals and collective interests. This could be a step towards unifying the workers in the industry; CONGA has given its enthusiastic support to the establishment of MOPICON. But whether a top-down initiative of this nature will work to the advantage of below-the-line workers remains to be seen.

## Training for the below-the-line workers

Training was high on the list as one of the benefits that those interviewed had hoped to gain from their guilds and a point on which they all expressed disappointment.

But the guilds themselves insist that training for their members does take place. Iyen Agboifo, the president of the Creative Designers Guild of Nigeria, for instance, pointed out that her guild provides requisite training for new members of the guild. In addition to this, there is a regular schedule of training activities, some of which are provided cost free and others for which members are required to pay (Iyen Agboifo, personal communication, 18 November 2009). Victor Eze-Okwuchukwu, the National Secretary of the Screenwriters Guild of Nigeria, stated that his guild organizes seminars, conferences and workshops for its members. However, he was quick to point out that those who want to gain from the guild 'must come in to work for the benefits' (V. Eze-Okwuchukwu, personal communication, December 2009).

Nevertheless, there are not too many training facilities for this grade of workers in Nigeria. The NFC gives a list of nine recognized institutions, six of which are based in Lagos (Nigerian Film Corporation 2007b). Training activities are also carried out in some other institutions not mentioned in the NFC list, such as the Lufodo Academy of Performing Arts, the Amaka Igwe Studios and Centre for Excellence in Film and Media Studies and the Edifosta Academy, all of which were established by notable film practitioners. However, the better known ones, which just about all the respondents made references to, are the National Film Institute, owned by the NFC; the ITPAN Training School, established by the Independent Television Producers Association of Nigeria (ITPAN); the Pencils Film and Television Institute, set up by the producer and director Wale Adenuga; and the Nigerian Television Authority TV College. Most of the respondents praised the quality of training received in the National Film Institute but were rather critical of the programmes of some of the other existing institutions. According to them, the products of these institutions were generally ill-prepared. However, Afolabi Adesanya, the NFC's managing director, noted that the programmes of such institutions are vetted by a regulatory body, the National Board for Technical Education. It is this same body, he adds, that designed the curricula for the approved diploma programmes in the institutions concerned (personal communication). Nonetheless, with the estimate of the Nigerian population standing at over 150 million, it is clear that the number of these training institutions is inadequate.

Given the small number of training institutions, it is valid to ask where or how the great majority of the technical workers obtain their skills. Many of them learn either on the job or through a mentoring process. Frank Cletus began his professional life working as a guard with a company that provided security services. A chance assignment to the main gate of a film-making company changed his life. He indicated his interest in working in the film industry to the owner of the company, who helped him secure the job of production assistant. He worked in that position for a year before, in his words, he was 'permitted to touch the camera as an assistant to the cameraman'. Two months later, he began truly handling the camera, setting and mounting it up. A year later, he was sent for a two-week training course at the then newly inaugurated ITPAN Training School (F. Cletus, personal communication). This mode of entry into the industry and the process of training is fairly common practice not just for cameramen. But there are many others who jump right in without the preparation of such mentoring or training. Leonard Nformi, for instance, spoke of cameramen with no formal training who began working in the industry on the merits of their previous experience in events coverage. Thus, the FountainHead research group concludes,

> Due to the lack of formal training institutes in filmmaking, the industry severely suffers from inadequacy in technically competent people. While the initial technical base of the workforce came from former employees of the [Nigerian Television Authority], there has been little scope for training and capacity development of the personnel involved in the industry. (FountainHead 2008: 133)

## Conclusions

In spite of the many achievements of the Nigerian video film industry, much remains to be done in terms of establishing a sustainable structure and improving the labour conditions of its workers. This widely recognized fact comes out clearly with regard to the corps of technical personnel. Not much attention has been given to providing training for technical persons in film production. Of course, the neglect of technical training is not peculiar to the film industry. There has been, to a large extent, a neglect of technical and vocational education because graduates of institutions of this nature are widely considered as inferior to university graduates. 'The public and even parents consider the vocational education track as fit for only the academically less endowed' (African Union 2007). This attitude is largely the source of the discriminatory treatment that some crew members claim to receive while on set, as well as what could be termed an inferiority complex that leads some of them not to stand up for their rights. Nonetheless, among those interviewed, there was a discernible sense of pride about their work which could be a step towards fighting such negative perceptions.

There is clearly a desire on the part of the technical workers for improved standards not merely with respect to their working conditions but in the industry as a whole. But they are currently not in any position to make these desires a reality. This is due mainly to the fact that, as a group, they are not sufficiently organized to present a common front. For instance, while trade unions in the public sector have been able to achieve many of their goals through industrial action, such a tactic would not work for the technical workers in the film industry given the weakness of the guilds. Individuals have to fight their own battles.

A lack of professionalism is what many identify as the cause of the problems which workers face. This lack of professionalism applies not just to those who form the crew but also to directors and producers. The increased relevance of the professional unions, the guilds, could help in improving standards in the industry. But many commentators have indicated the need for a larger overseeing body that would monitor the guilds, determine the requirements for entry into the industry and prescribe adequate training. MOPICON is a welcome development in this regard since it will have the authority not only to establish the levels of qualification required for entry into the various sectors of the industry but also to regulate the way the guilds that are active in the industry operate and to penalize those who do not conform to its standards. This, of course, would make it mandatory for all workers in the industry to belong to the relevant guilds. In this way, it is hoped that the guilds will come to play a more relevant role in terms of furthering the well-being of their members. The guilds should establish a unified structure of payments as well as a means for defending the rights of their members. But many of the technical workers are distrustful of those who head the guilds, and getting them into the fold would require winning their trust. Conversely, the change in leadership and focus that the technical workers desire of the guilds will only be speeded up by their own greater involvement in the affairs of the guilds.

## Bibliography

African Union (2007), *Strategy to Revitalize Technical and Vocational Education and Training (TVET) in Africa*, http://www.africa-union.org/root/AU/Conferences/2007/May/HRST/29-31/TVET_Strategy_english.doc [accessed 8 February 2010].

Ajeluorou, A. (2009), 'Unified Nollywood Gets Panel to Work on MOPICON Bill', *The Guardian*, 18 June, p. 68.

Cartelli, P. (2007), 'Nollywood Comes to the Caribbean', *Film International*, 5(4): 112–14.

FountainHead Research (2008), *Nigerian Media and Entertainment Industry: The Next Frontier, Making Steady Progress*, Lagos: FountainHead Group.

Haynes, J. (2007a), 'Nnebue: The Anatomy of Power', *Film International*, V (4): 30–40.

Haynes, J. (2007b), 'TK in NYC: An Interview with Tunde Kelani', http://postcolonial.org/index.php/pct/article/viewFile/659/409 [accessed 13 December 2007].

Haynes, J. (2007c), 'Nollywood in Lagos, Lagos in Nollywood Films', *Africa Today*, 54 (2): 131–50.

Haynes, J. (2007d), 'Video Boom: Nigeria and Ghana', http://postcolonial.org/index.php/pct/article/viewPDFInterstitial/522/422 [accessed 27 November 2007].

Künzler, D. (2006), 'The Nigerian Video Industry as an Example of Import Substitution', http://www.suz.unizh.ch/kuenzler/grey/Bergen1.pdf [accessed 30 November 2007].

Lobato, R. (2010), 'Creative Industries and Informal Economies', *International Journal of Cultural Studies*, 13 (4): 337–54.

National Film and Video Censors Board (2006), 'Classification Decisions', http://www.nfvcb.gov.ng/statistics.php [accessed 14 May 2008].

Nigerian Film Corporation (2007a), 'Film Associations/Guilds', http://nigfilmcorp.com/pdf/Index_Industry_Film%20Associations%20&%20Guilds.pdf [accessed 16 May 2008]

Nigerian Film Corporation (2007b), 'List of Film Schools in Nigeria', http://nigfilmcorp.com/pdf/Index_Industry_List%20of%20Film%20Schools%20in%20Nigeria.pdf [accessed 16 June 2009].

Ukadike, N. F. (2000), 'Images of the "Reel" Thing: African Video-Films and the Emergence of a New Cultural Art', *Social Identities*, 6 (3): 243–61.

UNESCO (2009), 'Analysis of the UIS International Survey on Feature Film Statistics', http://www.uis.unesco.org/Library/Documents/Infosheet_No1_cinema_EN.pdf [accessed 6 May 2009].

# Patronage and clientelism

# Fathers, patrons and clients in Kinshasa's media world

## Social and economic dynamics in the production of television drama*

KATRIEN PYPE

Just as media products vary depending on the social and cultural contexts in which they come into being, television worlds also differ across time and space. Despite the strong Western influence in the production of local television programmes, the generation of Kinshasa's television programmes partakes in local economic and political structures that define the notion of 'labour', hierarchical relations and work conditions.

Until now, very little research has been carried out on the economy of African television. Overall, audio-visual media produced, distributed and circulating on the African continent remain largely invisible in cultural studies. While most of the existing literature focuses on the issue of representation and tends to privilege reception, we must make serious attempts to make sense of the production modalities of African media texts. A culturally sensitive methodology, based on in-depth ethnographic research, is needed when studying the emergence of media products and the lifeworlds of media producers and consumers. The groundbreaking work by Birgit Meyer (2003a, 2003b, 2006) and Lila Abu-Lughod (2005) has allowed us to gain insight into the aspirations and negotiations that fashion the aesthetics and even the broadcasting modalities of Ghanaian witchcraft films and Egyptian melodramas. Anthropological research on Africa's media can now move into a new phase and take up the daunting task of identifying the various socio-economic vectors that undergird the making of soaps, serials, films and other genres such as talk shows and commercials.[1]

In this chapter, I want to make the argument that the patron-client relationship is the main social and political structure that undergirds the production of television serials (synonyms *maboke*, *télédramatiques*) in Kinshasa. This kind of relationship thrives upon obligations shared by both 'big men' and their dependants, the so-called 'small people' (*petits*). It derives to a large extent from the notion of 'wealth-in-people' (Miers and Kopytoff 1979; Guyer 1993), which has commonly been used in studies of slavery. In this context, the concept indicates the ability of leaders and elders to accumulate wives, children, clients and other dependants as wealth and as a vehicle to future wealth. The control over people (wives and dependants) was a more important source of wealth in pre-colonial equatorial Africa than ownership of land or goods. In postcolonial African lifeworlds, often characterized by insecurity and precariousness, hierarchical structures are maintained and young people remain to a large extent dependent on family relations and family obligations if they want to marry and participate in modern life. This certainly holds true in everyday life in Kinshasa, where children and youth depend to a large extent on the networks of their elder relatives in order to marry. Yet, in this urban context, youth are also able to carve out their own relationships and networks, and to provide in alternative ways for their own well-being and future. It could even be argued that in the current urban crisis, which has lasted since the early 1990s, the dependency has shifted: elders are now increasingly depending on the skills of their offspring, who are more successful in the informal economy (see Pype 2008).

I use the term 'patron' in two different ways. First, in the Kinois[2] sense, 'patrons' (Lingala *mokonzi* or *mopao*) are 'big men' (or 'big women') with a group of dependants around them. These terms denote a person with financial means who displays his or her wealth and consequently achieves high social status in the city. Their dependants are called '*petits*' (small people). Participation in *grands-petits* relations raises social power and esteem for both 'patrons' and 'clients', and constitutes networks of benefactors through the forging of ties of patronage and dependency, often with lucrative consequences. Second, in the anthropology of art, the concept of 'patron' is used to indicate wealthy individuals who commission works of art (Ben-Amos 1980; Vansina 1984: 44–7; Perani and Wolff 1999). In the social context of the Kinshasa's *maboke*, both senses are interlinked. The kinds of 'patrons' that these young actors are engaged with are men and women of importance who ask to have their names cited in an episode (see below), but they will never suggest a serial be created in order to enhance their social esteem.

The argument that the patron-client axis structures the production of television drama in Kinshasa will be supported by ethnographic material gathered during participant observation with Kinshasa's most popular television acting group, CINARC (Cinema-Arc-en-Ciel, 'Rainbow Cinema'). Most importantly, the teleserials facilitate not only the circulation of money but also the spread of reputation (*lukumu*) among extensive networks of youth and lineage groups, and also beyond them, since successful urban leaders such as politicians, religious authorities and musicians also contribute financially or otherwise to the production of the *maboke*. The social space in which Kinshasa's teleserials are produced and viewed is a zone in which both TV actors and others (fans and sponsors) cultivate simultaneously expressive and economic forms of sociality. Therefore, my discussion of Kinshasa's *télédramatiques* examines the degree to which artistic professionalism, economic incentives and social structures are tied together and configured within the boundaries of the urban setting. This means that I will discuss not so much the content of the serials but rather the production of authority and the circulation of reputation that is facilitated by the *maboke*.

# Kinshasa's media world

Since Mobutu relaxed his grip on local media and ordained freedom of the press in 1996, Kinshasa's media world has been ever expanding (see Pype 2009). It is beyond the scope of this chapter to offer a thorough introduction to the various television stations in Kinshasa (see Pype 2008, 2009). The number of local television stations rose from 23 to 41 between 2003 and 2009. All of these channels have at least one or two local drama groups that weekly prepare an episode of a serial to be broadcast the same week. In Kinshasa's economic context, it is difficult to speak about a 'television industry', since the very concept of 'industry' evokes notions of paid labour, organized and identified professional roles and the production of commodities, meaning goods exchanged for money. Kinois who appear in the television serials operate within Kinshasa's informal economy, where social relations are the main basis for the exchange of services, goods and money.

Despite the large number of television stations, filming in Kinshasa is still rather expensive. However, the digital video camera is relatively cheap and easy to use. Most troupes film their programmes with hand cameras, which the drama groups usually borrow from the television station they work for. Often, the same camera is used by different groups producing for the same channel. Since Kinshasa's television channels broadcast several serials produced by different troupes, there is a strict and rigid scheme that indicates which theatre company can use the filming equipment on which days. These schedules are, however, often interrupted by other employees who need the filming equipment, for instance cameramen who report for the television journal or for other programmes. These men often call the troupe's leaders and order them to drop the camera off within a span of a few hours at a certain location, thus leaving the troupe without filming equipment. To decrease their dependency on the channel's equipment, some leaders of Kinshasa's drama groups have bought their own cameras. When not filming for the *maboke*, some of their members are sent to wedding ceremonies, burial rituals or other festivities to film and thus to increase the troupe's income.

The owners of television channels select their drama groups on the basis of a limited set of criteria, namely initial dramatic skills and consistent storylines. None of the television patrons that I interviewed interfered in the production of the serials, in the outline of the scripts or in the selection of the actors. Contacts between actors and the television bosses are often minimal, and only when the popularity of the troupe is lagging, or when the troupe has committed a major social error, might the channel's boss exercise his editorial power.

Kinshasa's teleserials profess a Pentecostal message, and translate urban life-worlds in a religious way (Pype 2012). According to several owners of Kinshasa's channels, the recurrent Pentecostal message in Kinshasa's teleserials derives from a larger societal concern that not only influences the way in which life itself is experienced but also imposes itself on leisure activities and popular arts. As business directors, the channels' heads argue that the supremacy of Pentecostal-Charismatic Christianity in the teleserials guarantees a large viewing audience. Theatre companies producing Christian narratives are therefore offered more facilities, even on Kinshasa's so-called 'profane' channels.

Filming television serials does not take much time: usually the shooting of a fifty-minute episode takes between one afternoon and a day and a half to complete. Each week, a new episode has to be filmed. Illness, quarrels between actors or disputes with the owners of the compounds in which the serials are filmed render the recordings difficult, forcing the performers to respond in a creative and effective way. Some actors arrive hours late. Heavy rain or difficult public transport can make moving from one shooting location to another hazardous, and power cuts often disrupt the filming schedule. Sometimes certain storylines must be broken off, fictive relationships must be altered or fictional characters must be relocated to new sets.

The serials are shot in real houses, whose owners are acknowledged in the fictive narrative. There are no costs for attire, since the actors usually perform in their own clothes. If their personal wardrobe does not match their fictional character, they borrow costumes from relatives or from boutiques, for whom this is a way to advertise. Only a limited set of characters (the fool, the healer and the witch; see Pype 2010) need special items that are usually the private property of the artist.

Dialogue, improvisation and a striking openness of the narratives are the main components of the preparation and performances of plays in Kinshasa and also of the mass-mediated serials.[3] The openness of the *maboke* derives from or enables a multiplicity of 'authors'. Usually, the troupes' leaders conceive the scenario of one episode at a time. The script is put on one sheet of paper (*canevas*) that summarizes the key events of the scenes in a few sentences. The individual actors must then improvise their scenes. During the shooting period, the *canevas*, of which there is only one copy, is shared among the actors, who read the main idea of their scenes. Based on this minimal information, the actors then flesh out their scenes, usually without rehearsing. As there are no extensive directions or words to be pronounced, the rest of the creative process is very much in the hands of the young actors. The most experienced self-direct their scenes.

Another characteristic of Kinshasa's *maboke* are the multiple intersecting storylines. In the first episodes, different households are shown, each with its own difficulties. A general plot line seems to be lacking; the serials seem to go in all directions. The themes of marriage arrangements, tensions between village people and Kinois, the quest for money, illegitimate sexual affairs or the search for health assistance all take place in one episode. After some episodes, filming problems, the improvising abilities of the actors, remarks of the audience, the popularity of one particular character or other similarly uncontrollable events might influence the choice of which subplot should dominate and the direction of the serial as a whole. This abundance of plotlines and of intermingling realities may well be a characteristic of Kinshasa's contemporary society (Jewsiewicki 2004: 262). Jewsiewicki observed the same multiplicity of themes, images and stories in Kinshasa's popular paintings (*tableaux*). He confesses that this 'visual cacophony' might be the most unsettling aspect of Kinshasa's society for someone educated in the West. What he writes about

Kinshasa's *tableaux* can easily be transposed onto the *télédramatiques*: 'The accounts, the images are shown in simultaneity, but because their contents are usually well-known, one easily goes on from one to another, borrowing a kind of linearity in zigzag' (Jewsiewicki 2004: 261, author's translation).

Many Kinois speak more than one vernacular language, but the lingua franca among Kinshasa's inhabitants is Lingala, a language derived from the upper-Congo river people who used it prior to colonialism as their lingua franca (Burssens 1954: 27–30). KiKinois, the version of Lingala that Kinois use, is the dominant language in Kinshasa's teleserials. KiKinois is not the official version of Lingala but rather a pidgin, a mixture of Lingala, French, kiKongo and newly invented words. When representing adolescents and young men in the serials, Hindoubill is used. Hindoubill is a mixture of kiKinois with new words inspired by English (in particular from American rap), inversions of regular French and Lingala vocabulary. It contains a high degree of irony and machismo. The language is continuously reinvented to guard the boundary between the genders and the generations. Although Hindoubill originated during the colonial period (De Boeck 2004: 62), those who were young at the time cannot understand the version used nowadays. Furthermore, each male youth group (gang, *écurie*) uses its own version, thereby marking the unity of a particular group of young men.

Depending on the dominance of a certain ethnic group in the troupe, another local language may also be spoken. In the serials produced by Muyombe Gauche, for example, lengthy scenes are set in kiKongo, while CINARC serials often display Luba elders, speaking and singing in ciLuba. The degree of French in the serials depends both on the educational level of the actors and on the cultural worlds evoked by the fictive characters. Performers embodying the role of pastors often insert French words into their speech, a practice that indexes the importance of their social category. The performers' popularity depends to a great extent on their language proficiency. In several instances, viewers urged me to encourage a newly arrived actress in the CINARC company to use French in her roles. In contrast to the other CINARC performers who regularly inserted French words, she only spoke kiKinois. People interpreted that particular actress's lack of proficiency in French as an indication that she was less 'modern' or 'urban' than the other members of the troupe.

## The troupe

Drama groups involve a fluid number of young men and women – usually between twenty and fifty – who gather to enjoy comedy and artistic development. Ethnicity plays an important role in recruiting new members for the company, and it colours its cultural products. All theatre companies in the city are undoubtedly influenced more by some ethnic cultures than by others. This often depends on the ethnic identity of the troupe's director. In most cases, the leader's ethnic identity attracts individuals of the same ethnic group, and this inevitably shapes the troupe's cultural work. The CINARC leader, for example, is of Kongo origin while some of the troupe's more influential men have Luba roots. As a result, most CINARC members belong to either the Kongo or Luba groups. Unsurprisingly, the CINARC serials display a balance between Kongo and Luba practices; fictional characters often have Kongo or Luba names and speak kiKongo or ciLuba, and dances used in the serials are inspired by Luba or Kongo rites.

The majority of the acting groups in Kinshasa are inscribed within the urban form of the voluntary association, or the *écurie*. *Écurie* refers to a constellation of networks, obligations and hierarchy. Family members often occupy the most important positions in these associations. In most theatre companies (as in many other *écuries*), consanguinity remains an important factor in determining the distribution of power within the group. In the case of CINARC, its core consists of consanguine brothers and cousins, and many actors complain that consanguine relatives receive the most important roles. Without exception, the leaders perform the leading parts in the serials and because of this, they become very popular with the audience. Through their success and leadership of the company, the troupe's leaders become big men.

The patriarchal character of Kinshasa's society is reflected in the composition of the troupes, since women rarely lead theatre companies.[4] CINARC, the Evangelists (*Les Evangélistes*), the Lions (*Les Simbas*), the Stars of Africa (*Les Étoiles de l'Afrique*) and the Trumpet (*La Trompette*) are some of the theatre companies that appear on television. In general, these drama groups are better known as 'the group of [the screen name of its director]'. Some examples are troupe *ya Caleb* (the troupe of Caleb, referring to the fictional name of the CINARC leader), or *les baCaleb*, troupe *ya Muyombe Gauche*, troupe *ya Sans Soucis* and troupe *ya Devos* (*les Evangélistes*). The second most popular actor in any artistic association is generally a girl or woman who often plays the role of the wife of the director's fictional character. I will illustrate the positions of power by discussing the biography of the drama group CINARC, which is one of Kinshasa's most popular television troupes. During my fieldwork, the group twice received the award for best local television group (Mwana Mboka Trophy). The group also has an excellent reputation in the diaspora.

In 1999 Bienvenu Toukebana (then 28) founded a theatre company called Cinarne (*Cinema-Arche-de-Noe*), of which CINARC (*Cinema-Arc-en-Ciel*) would later become an offshoot. At the time of Cinarne's founding, this young man of Yombe origin (a subgroup of the larger Kongo group) had just returned from a long stay in Lagos. His mother had sent him abroad for five years during which time he engaged in petty trade buying mattresses, clothes, soap, radios and other goods for export to Kinshasa where she sold these items on the market. While in Lagos, Bienvenu became intrigued by Nigerian film and subsequently joined a group of actors whose skills, techniques and themes he quickly learned. Back in Kinshasa he tried to set up a theatre company of his own without much success. Things changed only after he had a dream in which God asked him for his help. Bienvenu would often repeat this dream narrative during television shows and at times when he sensed that his leadership in the theatre company was threatened:

> God asked me to work for Him. He knows that I love television, and He asked me to work as a dramatic artist for Him. Through the serials, we can show people the goodness and the love of God. We also have to let people

know that the devil is among us. God loves us, but we may not cooperate with His enemy. The morning after my dream, I started to pray, and there God revealed to me the strategies to find good actors.

To recruit actors, Bienvenu spread the word in his community (Lemba), his church (at that time *Arche de Noe*, led by the Prophet Dennis Lessie) and on several television channels. He also invited Chapy, his cousin (MoSiSo), with whom he was raised, and Jef Kabangu, his older brother. Jef was born out of an earlier relationship between their mother and a Luba man. The relationship did not last long, and after the break-up, Jef's father took his son with him. During their childhood, Bienvenu and Jef knew of each other's existence, though they never met. Only when Bienvenu began Cinarne did he search for and find his brother, who immediately joined the project. Though Bienvenu is the troupe's head, Jef has much authority because of his blood relationship with Bienvenu.

According to the foundation narrative, Bienvenu's leadership is based on a call from the Christian God. His authority in the artistic association is therefore founded on this divine gift, and his leadership can be defined as 'charismatic leadership' (cf. Weber 1947: 328–49). His authority over the CINARC members is also upheld by the way he has arranged his life. He is perceived as a courageous man (*un courageux*) who has managed to create a group of followers, namely the members of his troupe and his fans.

Bienvenu's leadership is sustained by 'the core' (*le noyau*) of the troupe, whose four members are also called, collectively, 'the elders of the group' or 'the *bampaka ya lingomba*'. A steering committee, the '*comité du directeur*', is made up of the four elders and includes two other young men with artistic seniority. These are all unmarried young men in their early thirties. The authority resides in them over the workings and members of the theatre company. They take the most important decisions with regard to the distribution of roles, internal disputes and who is to represent the company on any particular social occasion or mass-mediated activity. In addition, the other actors must ask their permission for absences from prayer gatherings or rehearsals or for leaving the shootings early. Other problems such as lack of money, health issues and spiritual difficulties should also be addressed to them, and here the elders decide what action the artistic association should take. A larger committee, the so-called '*comité directeur élargie*', is composed of the '*comité du directeur*' and the most important actresses in the theatre company. In practice, this group is never called together and the impact of the female 'elders' is therefore minimal. The remaining members of the troupe are subdivided into groups such as '*les bules*' (Hindoubill for *les bleus*, the new ones), '*les balikili*' (a military name for new recruits) and the 'elder siblings' (*bayaya*). 'Bules' are not paid for their work for the troupe. 'Bayaya' are those who have already been active in the company for some time; they may be younger than newly arrived members but, due to their artistic experience, they are considered 'older' in the artistic world.

Social rules concerning deference (Li. *bonkonde*), respect (Li. *botosi*) and taboo (Li. *ekila*), which structure social encounters in Kinshasa, also dictate intra-group relations. The troupe's leader requests total respect from the actors and actresses, and he is the only one who may sanction and reprimand them. Company members usually address him with the title 'president' instead of by his first or screen name. If someone shows him a lack of respect, he punishes the person by withdrawing him or her for a few weeks from the screen, no matter how important his or her role in the serial being filmed at the time may be. The older boys must be approached in more respectful ways by both girls and younger boys in the group. Furthermore, deriving from artistic seniority, those who arrived later in the group must be respectful towards those with longer membership in the theatre company. Petty conflicts constantly arise when one of the actors has gained more popularity due to a specific role he or she is playing at the moment or because of a shout[5] he or she has created. The most popular performers tend to neglect social rules of authority and respect, and this threatens the harmony (Li. *kimia*) and stability (Li. *bobongi*) within the company. The president is therefore frequently obliged to take steps to reinforce his authority over these young people whose sudden stardom can influence their behaviour. Sometimes, these decisions affect the teleserials: due to intra-group strife, a fictional character can be written out of the script for several episodes or even for the whole play.

## Artistic and spiritual kinship

Most performers join a theatre company without any prior artistic experience. Though some dramatic artists are also active in other types of cultural production (such as singing in a choir) or have taken part in cultural activities organized in their schools, they all have to learn techniques of improvisation and behaviour in front of a camera. For this purpose, the troupe's leader organizes rehearsal sessions over a period of several weeks at which new members can observe the dramatic work of the more experienced artists. When the junior artists finally begin to act, the troupe's director corrects them.

There is an interesting evolution in the roles attributed to new members. At first, they are allowed to perform in small scenes that disrupt the serials' narratives. These scenes, commercial shots for commodities like shampoo and food, but also for stores or firms with which the company's leaders have contracts, require minimal acting skills. Next, the actor is permitted to perform in a play where he or she is given the role of a sibling or a child of one of the protagonists. Once the troupe's director is convinced that the new performer has acquired the necessary dramatic skills, he then creates a serial for this player.[6] This move, however, often leads to conflicts with other more established artists who fear losing screen time and thus social prestige.

The transmission of artistic ability from the company's leader to the actors establishes his identity as an artistic father and constructs the others as his artistic children. The type of fatherhood exerted by a troupe's leader is not at all limited to the teaching of dramatic skills. The directors of drama groups help their children to socialize, adopt appropriate conduct in the urban space and train themselves for their future roles as adults. The company's leader takes full responsibility for his actors' behaviour both on and off stage, the latter probably being the more time-consuming task. As a result, troupe directors strive not only to mould the actors' artistic performance but also to influence their social life, social environment and behaviour in public spaces.

Feeding and housing[7] are two other main strategies by which metaphorical kinship is made real (cf. Carsten 2004: 139). Bienvenu's eldest sister cooks for the actors, and, in some cases, Bienvenu houses them. Ance, for example, who lives in a street dominated by one of Kinshasa's most notorious fighting gangs (Bana Bolafa), regularly seeks refuge in the home of his president when police and military men are out arresting any young boys they find near the Bana Bolafa's headquarters. Bienvenu also hosts some actors for a longer period. Patrick, for example, was living with the troupe's leader during fieldwork. He only saw his mother during the weekly services at the church of the Holy Mountain, which is just a few streets away from her house. Bienvenu took Patrick in after he had been informed about a new job Patrick had taken. Since the salary Patrick earned as a newly initiated CINARC actor was insufficient to cover the needs of his family, he had also accepted a job offer in the casino at Le Grand Hôtel (one of Kinshasa's biggest hotels located in the residential area of Gombe). As, according to Christians, this is a place where money, alcohol and prostitutes are found – a 'demonic' triad – Bienvenu ordered his actor to choose between working for God and continuing to serve the devil. If Patrick chose God, Bienvenu promised him to take him into his home and to feed and dress him. The choice was easy, and Patrick found new shelter. During his stay in Bienvenu's compound, Patrick performed all kinds of chores; he was Bienvenu's driver and was sent around town to pick up people or goods and at times also functioned as Bienvenu's bodyguard. Bienvenu's concerns with regard to the social circles in which Patrick moved thus inspired the troupe's leader to host Patrick. In order to keep Patrick away from a 'demonic' world, Bienvenu had to offer his artistic son the means to move out of it. Providing care for the spiritual security of his pupils is only one of the various tasks of social fatherhood that Bienvenu also exercises for his artistic children.

Relationships between the theatre company and the patrons of the television companies are also inspired by fictive kinship relationships. The directors of media enterprises are considered the 'fathers' of the troupes, and the artists are then their children. As a father, the patron of a television company should make sure that his children eat, are properly dressed and have the material needed for their work. A good leader of a television company makes sure that the troupe is paid and can use good-quality material. A television leader also exerts rights over his children. He can suspend the troupe, correct the artists on certain points and advise them to change their conduct both in public and private life. As his children, the actors should pay respect to their father. This means mentioning him from time to time in their serial (see below on citing patrons). Pius Mwabilu, the head of RTG@, told me, 'When you are in your father's house, don't you say the name of your father many times a day?', explaining why the CINARC actors had dropped his name several times in every episode of their serials since switching to RTG@. The channel's leader functions more like a distant father, or possibly a God, because contacts between the performers and the channels' heads are scarce. Only the troupes' leaders regularly meet the television bosses.

In an evangelizing drama group, an artistic father is often also a spiritual father. For most of the youth connected with the CINARC group, the troupe's leader is also a 'spiritual father' because he has preached God's word to most of the actors. The account of Bibiche Nsasi (fictional names Mambweni or Sylvie, age 26) illustrates this. This young girl, who is unmarried but has a child, became a member of the Christian theatre company at a difficult period in her life. Two years before she joined CINARC, everything seemed to go wrong in her life. She was studying at the University of Kinshasa (UNIKIN) but became pregnant by a fellow student who refused to marry her. Her parents, full of shame, agreed to host their daughter and her baby girl only if she would stop studying and find a job. She worked for several years until she lost that job. At that moment, out of work and raising a two-year-old daughter, she saw one of Bienvenu's advertisements on television saying that he sought people wanting to work for God through the medium of television. She immediately called Bienvenu and attended the group's rehearsals, without her parents' knowledge. They would have prevented her from joining, she said, referring to the immoral status female artists have in Kinshasa. During these initial meetings with the company, she sensed the Holy Spirit's presence, and she immediately knew that she had to stay with this group. Once in the group, she converted to Christianity. 'Bienvenu has brought God back into my life, and thanks to Him, I have become someone.' Her exact words were 'Nasalaki nkombo na ngai' – 'I have made my name.'

Other troupe members also exert spiritual fatherhood within the drama group. Since Bienvenu is so involved in the production process (writing scenarios, supervising the production of the serials) and public relations, he has given the task of caring for the spiritual welfare of the newer members to other CINARC actors who are actively engaged in the church's activities. These artists, Chapy and JC among others, are sometimes much younger than some of the members put in their spiritual charge, but their ardent faith and intense engagement with the group's church has accorded them the status of spiritual elders. At times, during the rehearsals, I observed how some performers would turn to one of these spiritual advisors who would heal them by laying their hands on their heads or aching body parts, while the others continued to practise or listened to the president's instructions. Members could in fact discuss any physical afflictions and social problems with these specific actors at any time.

Ultimate spiritual parenthood for the members of a Christian theatre company, however, resides with the pastor and his wife, who are considered to be spiritually responsible (Li. baboti ya Nzambe) for their followers. The importance of the pastor and his spouse is reflected in practices at the end of a service or other spiritual activity. It is expected that everyone who attended the gathering or ritual greet the couple. The pastor is allowed to ask private and, at times, unsettling questions of his children. He confronts them with their own doubts and indicates personal weaknesses where the devil could profit or is already taking advantage. As a result of these conversations, the pastor knows a great deal about the private lives of the members of his church.

For the drama group as a unit, the pastor is an important person as well: he prays for them and gives them spiritual advice during private encounters. The importance of the role of this spiritual leader was reflected in the way the artists welcomed me: while Bienvenu never took me to his relatives, he insisted that I meet *Pasteur* Gervais, the spiritual leader of the troupe, and speak with him.

## Distributing the money

Television acting groups earn a particular amount of money from the television station for which they work. Depending on the popularity of the troupe's work, a contract (which can always be renegotiated) can vary from US$800 to US$1,500 per month. This amount is transferred to the troupe's leader, although the money, which should cover the working costs, is meant to be redistributed among the artists. Because of the large number of actors a troupe can hold, not much money remains for the individual actors. An important strategy for the actors to increase the amount is to include private enterprises within the narratives. Scenes are shot in boutiques, in supermarkets and in commercial telegraph companies, while the serials' protagonists remain in character. Often, newly arrived artists receive their first scene in such a shot.[8] Usually, drama groups have an oral agreement with up to four or five of these economic bodies, usually receiving US$10 for each episode. In this way, US$40 to $US50 extra can be made. This does not mean that the whole amount is exclusively for the troupe, since the station's heads often demand a part of this money. Bigger enterprises such as telecom providers (Vodacom, Tigo etc.) and the two local breweries also invest a great deal in the production of local television drama, and their logos appear on screen. Usually for the breweries, the beer logos are displayed, though Christian groups forbid displaying brewery logos but allow soft-drink logos of the same companies.

Significantly, the consumer goods that are advertised in the serials all pertain to a Western consumer culture. In particular, modern communication technology and Western cosmetics and clothing styles are advertised, but there are no advertisements for traditional healers or traditional medicine, for example, or for so-called traditional cloth or local beverages such as the *lokoto* or other local drinks. These goods do not match the narratives and the worlds that are portrayed in the television serials, and they also do not reflect the world in which the artists themselves long to live. As I argue elsewhere (Pype 2012), many of the artists enter into the world of drama because it reflects a world to which they do not have access. It enables them to become consumers for a short time, after which they go back to their tiny homes, where they do not have access to lavish drinking and spending.

The troupe's leader invariably takes the biggest share of the money given by the channel as well as a share of the money gained by name-dropping for big men who have approached the drama group (instead of individual actors) and from advertising for various enterprises. Although this often raises discontent among the actors, hardly anyone objects to this. First and foremost, the exact income of the group is known only by a small number of the group's members. According to local rules concerning secrecy and discretion, a *petit* cannot ask these kinds of questions of a senior member, and a band's leader is never obliged to inform his dependants about the exact income or the expenses he has made. Furthermore, a band's leader spends a great deal of money on his artistic children. For example, a theatre company usually gathers in the leader's compound before rehearsals and filming and food is shared among them. Also, depending on the financial scope of the band, artists usually receive money to move from one shooting location to another. However, to minimize the costs, but also in order not to overwhelm the hosts with strangers in their house, only those artists who perform in a particular location are paid to go to that setting.

Distribution within the group is carried out according to rank. The main criteria are artistic seniority and personal affiliation with the band's leader, but another important criterion is the effort of individual actors to find additional sponsors.

## Ties with sponsors and fans: name-dropping

Small favours and exchanges between viewers and artists are a key aspect of the social dynamics in Kinshasa's media world. These are rendered possible by the closeness between television stars and Kinshasa's urbanites. Most performers use public trans-port, go to the market and visit churches just as ordinary people do. In contrast to the few major music groups whose lead singers or musicians earn enough money to pay for their own car and driver, television actors earn almost nothing and thus depend, like most city dwellers, on their social network to survive. The status of stardom makes one visible in the street and enables one to establish contacts with a range of people wider than one's own small horizon of neighbourhood, church community or lineage. Jef, for example, spoke in our first discussion about his reasons for participating in CINARC's serials, alongside those of his spiritual calling and his intention to evangelize the city:

> Contact with fans is very important. Sometimes people come up to me and say that they admire my work. One day, for example, a man told me that his children follow my work on television. He invited me to his house and we became good friends. I was writing my final paper for ISTA [engineering school] at the time. This man had a computer at home, and thanks to him, I could write my text.

These more fluid and temporary social relations are rarely the focus of research on sociality. Christine Helliwell (1996) describes anthropologists' tendency to privilege well-defined social groups when studying social relations. This is, she argues, a con-sequence of the visualism (the emphasis on the visual senses as a mode of gaining knowledge) of Western knowledge, a concept she derives from Fabian's influential *Time and the Other* (1983). Helliwell identifies the production of diagrams, charts and maps as the most exact means of analysis. She writes, 'Western anthropologists (and others) will tend to accord bounded social entities a higher facticity – to see them as more 'real' – than more fluid, relational forms of sociality' (Helliwell 1996: 129). In the following sections, I seek to highlight a particular connection in an artist's social world: contacts with 'patrons'. These contacts are expressed and sometimes established through the citing of individuals' names in the fictive narratives.

Name-dropping in the teleserials is a practice that publicizes people who have contributed financially in one way or another to the creation of that particular nar-rative. Examples are individuals who have given clothes or money, or allowed their house to be used as a location for a shoot. When watching a serial, one is often struck by the references to 'real' people, although these individuals have no impact on the fictional plotline. Actors, for example, prefer to open scenes with the mention of people they 'have just met' in the market, on public transport or in other public places. The citation of the name happens very quickly but is not at all trivial. People pay attention to the mentioned names and comment upon them; in other words, having one's name cited is an important way to become known in the city. It indicates that the artists have good relations with these individuals, and enhances the reputation of the person whose name is mentioned.

This practice of citing the personal names of real individuals is called 'throwing a name' (Li. *kobwaka nkombo*) or 'to do a *libanga*' (Li. pl. *mabanga*). The latter is Lingala for 'stone' or 'rock' but also refers to a diamond, and points to the economic struggle to survive.[9] For the actor, 'throwing persons' (i.e. mentioning names) confirms and creates personal networks that are socially and sometimes financially rewarding because the performance of the *mabanga* entails an obligation from the cited person, who, in turn, is expected to offer monetary or other material gifts for the work the actor has performed.

Some of the 'big men' thrown by CINARC actors during fieldwork were business men: a vice-minister, who gave money according to the way in which he had been thrown; the wife of a well-known journalist; the troupe's spiritual leaders; and some young fighting boys from Lemba (Kinshasa's district in which the CINARC group mostly filmed) who provided security during the troupe's cultural events. Sometimes Congolese in the diaspora contacted the dramatic artists, asking to be cited.[10] Due to the temporary nature of these contacts, the names that are dropped frequently change, reflecting shifts in the social relationships of the members.

Political and social elites often request to be named during the serials in order to enhance their personal prestige and reinforce their authority and position. Many successful men and women deliberately seek out relationships with the artists, whose 'power of the word' they can use for their self-promotion, precisely because the television celebrities have such a wide audience. Usually, Kinshasa's important people initiate the exchange. During a conversation I had with Muyombe Gauche (one of Kinshasa's most popular dramatic artists) spanning just a few hours, several bosses of local business companies called him, asking to be mentioned in the following episode. It is important to note that when citing business people, it is not the names of the companies that are mentioned but the personal names; in this way the individuals are honoured, and their personal social prestige is enhanced.

When the theatre company is in need of money, the actors spontaneously praise the city's big men on the assumption that these 'patrons' will have seen or heard the mention and will contribute money. Often, the young actors themselves try to become clients of big men and big women and present themselves, in phone calls and visits at their houses, as dependants of these 'patrons' in whose financial resources they hope to share. The young artists have much more to offer their potential 'patrons' than other youngsters: they can drop the names of their 'patrons'[11] in the televised episodes and other cultural performances, which of course allows their 'patrons'' names to be heard all over town (and beyond, in the case of serials diffused on national television channels) and thus raises the social esteem of the city's 'big men and women'.

As a result, the 'patron'-client relationship between 'patrons' and performers is more complex than a regular *'grand-petit'* relationship. As stars in the city, the artists occupy a privileged position that lifts them above the status of common people. For their viewers, the actors are themselves 'big men' while they happily perform the role of a *petit* in their relations with other big men and women who have won acclaim through commerce or politics. The players occupy dots, as it were, within a web of multiple relationships that bind them to both the 'smallest people' and the 'biggest persons' in town.

One could contend that the actor and his 'patron' are not so much engaged in a 'patron'-client relationship as in that of a praise singer and his 'patron'. This was well illustrated in the dropping of names during the weeks preceding the first democratic elections (2006). Politicians and military men have a tradition of being named in Kinshasa's popular culture, especially in music. Election fever slipped into the serials as well. Many candidates for the presidency or for parliamentary seats approached the actors to have themselves or their party mentioned. While in September 2005 the Commission of Censorship prohibited musicians from citing the names of political persons and military officials, no such ban was placed on serials.[12] During the months before the first elections, many television serials were filled with references to and praise for candidates.

## The politics of *mabanga*

There is, however, some secrecy around name-dropping (*mabanga*). First, face-to-face contact between the actors and these big men is rare. The latter often call the artists by phone, and after being mentioned send one of their *petits* with a thank-you message and some money. Second, the actors are somewhat ambivalent with regard to the phenomenon of praising or citing people. At first, during formal interviews, none of the actors would acknowledge that they actually 'threw' people. Some argued that this would amount to a 'selling of the art'. The actors responded to questions in this regard with the same sense of shame that White (1999) has noted while researching *mabanga* in popular music. Their front stage behaviour (Goffman 1971 [1959]) in our initial encounters demonstrated that they wanted to represent themselves as 'real artists'. They maintained that the references to 'patrons' 'ruined the story'. However, the actors always referred to other theatre companies where 'one could hear one *libanga* after another', thus questioning the quality of their colleagues' or competitors' serials. Sometimes the actors cited American films – most often *A Prince in New York*, starring Eddie Murphy – arguing, in their own defence, that these big actors 'drop' names: 'Eddie Murphy mentioned Arnold Schwarzenegger in this film. If [he] can do it, why can't we?'

Most of the artists who are already well known by the public seek to secure individual relationships with 'patrons'. Having one or more 'patrons' is something to be proud of. 'As artists, we must know how to use our language. Politicians need to do this too. Through words, we must win our market. This is one of the most important aspects of the power of the word, a power that God has given to us', an actor named Raph explained. He jokingly referred to the actors' ability to access high social strata as 'the inexplicable work of ants' (*mystique ya bafourmilles*), for 'ants get in everywhere'.

In the following, I discuss how Ance and Beti, two CINARC performers, met their 'patrons'.

## Beti, talking about her 'patronne'

Beti had just finished high school and was saving money to pursue higher studies. She wanted to study accountancy. In the meantime she earned some money by braiding hair and through her contacts from television appearances. Her main provider of money and luxury items (beautiful clothes, a mobile phone and credit for it) was Mi-Josée, an elderly woman who travels back and forth between Belgium and Congo. From time to time, Beti mentioned her benefactor's name in the theatre or sent her greetings to Mi-Josée when invited onto television talk shows. They knew each other through Beti's braiding work. As told by Beti, Mi-Josée was a friend of one of the women whose hair Beti used to braid. One day Mi-Josée noticed her work and, liking it, asked for her phone number.

Beti was very proud of Mi-Josée who, in her eyes, is a big woman, a status derived from her travels between Europe and Congo and the wealth she displays. Beti related, 'She lives in Brussels with her children and her husband and from time to time comes to Congo. In Europe, she buys cars that she sends to Congo. Now, she is in Boma to collect two jeeps she sent over here.' When Mi-Josée returns to Kinshasa, the word spreads, and Beti awaits her call. She invites Beti for a drink at her home, or she drops by to give Beti some money.

## Ance, talking about his 'patron'

It was thanks to Beti's network that Ance found his own 'patron'. Beti put Ance in touch with Mi-Josée's brother, Didier Mpeti. This man is a wealthy businessman referred to by some of Kinshasa's most popular secular musicians.

> He is 'the sultan of Brussels'. He is really a *grand prêtre*. I don't know exactly what he does in life, but I know that he has money. And he travels all the time. The first time we met he asked me, 'What do you want?' I had no mobile phone at the time, so I asked him to buy one for me. I know that he was surprised that I asked him for a phone at our first meeting. He told me to get into his car, where I saw some piles of money that he gave to someone in Kauka. When I got out of the car, he gave me 5,000 FC (about US$12 at the time). He told me, 'I am leaving for Europe very soon. I want you to "throw" my name during my absence. My brothers will call me. As soon as I get back, I will look for you.' I had no opportunity to 'throw' him for a long time, but as soon as he was back I called him and told him to watch the following Thursday evening. In 'Apostasy' I was in a shot with *frère* Patrice, who illegally arranged visas and travel to Europe. In the serial, I said, 'You are a fraud. The only one I trust is Didier Mpeti, the Sultan of Brussels.'

I tried to call Didier Mpeti in Europe, but could not speak to him. Last week Beti told me Didier Mpeti's younger brother had called her and encouraged me to continue 'throwing' him. I hope he will be here soon because I need money.

Didier Mpeti gave Ance a blue suit and designer sunglasses. At the time of my conversation with Ance, he had only been able to cite his 'patron' once. Ance, however, was convinced that in the future he would have more opportunities to mention him. Then, he planned to remind his 'patron' that he would like a mobile phone and maybe some money to start living on his own.

Since Beti had been instrumental in finding Ance a 'patron', Ance was in a position of dependency towards her. Opening up new networks entails obligations of gratitude towards benefactors. Beti complained that she was normally entitled to receive a portion of the money or goods that Ance received from his 'patron', implying that Ance did honour his obligations.

The politics of gender also cross-cuts the hierarchies between actors and influences the performance of mabanga. Gendered differences persist in these 'patron'-client relationships and determine the opportunities to establish them. Women are hampered in the search for individual 'patrons'. Due to their fear of losing honour or of being romantically linked by the audience and fellow actors to the persons mentioned, women are more reluctant to drop the names of 'big men'. They tend, rather, to restrict themselves to citing family members or friends who are socially harmless. Otherwise, like Beti, they search for big women whose names they might drop. Unfortunately, as there are fewer 'big women' than 'big men', the opportunities for actresses to access new networks are more limited.

Another restriction on the possibilities for citing people is inherent to the power relations of the drama group. First, mabanga reflects the internal hierarchal structure of a theatre company. 'Big men' are only mentioned by actors who are very successful or who have already established a 'name'. The 'bigger' the person to be named, the more important the actor doing the citing must be. In this way, the social esteem of both parties, the actor who mentions one's name[13] and the person cited, is enhanced. Second, the relationships between the actors, the cameramen and the image editors influence the final decision about whether or not to keep the mabanga in the episode. When an episode has first been broadcast, artists are often found expressing their discontent on learning that their libanga was cut. In several specific cases the actors complained that one particular actor, who was also responsible for production, intended to keep all the money, since his libanga always made it through the last cutting. Such occurrences often had repercussions on the relations between the actors and their 'patrons', as the process of exchange was interrupted. The latter, dissatisfied because their name had not been mentioned, would fail to live up to their obligations as 'patrons' while the actors were deprived of desperately needed services.

In conclusion to this section on the social significance of citing people, I turn to White's (1999) analysis of the mabanga phenomenon. Writing about the world of urban dance music, White describes *mabanga* as a violation of the moral order since the exchange of words for money does not occur between family members or people from the same educational level but rather between different social worlds. The case is somewhat different for the practice of *mabanga* in the serials. Actors sometimes refer to kin group members out of an interest in the collective welfare of family and the larger kin group. This may be an effort to smooth familial relationships, but it also may indicate simple tokens of respect and gratitude. From time to time, Ance mentioned the names of his friends from his 'old', 'pagan' period (before he became a born-again Christian), '[t]o keep in touch', he said. In the third episode of the serial 'Caroline and Poupette', Theresia (in real life, Anne) asked her fictional daughters whether her 'real' sister had come by. Anne did not receive any money for this *libanga* since she 'threw' her sister out of gratitude. Anne said,

> She takes care of my children while I work here for CINARC. Sometimes she gives me money to take them to the hospital. Last week, my son suffered from malaria, and I had no money to buy the medicine. Luckily, she bought all the drugs he needed, and now he is healed. As I have no money, this is my way of thanking her.

In addition, the need to smoothen social relations can also be a motivation for dropping a name. An example here is Nene's periodic mention of her fiancé's mother. Nene told me that her fiancé's family did not approve of her acting work, which they perceive as unworthy of a woman. In a bid to win the confidence of her fiancé's relatives, she mentioned her fiancé's mother's name from time to time.

## Conclusions

The main goal of this chapter has been to provide an alternative, ethnographic approach to the worlds in which television products emerge. In a society where an informal economy thrives, the television world is likely to be embedded in the structures and value systems that orient modes of production and labour in other sectors of that society.

Teleserials constitute a strong connective space between the economic dimension of daily life and the social dimension of identity formation. The urban milieu of Kinshasa powerfully shapes the strategies of economic engagement pursued by Kinois.

Crucially, the economic ties discussed above are not at all static. They are not produced on a long-term basis and, as is typical for urban networks, they are easily dissolved. Contracts with sponsors can be aborted for various reasons, among them being that the product has not been made visible enough, or that a personal conflict between the band's leader and the head of the enterprise has risen, or even that the artist who has initiated the contract has left the group. Still, there are so many different enterprises that long to collaborate with the drama groups that the loss of a contract is usually not a big issue. A politician's rival, or a rivalling company, will happily take over the sponsorship, which then means a symbolic victory in the extra-artistic world.

This is not at all limited to the world of television drama; the same dynamic occurs in, for example, the sponsoring of local musicians.[14]

Such data suggest that teleserials in Kinshasa are not produced so that the people involved in their production can become wealthy; rather, the production of social relations and the public expression of those networks are the major goals to which both artists and the viewers who are included in the serials aspire.

## Notes

\* This chapter was previously published in a monograph on the production of Kinshasa's teleserials (Pype 2012). It appears here with kind permission of Berghahn Books. The material for the research was gathered during fieldwork with Kinshasa's most popular drama group (seventeen months between 2003 and 2006). Fieldwork included interviews with Kinshasa's dramatic artists and observation and participation during religious events, the actual filming of the teleserials, and the interaction between television actors and their audiences in talk shows and beyond the studio. The research was funded by the Faculties of Educational and Psychological Sciences and of Social Sciences at the Catholic University of Leuven (Belgium). The chapter was written while the author was a Newton International Fellow (British Academy) at the Centre of West African Studies (University of Birmingham).

1 For an interesting introduction into African television worlds, see Bourgault (1995).

2 'Kinois' is the adjective of Kinshasa. 'Kinois people' are Kinshasa's inhabitants.

3 The making of the serials is reminiscent of the working modalities of the Yoruba artists Karin Barber describes in *The Generation of Plays. Yoruba Popular Life in Theater* (2000).

4 There are a few exceptions, one being Okapi, created in 2004. This group is headed by Shako, an important actress in Kinshasa's history of television serials. She first worked with Tshitenge Tsana in Groupe Salongo and later joined Sans Soucis. Since 2006, *Maman* Alingi heads the troupe Théâtre Toli. Hughuette Ntambikila leads the group Les Nanas Lumière.

5 A 'shout' is a catchy phrase that is often repeated in the serials and often takes hold in the 'real world'.

6 My participation in the CINARC group followed the same route: I first appeared in a commercial. Then, small roles like a church member or the secretary of a business patron were invented to insert me into the main storyline. After several months, Bienvenu created 'my serial' ('Back to the Homestead') with me in a leading role.

7 An example of the world of popular music: Lambio Lambio, the choreographer of Viva La Musica (Papa Wemba's group), hosts in his compound six girls whom he trains to become dancers. He teaches them how to dress, how put on make-up and how to behave in public.

8 This is, for example, also how I made my first performance in the CINARC serials. On the first day of my work with the troupe, they were shooting in the Balekaz Cosmetics shop in a side street of the main Boulevard in the city centre. Together with Bienvenu, the CINARC leader, two actresses and an actor who was also filming that day, we were waiting outside on the pavement until the costumers had left the small shop. Suddenly, Bienvenu asked me whether I was willing to play. I was going to be the vendor and would show Charlainne and her daughter, who were giving themselves a treat with a hair shampoo, the best available in Kinshasa. Bienvenu explicitly ordered me to say that these products came straight from Europe. He added that people would certainly believe the words of a white woman. Although I had no acting experience, and I was not acquainted with the overall storyline of the serial that the group was recording, I was immediately included in the group's work, which apparently not only produced Christian subjects but also modern consumers.

9 The creativity of the Kinois in the daily struggle for survival has generated 'new jobs' in the informal sector. Well-known examples of this are the *Khadafi*, who sell fuel; the *chargeurs*, who look for passengers for public transport; or the *bana ya vernis*, the pedicure boys from the townships who walk about the city all day long rattling their small bottles of nail polish and remover and calling out for clients.

10   These *mikilistes* use the *mabanga* in Kinshasa's popular culture as opportunities to promote themselves symbolically within their networks in Kinshasa and in the diasporic community, since copies of these serials also circulate in the Congolese diaspora. They wish their name to be heard throughout the city and be praised for being successful abroad.

11   The phenomenon of dropping names is not to be confused with the advertisements the groups or actors sometimes make for commercial ventures (shops, boutiques or cybercafés, for example), for special prayer events at a local church or for a school that a fellow spiritual leader has opened.

12   Many musicians expressed their objections at the time because receiving money from cited persons was the fastest and surest way to earn a living. In a city where CDs and audiotapes sell very poorly, the artists are forced to pursue other financial strategies. In the last month before the elections, cultural patronage on the part of the country's president became more visible. The sitting president invited bands – including Wenge Musica Maison Mère – and musicians – such as Tshala Mwana – to create songs in which Kabila's administration was lauded and in which Congolese, especially the Kinois, were called on to vote for Kabila. Other musicians took the initiative to create songs for Kabila in order to receive a piece of the cake. Other candidates for the presidency could not afford to have the biggest bands mention their names or to have songs written for their propaganda; instead, they hired smaller groups whose audiences tend to be very small. It is a long-standing tradition among Congolese musicians to create songs in praise of the political leader. Franco Luambo Makiadi, also known as 'Mobutu's bard', for example, wrote songs such as *Candidat na biso Mobutu* (Our candidate, Mobutu), *Cinq ans ekoki* (Five years of success) and other lyrics that acclaimed Mobutu's power.

13   Actors depend on the image editor, who is responsible for the final cutting and pasting in order to create a real story from the taped frames. One Thursday evening, while watching an episode together with some actors, I was astonished to see that the mixer had cut my *libanga*. There was no communication between the image editor and me. Afterwards he disappeared so I had no chance to ask him why he had not accepted this scene.

14   The two main breweries, for example, compete tremendously over the sponsorship of the main music artists such as Werrason and J. B. Mpiana. When Werrason ended his contract with Bralima, Bracongo soon became Werrason's main sponsor, and banners all over the city announced Werrason's '*change de frequence*', '*Bracongo supports Werrason*'.

## Bibliography

Abu-Lughod, L. (2005), *Dramas of Nationhood. The Politics of Television in Egypt*, Chicago: Chicago University Press.

Barber, K. (2000), *The Generation of Plays. Yoruba Popular Life in Theater*, Bloomington: Indiana University Press.

Ben-Amos, P. (1980), 'Patron-Artist Interactions in Africa', *African Arts*, 13 (3): 56–7.

Bourgault, L. (1995), *Mass Media in Sub-Saharan Africa*, Bloomington: Indiana University Press.

Burssens, A. (1954), *Introduction à l'Etude des Langues Bantoues du Congo-Belge*, Antwerpen: De Sikkel.

Carsten, J. (2004), *After Kinship*, Cambridge: Cambridge University Press.

De Boeck, F. (2004), *Kinshasa. Tales of the Invisible City*. With pictures by M.-F. Plissart. Ghent-Amsterdam: Ludion.

Fabian, J. (1983), *Time and the Other. How Anthropology Makes Its Object*, New York: Columbia University Press.

Goffman, E. (1971 [1959]), *The Presentation of Self in Everyday Life*, New York: Doubleday.

Guyer, J. (1993), 'Wealth in People and Self-Realisation in Equatorial Africa', *Man*, 28 (2): 243–65.

Helliwell, C. (1996), 'Space and Sociality in a Dayak Longhouse', in. M. Jackson (ed.), *Things As They Are: New Directions in Phenomenological Anthropology*, Bloomington and Indianapolis: Indiana University Press, pp. 128–48.

Jewsiewicki, B. (2004), 'Kinshasa: (auto)representation d'une société "moderne" en (dé)construction. De la modernisation coloniale à la globalisation', in P. Mabiala Mantuba-Ngoma (ed.), *La Nouvelle Histoire du Congo. Mélanges eurafricains offerts à Frans Bontinck*, C.I.C.M. Paris/Tervuren: Musée Royal de l'Afrique Centrale/l'Harmattan, pp. 251–66.

Meyer, B. (2003a), 'Visions of Blood, Sex and Money. Fantasy Spaces in Popular Ghanaian Cinema', *Visual Anthropology*, 16 (1): 15–41.

Meyer, B. (2003b), 'Ghanaian Popular Cinema and the Magic in and of Film', in B. Meyer and P. Pels (eds), *Magic and Modernity. Interfaces of Revelation and Concealment*, Stanford: Stanford University Press, pp. 200–22.

Meyer, B. (2006), 'Impossible Representations. Pentecostalism, Vision and Video Technology in Ghana', in B. Meyer and A. Moors (eds), *Religion, Media and the Public Sphere*, Bloomington: Indiana University Press, pp. 290–312.

Miers, S. and Kopytoff, I. (1979), *Slavery in Africa: Historical and Anthropological Perspectives*, Madison, WI: University of Wisconsin Press.

Perani, J. and Wolff, N. H. (1999), *Cloth, Dress and Art Patronage in Africa*, Oxford and New York: Berg.

Pype, K. (2008), *The Making of the Pentecostal Melodrama. Mimesis, Power and Agency in Kinshasa's Media World (DR Congo)*, unpublished dissertation, KU Leuven, Leuven.

Pype, K. (2009), '"We Need to Open Up the Country": Development and the Christian Key Scenario in the Social Space of Kinshasa's Television Serials', *Journal of Africa's Media Studies*, 1 (1): 101–16.

Pype, K. (2010), 'Of Fools and False Pastors: Tricksters in Kinshasa's Television Fiction', *Visual Anthropology*, 23 (2): 115–35.

Pype, K. (2012), *The Making of the Pentecostal Melodrama: Media, Religion and Gender in Postcolonial Kinshasa*, New York/Oxford: Berghahn Books.

Vansina, J. (1984), *Art History in Africa*, London and New York: Longman.

Weber, M. (1947), *The Theory of Social and Economic Organisation*, transl. by A. M. Henderson and T. Parsons, London: Hodge.

White, B. W. (1999), 'Modernity's Trickster: "Dipping" and "Throwing" in Congolese Popular Dance Music', *Research in African Literatures*, 30 (4): 156–75.

# Les chefs-opératrices

## Women behind the camera in France

ALISON SMITH

It is generally accepted that the last quarter-century has seen a vast change in the gender balance of those working in the cinema industry, in France as elsewhere. Especially in the high-profile field of directing, a new generation of talented young women entering the profession in the 1990s and 2000s established their presence with such assurance that it is hardly a matter worth remarking on any longer. Given the traditional emphasis on the 'auteur' as the figure of prime importance in French film-making, and the speed with which the extremely wide gender gap associated with the role was closed, it is perhaps understandable that rising numbers of women directors should be mistaken for a general feminization of the industry. The pattern, however, has not been replicated to the same extent in all sectors. While in some areas of the film-making process – editing and design, for example – women have always had a strong presence, others have been very firmly perceived as a male pre- serve, and none more so than cinematography. Although Agnès Godard, one of the best-known female directors of photography (DPs) in the country, told the review Positif in 2000 that she thought the French industry was exceptionally ready to accept a woman in the role (Audé and Tobin 2000), it is noticeable that in 2009, the 107 members of the prestigious Association Française des Directeurs de la Photographie Cinématographique (AFC) included only ten women, despite relatively large num- bers of aspirant female camera operators working at assistant level on film projects. To put this number into context, however, the AFC's US equivalent, the American Society of Cinematographers (ASC), counts only seven women among its 334 listed active members (its 161 associate members produce another seven). Although several eminent male names appear on both lists, no women have (as yet) become members of both organizations. The British Society of Cinematographers (BSC) has ninety-eight full members and only three women among them. The Associazione Italiana Autori della Fotografia Cinematografica (AIC) boasts three out of 106. France could thus be said to have a relatively good record, but with a strong emphasis on the 'relative'.

There is some evidence that the women who have become members of these bodies tend to be active members, but with such tiny numbers it is faintly ironic that Sue Gibson in Britain and Caroline Champetier in France were elected presidents of their Associations in 2008 and April 2009, respectively. It is also alarming that when the industry periodical *Film Français* enquired into the situation of women in the French cinema in 1999, their observations repeat almost exactly those mentioned above. In that year, they reported,

> Trente ans après les débuts à l'image de femmes comme Dominique Le Rigoleur ou Nurith Aviv, on trouve tout au plus une dizaine de chefs opératrices travaillant actuellement sur des longs métrages en France. Pas de quoi se vanter, même si la situation est beaucoup plus favorable qu'aux Etats-Unis, où l'ASC (American Society of Cinematographers) compte seulement cinq femmes sur les 315 membres de l'association.[1] (Dacbert and Caradec 1999)

Outside the eminent circles of the professional organization, the situation at first glance looks more even. A search on the Unifrance professional directory site for 'director of photography, female' yields 578 names. For the record, 2,945 names appear when the same search specifies male – a significant difference but a considerably better ratio than the ten to ninety-seven observed in the AFC.

However, that figure of 578 should not be taken too literally. There are a few list errors – Daniele Ciprì, for example, appears in this list as female, and lesser-known figures with ambiguous names may be harder to detect. The names include established directors such as Chantal Akerman and Agnès Varda, who, in very rare instances, usually for documentary projects, have been known to take charge of their own cinematography, but would no doubt be most surprised to be contacted by a director looking for a DP. In vast majority, the Unifrance list is made up of film students whose claim to experience as cinematographers is limited to one or two short films on which they also acted as director, writer and editor, and in some cases even these prove to boast a number of DPs. Although such entries may signal prominent careers to come, there is really no room for confident projections at this point, even if the position of DP were not itself in such flux that, at this small-scale level of production, director and DP are in all probability set to fuse even more in future.

In fact, on closer examination, only 128, or 22.4 per cent, of those 578 have ever been credited as cinematographer (or even co-cinematographer) on a feature film or a high-profile TV programme (Unifrance does not list TV credits, and my principal source for this information is the Internet Movie Database (IMDb), whose records of European television are not exhaustive, but which for that reason could be said to operate as a filter as regards the importance of the project). Many of the remaining 78 per cent are presumably at a very early stage in their career, but the scattered cases where birth dates are provided with the entry suggest that this is by no means always so.

Even those 128 names are not a reliable list. Seventeen are in the Unifrance directory on the basis of one French credit while their careers have taken shape and form in other countries. Forty-four of the remainder have worked as cinematographer only on a few small TV projects, or have single credits only as co-cinematographers. The latter usually prove to be on quite small-scale documentary projects, but there are several instances of women whose most high-profile credit proves to be a shared credit. For example, the female co-cinematographers who worked on Tranh Anh Hung's *Cyclo* (1995), Maurice Pialat's *Le Garçu* (1995) and Christian Vincent's *La Séparation* (1994), all very visible films made in the 1990s, never continued with a DP career or – in the case of Anne Nicolet, who worked on *La Séparation* – have remained at assistant level ever since. For the purposes of this chapter, the original 578 names supplied by Unifrance have been reduced to a sample of sixty-five who can unequivocally show at least one full-length feature film on their CV. The full list is given in an Appendix.

The first woman to be officially recognized as a DP in France was the Israeli-born Nurit Aviv, who attained the title in 1975. The ten AFC members (Aviv has never joined this body) are, in alphabetical order, Diane Baratier, Céline Bozon, Caroline Champetier, Crystel Fournier, Claude Garnier, Agnès Godard, Jeanne Lapoirie, Dominique Le Rigoleur, Hélène Louvart and Myriam Vinocour. Half of those (Baratier, Bozon, Fournier, Garnier and Vinocour) have become members since 2004. Outside that select group, there is Sabine Lancelin, a Zairean-born, French-based *chef-op* with a strong record of collaboration with the Portuguese director Manoel de Oliveira, and a few others with fairly substantial semi-mainstream filmographies to their credit. The absence of the popular commercial cinema from these titles is immediately remarkable on investigation; Catherine Pujol, whose nineteen credits include the popular Johnny Halliday vehicle *Jean-Philippe* (2006) along with the usual numerous shorts, stands out as an exception, but she worked on the film only as one of a partnership.

Dominique le Rigoleur, the most senior of the AFC's ten current female members, recalled that her year group at the French film school, Institut des Hautes Etudes Cinematographiques (IDHEC; now Ecole Nationale Supérieure des Métiers de L'Image et du Son (FEMIS)), which she attended from 1969 to 1971, constituted the first intake of women onto the 'Prise de vues', or 'Image' strand, which directed its graduates towards cinematography. 'Nous n'étions que 3 diplômées', she recalled in 2000 when the Women's Film Festival in Créteil staged a celebration of women behind the camera, 'et il est sûr que le fait d'être une femme dans ce métier ne m'a pas facilité les choses'[2] (Créteil 2000: 98), but she felt that 'aujourd'hui la situation se banalise'[3] (Créteil 2000: 98). If there is a recurring theme in recent interviews with France's most eminent women cinematographers, in fact, it is the insistence that the situation has improved to the point where there is little or nothing which is exceptional *now* in their position, despite the blatant lack of parity in fact. If anything, one can detect a certain understandable exasperation among highly skilled artists/ professionals if an interviewer shows a tendency to dwell on the matter to the detriment of discussion of their technical achievements or the more general challenges facing a rapidly changing profession. (It is perhaps symptomatic of this exasperation that an attempt to contact the ten AFC members at the start of my research for this chapter produced only one reply – from Céline Bozon, to whom I would like to extend my gratitude – and the interview that she very kindly accorded me confirmed my sense of a thematic insistence on the relative unimportance of gender except in very specific circumstances.) If one remains exercised by the contrast between individual confidence and collective scarcity, or by the large numbers of 'assistant camerawomen' who have never graduated to principal status, have worked only on short films or who have moved out of the field altogether, one is obliged to engage in a careful reading of the accounts these women have given of their professional experience, and to try to extract patterns and observations in the hope that, somehow, in any specificities and particularities that may be detected one may discover signs of a way forward for women behind the camera. This is what this chapter has set out to do. Of necessity I have relied largely on published interviews (which tend to be with well-established professionals, for obvious reasons) and on the observation of the career patterns visible among the larger sample of mostly younger women who appear on the Unifrance website. It seems to me, however, that there is little evidence of a dramatic change in career patterns between the 1970s and the 1990s and between the 1990s and the 2000s, even if overall numbers have risen slightly – there are only five non-AFC members in the attached list with full credits dating prior to 1990. This study has been carried out on a relatively strong national cinema industry with a well-established infrastructure and by that token a clearly defined sense of its 'establishment', an industry viewed by those women working in it, with some justification, as relatively open, 'easier' than other contexts, but nonetheless an industry in which the profession of cinematographer is nonetheless overwhelmingly male-dominated almost forty years after women began to enter it.

## The structure of the profession

In the 'normal', professionalized structure of a film team as it is constituted in mainstream production in a major industry, the cinematographer, or DP (in France, most commonly, the *chef-opérateur*, although the term *directeur de photographie* is gaining momentum, in part because it seems more easily amenable to feminization), holds a central, but also a complex, position. On the one hand, the work is understood to be technical: it requires, or always has required in the past, specialist training and also practical experience in the handling of sophisticated equipment, and a degree of scientific expertise unavailable to anyone else on set including (especially) the director; it usually involves responsibility for, and up to a point training of, a team of collaborators who constitute the 'camera unit' (*cadreurs*, *opérateurs* etc.), and at some level, at least until very recently, it has also involved heavy physical labour, since even so-called 'lightweight' or 'portable' movie cameras are bulky objects. Being a technician has implications for the relationship of the DP to the production: the cinematographer is part of the hired crew, often subject to union rules and without any authorial stake in the finished product. On the other hand, the work in practice involves creative responsibility which may be very considerable. Although the majority of cinematographers are at pains to stress that they expect the director to have a visual conception of their project and to be able to transmit it clearly, the DP is, ultimately, responsible for the realization of the image. The eye behind the camera as it turns is hers (or his), and, perhaps even more importantly, so is the sense of what will be imprinted on the film as a result of the camera's processing of what its eye sees. As a result, the working relationship between director and DP on set is inevitably a close and continuous creative partnership, which involves some sense of shared ownership on the part of those concerned, as Caroline Champetier has force-fully argued (Guérin, Strauss and Toubiana 1996: 95). A project's DP will therefore not be selected on the basis of mere substitutable technical competence but with an eye both to personal and stylistic compatibility. Many auteur-directors – those with enough influence over their film projects to be able to select their own collaborators freely – have established long-term working relationships with 'their' cinematogra-phers, and DPs at the top of the profession can afford to choose projects that interest them creatively; they may even decide to set their remuneration at a rate appropriate to the film's resources and artistic attraction, thus becoming effective stakeholders in the production.

At entry level, however, the consequences of this 'hired partner' status can lead to considerable difficulty in launching a career. The familiar dilemma of many young graduates, 'without experience no work, without work no experience', is exacerbated since, on the one hand, it is not part of the work of the cinematographer to initi-ate a project and, on the other, the collaboration required is so close that personal rapport with the director becomes almost part of the job specification. Inevitably, while training and its documented proof, qualifications, are increasingly becom-ing an entry requirement, early development of a career depends to a very large extent on personal relations and recommendations. There are two main roads to the acquisition of experience: one is the more traditional and still significant route, which is to work one's way up through junior roles on camera teams, in the process establishing working relationships with more established *chef-ops* and directors; the other, increasingly attractive in an industry where access to the means of production is increasingly envisageable, is to work within a peer group on small-scale student or graduate projects, usually short films or documentaries, in the hope either of attracting attention individually or establishing a viable collective production team. The latter strategy offers a greater opportunity for renewing professional structures, as well as being relatively congenial to new digital working methods, but it is also a hazardous business with a high failure rate, even in the French system with its inbuilt encouragement of small, innovative projects. The above considerations apply, of course, to both men and women, but the high proportion of such projects in the career structures of the young women on the Unifrance database is very noticeable.

## From assistant to *chef-ops*: working with established DPs

For the first generation of women cinematographers in France, the importance of personal contacts – often male personal contacts – in facilitating their first steps in the industry is evident. Certainly the vast majority, including Aviv, are graduates of the IDHEC/FEMIS, although not necessarily through courses in cinematography. Even that is not quite universal. Diane Baratier, for example, entered the profession through family connections – her father was the director Jacques Baratier – and trained on the job, working as a photographer and assistant camerawoman. She recalls (Bouhon 2004), 'Je voulais réaliser. Mon père m'a conseillé, pour apprendre le métier, de commencer à travailler comme assistante à la caméra plutôt qu'à la realisation.'[4] Nonetheless, it was only after a hiatus, during which 'je me suis retrouvée femme au foyer au Brésil'[5] that she decided to adopt the career definitively, and followed up her earlier training with evening classes at the École nationale supérieure Louis-Lumière.

But for Baratier, as for several of her most eminent colleagues in the AFC, evoking her early development involves, immediately and almost synonymously, recalling the vital role played by periods of assistantship to male 'stars' of an earlier generation. Baratier's mentor was Raoul Coutard, famous for his collaboration with Godard at the beginning of his career. Interviewed by *Cahiers du Cinéma* in 1996, when *Conte d'été* appeared at Cannes, she confessed, 'chaque fois que j'ai une difficulté, je l'appelle'[6] (Auger, Burdeau and Lounas 1996: 50). For Champetier, the essential influence, and explicit 'father figure', was William Lubtchansky, with whom she worked for some time at the beginning of her career. She told *Cahiers du Cinéma*, 'J'ai appris par les maîtres, les pères étaient les maîtres, ou l'inverse. J'ai assisté 8 ou 9 ans William Lubtchansky, à la sortie de l'Idhec,' adding, 'Parfois j'envie ceux qui ne sont pas dans l'amour et le respect du père'[7] (Guérin et al. 1996: 91). Agnès Godard has often recounted her debt to Henri Alekan, her tutor at IDHEC with whom she worked, memorably, for Wim Wenders on *Die Himmel über Berlin* (see for example Audé and Tobin 2000: 132). Jeanne Lapoirie's formative first work was with Thierry Arbogast, Luc Besson's collaborator; Dominique Le Rigoleur's with Nestor Almendros, who brought her with him into the ambit of the Nouvelle Vague. These, it should be noted, are very prestigious names indeed, although by no means all of their regular assistants (the majority of whom were male, as one might expect given the career structure in the field) went on to distinguished solo careers. The prevalence of this pattern highlights the importance of establishing relationships not only with like-minded directors but also with highly regarded 'masters' of the field, a career pattern which is replicated in the procedure for entering the AFC, which requires patronage (*parrainage*) by an established member who will speak for your professional competence. Since we can now see a first generation of women cinematographers well established and respected, the *parrainage* may sometimes be undertaken by *marraines* (godmothers), although the phenomenon, and the word, still seemed unusual enough for Diane Baratier to remark on it when she took on the role for Wilfrid Sempé in 2007 (Baratier 2007).

We might also expect to see early assistants to Champetier, Le Rigoleur or Godard beginning to make their mark as cinematographers on their own account. However, this does not seem to be the case. Among the sixty-five names on our sample there is only one case of a strong female 'apprenticeship' pattern lasting over several films (that between the relatively young Céline Bozon and Claire Mathot) and only six such pairings all told, even for one film (the others are Louvart/Bailly du Bois (2), Lapoirie/Cadet, Godard/Durand (2), Champetier/Filatriau, Godard/Mizrahi). Even if career development is inevitably slow (Champetier's 'eight or nine years' as assistant camera operator is fairly typical even of the most successful CVs), and uncertain for men and women alike, it would seem that the new generation of women most advanced in their career do not owe that advancement to their older sisters (although apprenticeships to men still play a part; Irina Lubtchansky is only the most obvious example). Céline Bozon claimed in an interview to have a slight preference for working with a woman as assistant, on the grounds of the *proximité* to be established with this close collaborator, but this is by no means universal, and even where enough time has elapsed to make meaningful observations there is not much sign of a new wave of young women being offered their own projects after training with their older female colleagues.

Although the lingering prejudice in the late 1980s and early 1990s (Godard recalls without rancour that in 1987, Henri Alekan felt obliged to double-check with Wenders that he was happy to employ a woman as first assistant (Audé and Tobin 2000), and that the producers of Claire Denis' first feature, *Chocolat*, refused to accept Denis' request to hire the young assistant as her principal *chef-op*) makes it easy to see why the insurance offered by association with an established 'master' was important, and perhaps essential, to the launching of many camerawomen's careers, there were exceptions to this even from the early days. It is interesting to observe that Nurit Aviv *began* her career in France as a principal cinematographer, working on documentaries and in the politically committed alternative sector which flourished briefly in the early 1970s, and that, despite the long abeyance of a strong alternative cinema, scanning the individual credits of the women on the Unifrance list one can easily observe the importance of the documentary genre in providing a first feature opportunity. For no less than twenty-one women, their first (and sometimes only) feature experience was documentary; to this list should be added a small number of others, not listed, who have so far achieved only co-DP-hood on one documentary. To some extent, this renewal of the documentary route to success may be linked to the importance and increasing openness of TV (a subject too large to be covered by this chapter). It is very rare indeed, however, that a young cinematographer starts her career as DP with TV work. Just as much as, if not more than, in film, French television relies on an apprenticeship system. Assistant camerawork is relatively easy to come by, but personal responsibility comes only after a trial period.

Twenty years after Aviv's formative period, Hélène Louvart came to prominence during the 1990s without ever acting as assistant thanks to a favourable climate for young directors, particularly those graduating from the film school. Louvart worked on the short projects of her peer group and was fortunate, or perspicacious, enough to pair up with Sandrine Veysset for Veysset's first feature, *Y aura-t-il de la neige à Noël?* (1996), which proved one of the great early successes of this new Jeune Cinéma, a movement frequently compared, then and subsequently, to a new Nouvelle Vague. Like Lubtchansky or Nestor Almendros in a previous generation, Louvart thus became associated with a new current in cinema, highly regarded critically and professionally. She is one of the rare success stories of the hazardous second route to professional entry. But even the Jeune Cinéma was a small-budget, independent, strictly art-house movement, which brought professional prestige but little or no recognition from big production houses, and its dynamic youthfulness quickly fell into abeyance. Some successful film-makers associated with it have remained in the public eye, but many others – and, it seems, more often the women than the men – have dramatically reduced their production. This lack of impetus is surely visible in the tentative career paths of many of the young women who appear on the Unifrance list – and this flags an overwhelmingly dominant pattern in the careers of women behind the camera.

## The importance of the 'auteur' sector

For all the AFC women, even the most eminent, professional acceptance came via the art-house and auteur sectors, and the pattern continues to this day. The mentors they cite are indications of this. Coutard, Lubtchansky and Almendros were all DPs closely associated with the Nouvelle Vague and its inheritance, who could introduce their assistants to Rohmer, Rivette or Jean-Luc Godard. Although Alekan had been associated with mainstream French production in the 1940s and 1950s, his renewed prominence in the 1980s, when Agnès Godard[8] worked with him, was due to his col-laboration on the artistic projects of Raoul Ruiz or Wim Wenders. Thierry Arbogast, on the other hand, followed his 'personal' director, Luc Besson, into superproduc-tions such as The Fifth Element (1997), but Lapoirie worked on only one Besson film, the breakthrough thriller Nikita (1990). She and Arbogast then collaborated again on André Téchiné's contribution to the mid-1990s Jeune Cinéma, Les Roseaux Sauvages (1994), and Lapoirie's subsequent career separated from Arbogast's at this point, developing through her encounter with Téchiné, with the young actor and aspirant director Gaël Morel, who played in the film, and eventually, through Téchiné and Morel, with François Ozon, into an exemplary trajectory for a successful art-house cinematographer. The art-house sector, with its will to adventurous creativity and its close personal collaborations, no doubt offers particular satisfaction to an image-maker, but the fact remains that a budgetary glass ceiling appears to exist above which the place behind the camera is reserved for men. The observation was already being made in 1999, when the Jeune Cinéma – which had also brought prominence to a number of young female directors – was at its most visible. Caroline Champetier told Film Français then: 'Il est clair que l'on ne va pas nous proposer Astérix. Nous avons beau avoir fait nos preuves sur nombre de films, quand on arrive à un certain niveau de budget, on sent des réticences ... Quand on est en compétition sur ce genre de films, on constate seulement qu'ils nous échappent systématiquement.'[9]

Eleven years on, the women of the AFC have still not been offered Astérix. Neither has any other woman, at the DP level. As assistants, camera operators or second unit teams, the story is somewhat different: although among the large numbers mobilized for these mega-projects women behind cameras are a tiny minority, they do exist, and CVs of assistants regularly boast such highly commercial projects as Les Visiteurs (1993)

(Brigitte Barbier), *La Reine Margot* (1994) (Francine Filatriau, Anne Nicolet, Myriam Touzet), *The Fifth Element* (Sophie Bosquet) and indeed *Astérix* (Eleonore Huisse on *Les Jeux Olympiques* (2008), Catherine Pujol on *Mission Cléopâtre* (2002)). Besson's *Arthur et les Minimoys* (2006) employed two women from the Unifrance directory on the camera team (Stella Libert, Anne Nicolet) and, in a development that may be a sign of career paths to come, no less than seven who advertise themselves on Unifrance as aspiring DPs participated in this film on the immense CGI team. But as *chef-opératrice*, even Catherine Pujol's co-acquisition of a relatively small-scale 'popular' project like *Jean-Philippe* is exceptional enough to be remarkable.

In the director-driven French independent sector, success as a DP has been strongly associated with close partnerships with individual directors. This pattern began in France with the success of the Nouvelle Vague and its modes of production in the early 1960s. The New Wave innovations increased the relative importance on the set of both the director and the cinematographer. The former became the acknowledged creative lynchpin of the project, the legal author of the film (from 1958), and the sole holder of day-to-day responsibility for its progress. However, the new approach to cinema championed both the vital importance of the image, completely eclipsing the script, and the right of visionary cinephiles to aspire to direct films with little or no technical experience. The new directors were thus highly dependent on skilled cameramen able to translate their ideas into arrangements of light imprinted on celluloid, while their working method in turn posed inspiring challenges to adaptable image-makers willing to experiment. In other words, the emphasis in the 'hired partner' status of the cinematographer swung dramatically from the 'hired' to the 'partner'. For those entering the profession at the time, it was an extremely exciting development. As Philippe Rousselot wryly recalls,

> J'ai commencé à travailler dans les années soixante quand le métier connaissait une fracture importante, léguée par la Nouvelle Vague. Les Nuyten [sic], Lafaye, Robin, moi-même, et bien d'autres, se sont engouffrés dans cette brèche avec une arrogance et un mépris des règles que nos ainés nous ont certainement reprochés, et avec juste raison sans doute.[10] (Champetier 2010)

By the time the first women began to enter the profession, this situation was a given. Quite as much as the direct transmission of skills and professional attitude, assisting Coutard, Almendros, Lubtchansky, Alekan or Arbogast meant an introduction to 'their' directors; working with one's peer group on student films meant testing professional relationships that, in case of affinities and success, might become the backbone of a career. Again, these considerations applied to both men and women, but when opportunities for work are more or less limited to the auteur sector, their significance increases. There seems no sign of this association diminishing – the only shadow over the development of directorial partnerships is the increasingly fragile career-path status of the independent, artistically minded director.

Naturally, since the cinematographer's full-time involvement with a film project is limited to the period before and during the shooting, a fully employed cinematographer will work on more films than a fully employed director, but the vast majority of the most established women cinematographers, especially those of the 'second generation' who began solo work in the late 1980s and early 1990s, have particular associates with whom they have shared a significantly greater number of projects than any others. Agnès Godard's association with Claire Denis, one of the best-known examples of director/cinematographer symbiosis in the industry, covers fourteen of the director's twenty recorded projects, 70 per cent of her output, and Godard also worked as an assistant on two others. Similarly, although with less international celebrity, Céline Bozon has worked on seven of the eleven films directed by Jean-Paul Civeyrac, an interesting director who came to some modest prominence during the Jeune Cinéma period with his critically acclaimed first feature Ni d'Eve ni d'Adam (1996) (photographed by Bozon). Such quasi-auteurial identification over a director's whole career is certainly unusual, but we see many other examples of a consistent rapport which offers evidence of a significant mutual exchange between director and cinematographer. Diane Baratier was Eric Rohmer's cinematographer on all his projects since L'Arbre, le maire et la médiathèque (1991), which was her first film as DP. From 1986 to 1993, moreover, the relatively young Caroline Champetier collaborated seven times with Jean-Luc Godard, an association that assured her critical attention as well as forming her outlook on the profession: 'Si je n'avais pas eu cette chance, ce temps d'apprentissage avec JLG, j'aurais sans doute été piégée par le naturalisme',[11] she told Cahiers in 1996 (Guérin et al. 1996: 98). Although Jeanne Lapoirie has only photographed five films for François Ozon, those five – from Gouttes d'eau sur pierres brûlantes in 2000 to le Temps qui reste in 2005 – constitute a significant corpus of feature films with which director and cinematographer each emerged definitively from an apprenticeship period characterized by short projects. Nurit Aviv's border-crossing career contains two defining associations, first with Agnès Varda – six projects from 1974 to 1985, including two films made in Los Angeles – then with Amos Gitai – ten films between 1982 and 1998, almost half his output during that period. Although Hélène Louvart's filmography covers a large part of the landscape of the Jeune Cinéma, two names stand out, Dominique Cabrera (seven collaborations since 1993, 70 per cent of Cabrera's work in the period) and Sandrine Veysset, with whom she has worked on the four feature films which constitute Veysset's entire output.

Reading further into this brief summary we may perceive subtle changes in the pattern of expectation. For Nurit Aviv and Dominique Le Rigoleur, the 'pioneers' of women's cinematography during the 1970s, solo projects were hard to come by. The post-1968 impetus to reform outdated structures and open alternative pathways to cinematic expression had created a small space for newcomers to make films, but even this sector was very male dominated. For both Aviv and Le Rigoleur, important openings came through the few women who were then involved in direction. Varda, whose commitment to feminist issues in the early 1970s brought her into the ambit of the cinema of protest and political renewal, became a close associate of Aviv until the mid-1980s; and Aviv's filmography in the late 1970s and early 1980s is full of small, often documentary, projects undertaken with women in Italy, the Netherlands, Israel and France. Although Le Rigoleur, as assistant to Nestor Almendros and others, was working on prestige projects for Robert Bresson, François Truffaut or Eric Rohmer in the 1970s rather than in the alternative sector, her first principal contracts, at the turn of the 1980s, came to her through Marguerite Duras, Aline Issermann or Yannick Bellon. None of these collaborations led to a lasting association, however. Duras and Bellon, major directors of an intellectually ambitious women-oriented cinema during the 1970s, directed very little in the 1980s, while the younger Issermann, with whom Le Rigoleur worked three times, seems to have had difficulty funding projects and turned increasingly to television. Le Rigoleur's subsequent career has not led her to associate herself for long with any single director; in this respect she is unique among those women who have been DPs for more than ten years.

It is among those who entered the profession between 1980 and 1995 that there is the clearest evidence of careers formed around strong identification with a director, although here too there is a divergence and a double pattern. While Champetier and Baratier, inducted by Lubtchansky and Coutard respectively into the art-house establishment, 'inherited' the leading lights of the Nouvelle Vague, now very much more experienced than these young DPs, for Agnès Godard, Jeanne Lapoirie and Céline Bozon the defining encounters were with directors of similar age and experience to themselves, with whom their careers could develop for a shorter or longer time through a process of exchange, according to the model pioneered, precisely, by the Nouvelle Vague. The publication in 2001 of Dominique Maillet and Sylvie Biscioni's collection of director interviews, *En lumière: les directeurs de photographie vus par les Cinéastes*, in which three women are selected to feature among thirty-seven DPs represented, is an indication of the degree to which this auteurist career model was perceived as the norm for a critically successful DP at the turn of the millennium.

Apart from Céline Bozon, however, the most recent wave of young women to make their mark as DPs have found it harder to acquire any such perceptible auteurist 'partner'. If anything, one can perceive the strongest director/DP relationships of the 1990s/2000s in TV work, where, for example, Myriam Vinocour has been associated with Richard Monnet. TV directors as a rule do not command the same public and critical attention as Rohmer, Denis or even Civeyrac, but the speed and economy of TV work requires a tight team, and partnerships that work are likely to be precious. The relative decline in the importance of auteur-directors in developing DPs' careers, however, seems at least credibly to point to a crisis in the *auteur* system itself. It is worth pointing out that if Sandrine Veysset or Dominique Cabrera had made as many films, with as high a public profile, in ten years as Claire Denis has been able to, then the shape of Hélène Louvart's career might be very different. Although Jean-Paul Civeyrac has been prolific, the visibility of his films has been fairly low and, in general, with one or two exceptions who are almost exclusively male (Despleschin, Honoré, Dumont, perhaps Ozon) the Jeune Cinéma has not provided its directors with the fortune that the Nouvelle Vague offered its founders. To seek to probe the possible reasons for their difficulties would be to take us a long way from our central subject – see, for example, Pascale Ferran's speech at the Césars ceremony in 2007 (Ferran 2007). The fact remains that the movement has not furnished the hoped-for auteurist opening for a new generation of *chef-opératrices*, while as we have seen the producer-driven popular cinema remains largely closed to them. Although within professional circles a female presence is now not only accepted but often enthusiastically foregrounded – as the figurehead position occupied by Champetier may indicate – one should probably beware of over-optimism regarding the career prospects for the current generation of assistant camerawomen, all the more in that a digital revolution is promising a shake-up of professional certainties at least as dramatic as that initiated by the Nouvelle Vague (Champetier 2010). (This may, of course, prove to be a productive crisis, but there is certainly a possibility that the importance of the DP on set may decline as a result of it.)

## The nature of the auteurist association

However important individual directors prove in individual careers, the work of a DP still involves close cooperation with every director they work with, cooperation based on expectations and preferences on both sides. The hypothesis that women prefer to work with women, often evoked when *chefs-opératrices* are interviewed and their careers are discussed, needs testing. If true, it could prove either supportive or problematic, or in different ways both, in establishing the female DP but, as we have already seen, several of the women under consideration have established their most important partnerships with male directors. We have also seen that, in the 1970s and early 1980s, to employ a woman as cinematographer was something of a political choice, and working with women (or with men with a feminist consciousness, like Bernard van Effenterre) was vital to Aviv and Le Rigoleur when they were starting out. Their successors did not find themselves similarly reliant on feminine or feminist solidarity to find employment. Nonetheless, the hypothesis finds some confirmation when we examine career profiles closely. All the AFC directors have worked with women several times, and made at least one feature film with a woman director. More than 50 per cent of Fournier and Godard's total feature films have been for women, while Hélène Louvart has worked with more women than men, across all her projects as well as on the features she has made. By a very approximate calculation, on average 35.5 per cent of these women's careers have been in collaboration with other women. Given that women have still not achieved parity even in the director field, this is a fairly high percentage.[12] However, several of the highest-profile women directors in France do not appear in their filmographies – Catherine Breillat, for example, has never worked with a woman cinematographer, Coline Serreau's association with Jean-François Robin is close enough to figure in the Maillet book, while Chantal Akerman has one early credit with Champetier and one with Sabine Lancelin, but has certainly not made a point of working with women.

The subject can be a sensitive one on both sides. Coline Serreau's association with Robin dates back to her first, feminist, films, and she found herself required to justify her choice to her collaborators, particularly on the interview-based documentary *Mais qu'est-ce qu'elles veulent?* She told Dominique Maillet,

> Beaucoup de filles me reprochaient d'avoir choisi un chef-opérateur homme. Sauf que Jean-François avait une idéologie et une politique dans la tête: il était d'accord avec ce que je faisais, il pensait comme moi qu'il y avait un nombre incroyable de choses à dire sur l'oppression des femmes.[13] (Maillet and Biscioni 2001: 196)

Nurith Aviv, in her interview with *Cahiers du Cinéma* in 1977, went to great lengths to frame her comments about directors in such a way that the gender appears to be feminine, principally by referring to them as '*la personne*' (the person). (Intriguingly, when the catalogue for the Créteil Films de Femmes Festival in 2000 quoted this interview, it altered her wording, substituting '*le réalisateur*' (the director, male) for '*le(a) réalisateur (trice)*' and an '*il*' (he) for an '*elle*' (she).) Nonetheless, her ideal director at this stage in her career, in terms of her relationship with him as DP, is not Varda (of whom she's even good-naturedly critical) but René Allio. In general, the predilection for working with women directors seems to be something that interests commentators more than the DPs themselves. The Créteil catalogue, for example, posits that Agnès Godard 'semble favoriser un cinéma "au féminin", ce qui ne l'empêche pas de participer à des succès plus éclectiques [sic] comme *La Vie rêvée des anges* ou *L'Arrière-pays*'[14] (Créteil 2000: 97). Stefano Masi makes a similar observation regarding Lapoirie's filmography and the number of first films by women that it contains (Masi 2003: 223): 'as if Jeanne had become the perfect travelling-companion for up-and-coming filmmakers needy of female solidarity [*bisognose di solidarietà femminile*]'.[15] Lapoirie herself, however, makes no such claim. Her principal referent in discussing her preferred working relationship is (unsurprisingly) Ozon, and when referring generically to directors, she uses the masculine gender without hesitation. Although Godard's particular career path means that when discussing collaboration, she refers constantly to Denis, her emphasis on their personal rapport is never – as far as I'm aware – attributed explicitly to shared gender. When her attention is drawn to the predominance of women directors in her filmography, she recognizes it, but is inclined to attribute it to her association with one particularly prominent example rather than to a general preference (Dirse 2000).

When discussing their ideal director, it is more important to these DPs that he or she should have a personal vision ('D. D. and S. L. P.' 1977: 31; Auger *et al.* 1996: 51; Guérin *et al.* 1996: 96–7; Strauss 1999: 66). It is a general characteristic of *chef-op* interviews, male or female, that they emphasize their own adaptability and their preference for being guided by a congenial directorial eye (Smith 2004) coupled with openness to discussion.[16] When not specifically pushed by interviewers, directors also tend to evoke criteria for choosing a DP that are not, or at least not directly, gendered. Xavier Beauvois cites Champetier's ability to put actors at ease and her commitment to her work – 'elle est profondément passionnée, elle est véritablement amoureuse de son métier' – and as a result she is neither a frustrated director ('Avant Caroline, j'avais travaillé avec un chef-op qui avait le désir de devenir metteur-en-scène et cela m'énervait un peu') nor a rigid technician ('elle est une vraie artiste'[17]). This latter consideration also commanded Philippe Grandrieux' positive assessment of his work with Sabine Lancelin:

> Sabine a tenu courageusement ce parti-pris [to underexpose the negative]. Souvent les techniciens cinéma sont dans des soucis qui ne sont pas ceux du film mais de place, de corporatisme, de carrière. Ils ont une sorte de comportement enfantin; ils se demandent si les producteurs vont être contents, si dans le milieu on va bien parler d'eux. [...] On s'aperçoit qu'à travers ce corporatisme, ce savoir faire technique, le cinéma disparaît. Je voudrais des techniciens qui ne se protègent pas et s'engagent dans l'idée du cinema.[18] (Du Mesnildot 2009)

Ozon's appreciation of Lapoirie emphasizes personal rapport ('we have the same tastes') and efficiency (Maillet and Biscioni 2001: 156), while Denis' association with Godard seems to go without saying. That their friendship includes feminine solidarity is clear from their reactions to recalcitrant producers and other gendered problems encountered on set, such as the physical strain of using a hand-held camera, but neither attributes their special understanding to the other's being 'a woman'. And while a woman director, especially one with a feminist conscience, may express a certain sense that she 'ought' to find a woman to operate her camera, an all-female team is no guarantee of harmony: Anne Fontaine's collaboration with Champetier was evidently a traumatic experience for the novice director (Guérin, Strauss and Toubiana 1996: 97), which translated for Fontaine into a stressful atmosphere that even imbued her with a 'fear of the technician'.

## A female gaze?

Gender, then, is certainly not always a criterion for selection of a cinematographer, at least not avowedly so, although there are directors, such as Catherine Corsini, who seem to make a point of seeking a female collaborator. I have not yet encountered an example of a director who has explicitly said that he would not consider a woman, but the attitude is unlikely to have been eradicated. But is there a gendered experience of the work of the chef-op? To what extent does an awareness of the implications of gender affect the actual process of handling the camera? Again, this is a question that regularly exercises interviewers and which sometimes seems unwelcome to interviewees. Nonetheless, they generally do not refuse to talk about it when pressed, and occasionally reflections on their approach to the work generate relevant responses unbidden.

The practical problems involved in the situation are not entirely taboo. Apart from early issues with acceptance, the sheer physical effort required occasionally sparks comment. In fact – and rather to my surprise – this was the first issue that Céline Bozon raised in response to a question about the specificity of a female DP's position: there is, according to her, an absolute necessity to have men actually manipulating the cameras, in 2009 as much as in the 1970s. This is of course not the primary responsibility of the DP, whose most important duty is to regulate the pattern of light imprinted on the film, but it involves dependency, which may well be seen as a restriction. Its significance, however, is not always unquestioned. For example, the camerawork on *S'en fout la mort* (1990), exclusively hand-held and very mobile, has been recalled, separately, by Claire Denis and by Agnès Godard. Denis remembers principally the implicit effort it involved for her cinematographer, who had recently given birth:

> Agnès portait une ceinture lombaire et on lui avait installé un harnache-ment de varappeur pour lui soulager le dos. ... Sur ce film, je pensais qu'il était préférable pour Agnès de faire uniquement le cadre tellement le tournage allait être physique.[19] (Maillet and Biscioni 2001: 124)

In fact, the 'cadre' (framing) is probably the most strenuous work required of a *chef-op* using a hand-held camera, even if it is considered subordinate to that of the lighting director. Nonetheless, Godard's own recollections of the physicality of *S'en fout la mort* sound a very different note. Exhilaration and engagement predominate.

> Je me suis rendu compte [sur *S'en fout la mort*] qu'avec la caméra à l'épaule, je filmais avec tout mon corps. C'était comme danser, quelque chose de vraiment grisant. Je me suis raconté que j'étais un personnage du film qu'on ne voyait pas. Bon, c'était un peu intellectuel! Mais quand les deux comédiens ont commencé à jouer avec la caméra, c'est-à-dire quand ils ont été complètement habitués à ma proximité, à mon regard, c'était comme s'ils jouaient avec moi, et j'aurais pu le faire sans limite.[20] (Strauss 1999: 66)

The idea of being an invisible character in the film recalls an observation that Champetier attributed to Louis Malle and also applied to herself: 'Les directeurs de la photo, relevaient ... de l'interprétation, au même titre que les acteurs. J'ai souvent ce sentiment-là, d'être mise en scène, mise en situation'[21] (Guérin et al. 1996: 93). It also underlines the close association between the DP and those in front of her camera, which may be quite as intense, fraught and significant as that with the director. It is indeed this exchange that seems most significant to the idea of a putative 'gendered gaze'. With documentary work, where the camera's subjects are non-professional and unprepared, the appearance of the person behind the camera can be directly significant. The only real difficulties that Céline Bozon recalled involved documentary shooting in 'milieux masculins', while Nurith Aviv told *Cahiers* that her gender and stature had helped to tame the intimidating camera for some of her subject:

> J'ai l'impression que pour obtenir des plans comme ça [an 11-minute documentary shot of an African mother and her children], le fait que je sois femme et *petite* aide beaucoup, les gens se sentent plus à l'aise, moins violés, peut-être. On l'a senti très fort en tournant *Daguerréotypes*, avec Agnès Varda, elle aussi femme et petite.[22] (D. D. and S. L. P. 1977: 29)

The potential 'violation' associated with the camera's gaze, a very familiar con-cept in film studies, might be expected to arise occasionally when women discuss their camerawork. Caroline Champetier confessed to a certain discomfort with the implicit fetishization of the camera in a fairly early interview (Derouet 1992), but direct self-questioning is quite rare. Godard's attitude is that approaches to the camera are individual and not gender determined, and her own descriptions of her extremely tactile camerawork, which recall Marks' partly gendered notion of a haptic cinema (Marks 2000), are indeed unique. Of all the women discussed in this article, she is the one who has most clearly developed her own distinctive, almost 'auteurial', style, which involves both vision and working method. She has done so by dint of a close and celebratory relationship with the camera and its magnetic 'central vision' (Audé and Tobin 2000: 134), which emphasizes dynamic and sensual contact without sexualization. In contrast, when Dominique Maillet asked Xavier Beauvois his opinion about his cinematographer's female gaze,[23] he offered a firm – if possibly ironic – counter-perception:

> Je trouve de toute manière que la caméra a quelque chose de féminin. La lumière, c'est comme un sexe masculin qui viendrait pénétrer la caméra et féconder la pellicule pour donner naissance à l'image ... Donc, le fait qu'une femme soit à l'œilleton me semble logique.[24] (Maillet and Biscioni 2001: 60)

What Champetier thought of this simile is not recorded.

Be it masculine, feminine or ungendered, there does seem to be a consensus that the camera is a source of potential disquiet for actors, that it has a rather daunting control over their image, that the relationship between them needs careful management, and that women may be perceived to be more skilled in this department, and themselves perceive it as fundamental to their professional identity. Beauvois, having fertilized his film with light, continues by suggesting that a woman's gaze provides 'reassurance' ('women are more sensitive'), returning once again to the importance of proximity and sensitivity. Denis, unbidden, says the same of her collaboration with Godard, associating herself and her cinematographer as observers careful to avoid abusing their powerful position: 'Nous sommes vraiment avec les comédiens et leur présence physique sans jamais être des voyeuses'[25] (Maillet and Biscioni 2001: 126). Ozon, meanwhile, emphasizes Lapoirie's ability to bring out the beauty of actors and especially actresses in a way that corresponds to his own desired vision of them (Maillet and Biscioni 2001: 154). Just as interviewers and commentators tend to emphasize women's collaborations with women directors, so the particular talent of women cinematographers for filming actresses seems to be a favourite anchor for observers. Cahiers' interviews with Godard and Champetier both insist upon it (Guérin et al. 1996: 90; Strauss 1999: 62). The interviewees themselves bear this out to a certain extent: Champetier recalling her work with actresses under Jean-Luc Godard's direction and with Sandrine Kiberlain in En avoir (ou pas) (Laetitia Masson, 1995) as emblematic of her approach; and Godard (Agnès) using her filming of the faces of Elodie Bouchez and Natacha Régnier in La Vie rêvée des anges to explain her criteria for selecting lenses. It is not, however, merely a matter of filming women, but rather a sensitivity to the person in front of the camera, and the establishment of a rapport with them, that emerges from the majority of chef-opératrice interviews.

Dominique Le Rigoleur summed up the ultimate professional satisfaction as the perfect realization of that rapport:

> On est toujours surpris, parfois comblés par ce qui semble être le hasard mais qui est peut-être l'intuition réciproque de celui (celle) qui filme et de celui (celle) qui est filmé. Parfois c'est magique, vraiment.[26] (Créteil 2000: 98)

*Celui* or *celle* have equal weight in this description, but a brief article that Champetier wrote in 2005 reveals that she continues to reflect on the camera's relationship to actors in a specifically gendered way. Entitled 'La différence des sexes est-elle visible au cinéma?', this is an editorial piece written by Champetier in her capacity as staff writer for *Cahiers du Cinéma*, and thus not explicitly concerned with her experience behind the camera: it is nonetheless revealing of the sensitivities of a camera opera-tor still troubled by the paradoxical gender relations that her position entails.

> C'est paradoxal d'être, pour un homme, acteur de cinéma, de s'offrir au regard, d'être l'objet du désir d'un metteur en scène et d'y répondre ... d'où vient que certains rejoignent, non sans une séduction proprement masculine, l'état féminin de proie filmée ... quand d'autres résistent à cela comme un marbre sur lequel l'eau glisse.[27] (Champetier 2005: 42)

The acceptance on the part of the camera operator that the female condition is that of 'filmed prey' is perhaps somewhat troubling – it is hard to imagine Agnès Godard describing any of her subjects like this – but that actors may feel the same way about their relationship to the camera is indicated by Roschdy Zem's response to Diane Baratier when she conducted a rapid enquiry among festival-goers at Cannes 2009 as to their understanding of what a DP did (with depressing results, it should be said; see Baratier 2009). For Zem, the DP is thus 'la personne qu'il faut premièrement séduire sur le tournage'.[28] It is tempting to wonder if he would have said the same thing to Raoul Coutard.

## Conclusions

If there is any sign of a specific feminine approach to the work of DP, then, it perhaps lies in this sensitivity to their human subjects, be they charmers, 'quarry' or fellow cast members. In addition, the still marginal position of women in the industry has perhaps preserved them from the 'corporate' mentality of which Grandrieux complains, and this may well be an advantage at a time of rapid and unpredictable change. The possible effects of the digital revolution on the position of the DP are still uncertain. In 2006, when the AFC put together its first charter on the subject, the mood was optimistic but also relatively relaxed. A round table convened by *Cahiers du Cinéma* (*Cahiers* 2006) boasted the enthusiastic title 'L'image numérique est fantastique' ('the digital image is fantastic' but also possibly 'fantastical, unreal'), but Champetier, an active participant, nonetheless opined that 'Je crois que ma vie de DP s'arrêtera avant celle de l'argentique, mais qu'il me reste du temps'[29] (*Cahiers* 2006: 12). Her editorial for the AFC newsletter in January 2010 – largely entrusted to Philippe Rousselot – sounds a rather more worried note, predicting a period of 'chaos' (Champetier 2010). In conclusion, however, Rousselot's article offers a note of renewal: 'Je voudrais trouver un peu de consolation dans la croyance qu'une nouvelle génération trouvera sa façon d'être au monde et sera à même de rétablir les règles d'une possibilité de faire encore du cinéma, et d'en vivre.'[30] If this is to be the case, perhaps adaptation will favour the kind of independence of spirit and engagement with their subject that has been associated with those women so far determined to take up the camera.

## Notes

1  Thirty years after women such as Dominique Le Rigoleur and Nurith Aviv began their careers behind the camera, there are at most about ten *chefs-opératrices* currently working on feature films in France. Not a proud record, even if the situation is much more favourable than in the United States, where the ASC numbers only five women out of its 315 members.

2  We were only three graduates, and it's certain that being a woman in this profession didn't make things any easier for me.

3  Today the situation is becoming normal.

4  I wanted to direct. My father advised me to learn the trade by starting out as an assistant camera operator rather than in direction.

5  I found myself a housewife in Brazil.

6  Every time I have a difficulty I call him.

7  I learnt from the masters, the fathers were the masters, or vice versa. I assisted William Lubtchansky for eight or nine years, when I came out of the IDHEC. ... Sometimes I envy those who don't feel this love and respect for the father.

8  Is this the appropriate moment to specify that there is no connection between Agnès Godard and Jean-Luc, although the coincidence of names has escaped no one? Agnès recalled (to *Cahiers* in 1999): 'On m'a souvent demandé si j'étais sa fille. Quand j'ai passé le concours d'entrée à l'Idhec, on m'a raconté que ceux qui corrigeaient les épreuves étaient pliés de rire. Maintenant, on me demande si je suis sa soeur parce que j'ai les cheveux blancs' [I've often been asked if I was his daughter. When I took the Idhec entrance exam, I'm told that the markers were doubled up laughing. Now I'm asked if I'm his sister because I have white hair] (Strauss 1999: 63). They have never worked together.

9  It's obvious that we're not going to be offered *Astérix*. However much we've proved ourselves on plenty of films, after a certain budget level you can feel a hesitation ... When we're in competition for this kind of film, we can only observe that we systematically don't get them.

10  I started working in the 1960s when the profession was experiencing a major split, as a result of the Nouvelle Vague. Nuytten, Lafaye, Robin, myself and many others plunged into the breach with an arrogance and a disrespect for the rules which our elders certainly complained of, no doubt quite rightly.

11  If I hadn't had this good luck, this apprenticeship with JLG, I would certainly have fallen into the trap of naturalism.

12  This is a result of amalgamating two sets of figures: the percentage of women among all the individual directors for whom the DP has worked and the percentage of their feature-length films (including documentaries) which were female directed. The highest percentage was for Agnès Godard's feature films (60 per cent), the lowest for Claude Garnier's (9 per cent, one out of eleven). When younger and less experienced cinematographers are included, the first percentage is noticeably less, but some 33 per cent of their (relatively much rarer) feature-length films have been directed or co-directed by women.

13    Many girls reproached me for choosing a man as *chef-op*. But Jean-François had an ideological and political way of thinking: he agreed with what I was doing, he thought as I did that there was an incredible number of things to say about the oppression of women.

14    Seems to favour cinema 'in the feminine', which hasn't prevented her taking part in more eclectic hits such as *La Vie rêvée des anges* or *L'Arrière-pays*.

15    This is a bilingual Italian/English text: the English is evidently a translation however, so I include the Italian phrase when the English sounds awkward.

16    See especially Guérin *et al.* (1996, 97): 'Le fait que j'intervienne, que je parle du film comme un objet à partager, est mis en cause, surtout par des gens avec qui je n'ai jamais travaillé', and Lapoirie in Masi (2003: 224): 'I follow the director's ideas but, above all, I follow the film. At times the film overrides the director, it's like it takes on a life of its own', perhaps the nearest approach to a claim to independent vision put forward. However, Lapoirie also says that she appreciates Ozon's tendency to get behind the camera himself: essentially, to do his own framing.

17    She's deeply enthusiastic, really in love with her work ... Before Caroline, I worked with a *chef-op* who wanted to be a director and that rather got on my nerves ... She's a real artist.

18    Sabine bravely carried out this decision. Often cinema technicians have concerns which are not to do with the film but about position, corporatism, career structure. They behave rather like children: wondering if the producers will be satisfied, if they'll get talked about in their profession ... You realize that amidst this corporatism and technical know-how the cinema is getting lost. I want technicians who don't protect themselves and who are committed to the idea of cinema.

19    Agnès wore a lumbar belt and we rigged up a rock climber's harness to take the weight off her back ... On this film, I thought it was preferable that Agnès only do the framing since the shoot was going to be so physical.

20    I realized that with the camera held on my shoulder, I was filming with my whole body. It was like dancing, really intoxicating. I told myself that I was a character in the film who couldn't be seen. OK, it was a bit intellectual! But when the two actors started playing with the camera, that is to say when they were completely used to my being close to them and watching them, it was as if they were playing with me, and I could have gone on for ever.

21    DPs were part of the cast [rather than the crew], just like the actors. I often feel that way, as if I'm being directed, put on stage.

22    I have the impression that to get shots like that, the fact of being a woman and *small* is very helpful, people feel more at ease, less violated, maybe. We felt that very strongly when I was making *Daguerréotypes* with Agnès Varda, who's also a woman and small.

23    Maillet asked both Beauvois and Ozon this question, but not Denis!

24    In any case I think the camera has something feminine about it. The light is like a male member which penetrates the camera and fertilizes the film to give birth to the image ... So the fact that there's a woman at the viewfinder seems logical to me.

25    We are really with the actors and their physical presence without ever being *voyeuses*.

26    One is always surprised and sometimes delighted by what seems to be chance but is perhaps a matter of mutual intuition on the part of the person filming and the person filmed. Sometimes it's magical, really.

27    It's paradoxical for a man to be a film actor, to offer himself to the gaze, to be the object of a director's desire and to respond to it ... and it means that some conform, although with a specifically male form of seduction, to the feminine condition of filmed prey [!], while others resist that like marble which water slides off.

28    The first person you have to charm on set.

29    I think my life as a DP will end before nitrate film does, but that I have time left.

30    I would like to console myself somewhat in the belief that a new generation will find its mode of existence in the world and will be able to re-establish the rules that will make it possible still to make cinema, and to live by it.

# Bibliography

Audé, F. and Tobin, Y. (2000), 'Agnès Godard: regarder jusqu'à vouloir toucher', *Positif* 471 (May): 131–6.

Auger, C., Bureau, E. and Lounas, T. (1996), 'Entretien avec Diane Baratier et Pascal Ribier', *Cahiers du cinéma*, 503 (June): 51–2.

Baratier, D. (2007), 'Wilfrid Sempé ou Marraine-moi', http://www.afcinema.com/Wilfrid-Sempe-ou-Marraine-moi.html?lang=fr [accessed 10 January 2010]. First published in *La Lettre de l'AFC*, 164, April.

Baratier, D. (2009), 'Diane recherche désespérément ...', filmed interviews with Cannes festival-goers, available on the AFC site at http://www.afcinema.com/Diane-recherche-desesperement.html?lang=fr and subsequent pages [accessed 1 March 2012].

Bouhon, J. J. (2004), 'Un nouveau membre actif à l'AFC: Diane Baratier', http://www.afcinema.com/Un-nouveau-membre-actif-a-l-AFC.html?lang=fr [accessed 10 January 2010]. First published in *La Lettre de l'AFC*, 135, September.

*Cahiers du cinéma* (2006), 'L'image numérique est fantastique', round table discussion, *Cahiers du cinéma*, 510 (March): 10–16.

Champetier, C. (2005), 'La différence de sexes est-elle visible au cinéma?', *Cahiers du cinéma*, 607 (December): 42–3.

Champetier, C. (2010), 'L'éditorial de la Lettre de janvier 2010', *La Lettre de l'AFC*, 194 (January), http://www.afcinema.com/L-editorial-de-la-Lettre-de,6003.html?lang=fr [accessed 10 January 2010].

Créteil Films de Femmes Festival (2000), dossier 'Les chefs-opératrices: une esthétique du regard', festival programme: 94–9.

'D. D. and S. L. P.' (1977), 'Rencontres avec des techniciens (1)', *Cahiers du cinéma*, 283 (December): 28–9.

Dacbert, S. and Caradec, P. (1999), 'Les Femmes cinéastes', http://archives.arte.tv/cinema/venus/ftext/femmes.htm [accessed 5 January 2010]. First published as 'Les femmes sont-elles des hommes comme les autres?', *Le Film français*, 2796, 8 October.

Derouet, C. (1992), 'Mémoires d'aveugle: entretien avec Caroline Champetier', 24 *Images*, 61 (summer): 28–31.

Dirse, Z. (2000), 'Women on Camera – Les Chefs-Opératrices: French Women Cinematographers Speak Up', *Canadian Society of Cinematographers Magazine* (September), http://www.csc.ca/news/default.asp?aID=841 [accessed 10 January 2010].

Du Mesnildot, S. (2009), 'Entretien avec Philippe Grandrieux (La Vie Nouvelle)', 16 April, http://lesfilmsliberentlatete.blogspot.com/2009/04/entretien-avec-philippe-grandrieux-la.html [accessed 11 January 2010].

Ferran, P. (2007), 'Violence économique et cinéma français: Tribune de Pascale Ferran, Césars 2007', *Le Monde*, 26 February, http://www.cip-idf.org/article.php3?id_article=3277 [accessed 10 January 2010].

Guérin, M. A., Strauss, F. and Toubiana, S. (1996), 'Le Goût de la lumière', interview with Caroline Champetier, *Cahiers du cinéma*, 500 (March): 90–8.

Maillet, D. and Biscioni, S. (2001), *En lumière: les directeurs de photographie vus par les cinéastes*, Paris: Dujarric.

Marks, L. (2000), *The Skin of the Film: Intercultural Cinema, Embodiment, and the Senses*, Durham and London: Duke University Press.

Masi, S. (2003), *La memoria del cinema: L'Abruzzo e i mestieri del cinema*, Afragola: Collana di Studi Abruzzesi 46.

Smith, A. (2004), 'The Other Auteurs: Producers, Cinematographers and Scriptwriters', in M. Temple and M. Witt (eds), *The French Cinema Book*, London: BFI.

Strauss, F. (1999), 'Filmer, c'est regarder intensément quelque chose qui va disparaître', interview with Agnès Godard, *Cahiers du cinéma*, 538 (September): 62–6.

# Creative agency

# Cornel Lucas

## Stills photography and production culture in 1950s British film

LINDA MARCHANT

chapter

# 10

Imagine the bombshell curves of Diana Dors, the smouldering starlet eyes of a young Joan Collins, or a cheeky and infectious Norman Wisdom grin. Chances are, the images of these British stars that you see in your mind's eye come not from the films in which they appeared but from still portraits created by studio photographers. Large numbers of still images were produced at the pinnacle of British film production in the 1950s, from stills depicting movie action to the carefully crafted glamour portraits of the stars. Many of us are familiar with them from film ephemera, books, DVD covers, magazines and newspapers. However popular these images are, the photographers themselves have received little acclaim or attention, and their working practices have largely remained hidden behind the lens. David Campany points out that 'film stills are a neglected chapter in the history of 20th century photography' (Campany 2007: foreword); this also holds true for the field of film studies.

British film production entered one of its most successful eras in the 1950s, when photographers were employed or contracted by the film studios to support and promote film production. The largest of the British film studios, Pinewood, was owned by the Rank Organisation. In 1949, Rank's new managing director, John Davis, sanctioned the setting up of a new state-of-the-art stills studio to be opened in 1950. He employed the photographer Cornel Lucas as head of the operation. Lucas had previously worked as a photographer within the film industry and had built his reputation photographing stills and the starlets of the Rank Charm School before moving on to more established film stars. He ran the studio at Pinewood successfully until the end of the 1950s, working with fellow photographers and behind-the-scenes workers to produce the film stills, promotional images, event photographs and star portraits that were required by the Rank production machine over the decade.

Lucas's work has received more exposure than that of many of the other stills photographers of that era. As head of the stills or 'gallery' studio, he was able to specialize in making studio portraits and creative publicity shots rather than the more everyday action or 'unit' stills that formed a larger part of many photographers' workloads. These glamorous portraits of well-known faces led to a solo exhibition of his work in London in 1958 whilst he was still head of the photography studio at Pinewood, 'the first one-man exhibition of a photographer in the film industry' (Cine Technician, May 1958: 270). Lucas continued working as a photographer well into the 1980s. In 1988, his first book of portraits, Heads and Tales, was published. It included many portraits from the fifties and reignited interest in his work. In the book, reproductions of the portraits are accompanied by Lucas's reminiscences of that particular star, or that photo shoot, or the film they were working on at the time. Ten years later, Lucas also received the accolade of being the first stills photographer to be given a British Academy of Film and Television Arts (BAFTA) award for his services to the British film industry. A second book of his work was published in 2005 to coincide with a major retrospective at the National Portrait Gallery in London, and his work is held in a number of major UK photographic collections, including the National Portrait Gallery, the National Media Museum and the Photographers' Gallery. Another solo exhibition in 2011 at Chris Beetles Fine Photographs Gallery in London situated Lucas's work within a commercial fine art context.[1] This broad exposure of his photographs in national and commercial galleries, along with published reminiscences and interviews, has made him unique amongst the stills photographers of the era.

The material relating to Lucas's work provides a glimpse into the world of the stills photographer and gives some indication of how this sector of behind-the-scenes film workers functioned. Starting by looking at similarities in working practices of the Pinewood photography studio and the Hollywood model of production upon which it was based, I will argue that the use of photographs across the chain of production is what links the two systems. Few studies of labour conditions in the British film industry have explored the nature of creative agency in the context of a system of production that prioritized standardization over innovation (notable exceptions are Chanan 1976 and Stollery 2009), and none have looked at it in relation to stills photography, which is central to, but not part of, film production. I will use Lucas's work to investigate the conflict between industrial constraints and individual creativity in the field of stills photography before finally moving on to examine the position of stills photographers in general, and Cornel Lucas in particular, within the hierarchy and networks of film production in 1950s Britain.

Before starting to examine the working practices and environments of the stills photographer of this era, it is useful to situate the role and output of the stills photographer in a wider historical context. The stills photographer has played an important role in film production and promotion ever since the birth of the commercial cinema, providing valuable exposure for stars, films and the studios themselves. That stills and star portraits were perceived as important to the filmmakers and stars is rooted in the history of the evolution of the photographic studios in Hollywood.

# Still photography in the context of film-making

Still photography played an important role in film production in the United States from a very early stage in its development. From the silent era onwards, the cameraman, eventually a *specialist* stills photographer (Finler 1995), would respond to the 'cut' at the end of a take with a shout of 'Still!' and preserve the scene for posterity and for continuity purposes. This was not the only function of the still photograph, however. With the emergence of the Hollywood star system, leading screen performers quickly recognized how important disseminating the 'right' image would prove to their film careers and their relationship with the film-going public. In the 1920s, for example, Mary Pickford spent US$50,000 per year on obtaining the finest publicity photographs and portraits from commercial photographic studios to enhance her star persona and advance her career (Fahey and Rich 1998: 13). Producers were also quick to recognize the contribution that portrait photographers could make to the commercial success of their in-house stars and their films. In the early 1930s, film studios responded to the dual usefulness and commercial potential of the still image by creating their own 'gallery studios' to shoot both 'portrait stills' and 'unit stills'. The portrait photographers would work in the studio making studied, constructed, glamorous portraits of the stars, whilst the unit stills photographers would, according to Finler, do almost everything else – photographs to assist in location finding, casting, costumes and set continuity, publicity shots, anything. Finler outlines how photographers were used at almost every stage of the film-making process and points out that in smaller Hollywood studios the roles of unit and portrait stills often crossed over. In this way, the term 'stills photographer' is commonly used to cover all aspects of non-moving images associated with film-making, not just the stilled action shots.

By the 1930s, all of the major Hollywood studios had established gallery studios. John Kobal argues that photographers were employed by them not simply to ensure that the studios were not paying large sums for the volume of images they needed for publicity purposes, but also to produce 'a look for their stars that would become associated in the public's mind with the particular studio that employed them' (Kobal 1980: 48). The work of the photographers within these galleries was distributed widely to cinemas, film magazines and, perhaps most importantly, the burgeoning fan magazines. Although it was the images rather than the photographers that received more attention at the time, collectors and galleries have subsequently drawn attention to a small number of photographers whose work from the height of Hollywood star worship created the images that today are seen to depict and typify the glamour of the Hollywood studio era.

Two of the most celebrated are Clarence Sinclair Bull, Head of Stills at MGM, and George Hurrell, Head of Portraits at MGM, both of whom have received widespread critical acclaim for their creative vision and the quality of their work. MGM in the 1930s and 1940s set the standard for stills photography within the film industry. Echoes of MGM production environments and practices, hierarchies and creative qualities can all be found in Cornel Lucas's work and practices at Pinewood. MGM's system of photographic production was efficient and generated images that were appropriate, useful and valuable to the film studio. As such, many aspects of the production environment were embraced, albeit in a scaled-down version, as a model of practice by Rank in Britain in the 1950s. 'The Pool Studio', as Pinewood's photographic studio was called, was purpose built with an eye to Hollywood-style success.

## Hollywood reflected in the pool

Although Pinewood's photographic studio was developed twenty years after that of MGM, there were similarities in circumstances, production environments and output that indicate why the MGM working model might have proved a useful one for adoption at Pinewood. As with MGM, Pinewood was the largest of the national film studios, with the highest number of in-house stars. MGM in the 1930s was investing to counteract the Great Depression and stock market crashes, whilst Pinewood in the late 1940s was operating in an economic context defined by Britain's indebtedness in the wake of the Second World War. Patricia Warren's analysis of British film studios points out that 'the Rank empire appeared to be collapsing' (Warren 2001: 120), with debts of £16 million having led to the closure of studios in Islington and Shepherd's Bush and the leasing of Denham Film Studios. The government view that film-making needed to be streamlined was expressed in a Cabinet meeting on 24 March 1949: 'Under present conditions the aim should be to build up a healthy film-producing industry rather than to prevent unemployment. The industry is overstaffed at present and undesirable restrictive practices are supported by both employers and workers. ... [T]he opportunity should be taken to ensure that the industry is purged of its extravagant tendencies' (Government Papers 1949).[2] Having concentrated production at Pinewood, Rank employed John Davis to 'slash budgets, lay off staff and reduce the salaries of the remaining executives' (Warren 2001: 120) in an attempt to turn the business into a profitable concern. One particular manifestation of this was the consolidation of the production of still images for the company at Pinewood.

According to one commentator, 'When the British film industry modelled itself on Hollywood lines and nurtured its stars, the key figure was the studio stills photographer. He was given all the studio space and technical resources needed' (The Sunday Times, 28 August 1983). The photographer was useful to the studio in terms of profitability, and so Rank's investment in the construction of a studio reflected this importance. The specially constructed gallery studio at Pinewood, built over the swimming pool in the former stately home (hence the 'Pool Studio' title), was unique amongst the film studios in Britain at the turn of the 1950s in being purpose built and relatively well equipped and staffed. It occupied a central position in the building, situated next to the dining room and bar, enabling easy access for the actors and actresses, directors and other stakeholders in the production of the image. The central location and exotic design increased its visibility and profile, adding a touch of Hollywood glamour for anyone visiting Pinewood.

Considerable investment was made in building, equipment, processes and the establishment of a 'house style' to ensure that the photographic studio at Pinewood was able to support the work of the film studio. Considering emigration, Cornel Lucas had travelled to the United States after the war to develop his skills[3] and to observe and learn from acclaimed photographers. On his return to the United Kingdom after the two-month visit, Lucas 'realised just how technically advanced the Americans had become and how dilapidated the equipment in the United Kingdom was in comparison' (Lucas 2005: xi). Lucas was asked to head the studio following his success in photographing Marlene Dietrich and his credited role as 'special stills photographer' on Powell and Pressburger's The Red Shoes (1948), in a similar career trajectory to that of George Hurrell at MGM. Interviewed in The Veteran magazine in 2005, Lucas recounts how he was told to 'equip the [Pool] studio as you want to equip it' (Eyles 2005: 17).

In the interview, he talks of the shortages of modern equipment due to rationing, the war and the difficulty of importing, but points out that he was able to use some of his own state-of-the-art equipment: '[F]ortunately, I had purchased two wonderful portrait lenses and shutters in America. ... They were a great asset to me. ... It was a wonderful studio' (Eyles 2005: 17). Lucas provided not only his lenses but also his own camera – the Kodak Studio Camera No. 3, an impressive 10 × 12 format adapted to take 10 × 8 film. This camera, dated 1946,[4] was one of only three manufactured by Kodak. His growing reputation and the equipment and expertise he brought with him made Lucas an asset to the studios. Having worked at Rank's Charm School prior to the 1950s, he was already familiar with many of Rank's young stars. He had also worked with major stars and directors, and was familiar with British and American film studios and practices.

The images that Lucas and the other Pinewood photographers produced during his time at the studios were made for the same purposes as those made for the Hollywood studios in the preceding decades. Bull and Hurrell had developed many of the pre- and post-production techniques and processes used to generate the Hollywood glamour portrait style of soft focus, well lit, elegantly posed close-ups of porcelain-skinned models. The studio system they worked within was designed to maximize output and efficiency across all areas of production, such as wardrobe, scripts, marketing and photography, whilst maintaining and setting quality standards. The processing and printing machines at MGM turned out 25,000 negatives and 14,000 prints per week in 1930–1 (Vieira 1997: 26).

The role of the photographer in the Pool Studio in the 1950s was to produce similar types of output and to keep the photographer, as a studio employee, working at maximum capacity and for maximum profitability. Two valuable resources can help us build a picture of these roles and working conditions. The first is Lucas's first-hand retrospective recollections, published mainly in Heads and Tales (1988) and Shooting Stars (2005). Although it is clear that the use of first-hand reminiscences is problematic due to the subjective nature of the accounts, in this instance they are a rare and personal glimpse into an unseen industry. The second resource is Cine Technician, the film worker's union trade journal. Published monthly throughout the 1950s, it provides some balance to Lucas's first-person narrative, although clearly it presents a union perspective. Both sources help to provide a picture of the role and working conditions, and give some idea of the importance and centrality of the work undertaken by photographers despite their behind-the-scenes profiles.

## Stills production

It is difficult to determine how many stills photographers, and associated workers such as finishers and printers, worked within British film studios during the period. However, in the 1950s, no more than 130 people belonged to the Stills Section of the Association of Cinematograph Technicians Union (ACT),[5] which was originally set up as the Stills Camera Section, but later admitted stills-processing technicians.[6] A report on the British film industry published by PEP (Political and Economic Planning) in May 1952 described ACT as enforcing a 'strong closed shop' to protect its workers and industry, so it can be assumed that this figure covers the majority of stills workers. Lucas himself was a member of ACT and described how he was protected by the Union steward in his very early career when he had caused costly damage to a film in processing. The steward pointed out that he was underage and should not have been operating the machine, thereby saving his job. That he remained a union member during the 1950s can be inferred from his inclusion in the BECTU History Project, a rich archive of recordings of oral histories of many union workers.[7]

The two major film companies, Rank and Associated British Picture Corporation (ABPC), had multiple stills photographers contracted to them, and were able to bring in extra photographers if necessary. Approximately a dozen photographers' names appear either in listings or on the reverse of images made at Pinewood during this period. Other photographers were either contracted to a studio or worked free-lance, but even in the latter case, listings in the Cine Technician as a 'Guide to British Film Makers' reveal that particular studios tended to work repeatedly with the same photographer. These listings are not complete as they do not include all film productions. Examples, however, include Robert Penn, who did most of his work at Ealing but also produced images for ABPC Elstree, Merton Park Studios and MGM British, and John Jay, who undertook most of his work at Bray Studios but who is also found listed for images taken at Southall and Riverside Studios Hammersmith. In this way, stills photographers' names often appeared connected with specific film studios, even if they were not necessarily directly employed by them. They formed a network of workers who frequently crossed paths or worked together on productions.

Working conditions were set by agreement between the union and the British Film Producers Association (BFPA). Allowances were payable for after-hours work and meal expenses, at least for Rank technicians as the Rank Organisation were members of the BFPA. The working week decreased across the 1950s from a 44-hour week at the beginning to 42.5 hours mid-decade and down to 40 hours by the end. Pay claims from the union were commonly reported by Cine Technician, which frequently described them as 'reasonable' in light of increasing profits made by the studios over the decade. Pay was described as relatively high in the 1952 PEP report into the British film industry, to compensate for the lack of steady work, high unemployment rate among union members and irregular nature of the work (PEP 1952: 279).

The union insisted that a stills cameraman was needed for every production, an example of the 'restrictive practices' referred to in the above report. In February 1956, however, *Cine Technician* reported unrest from the Stills Section, which had refused to meet with other sections of the union to discuss a resolution relating to the production of still images. The Stills Section felt 'that the Still Cameramen were the only people who should take stills of any description relating to any film production' (*Cine Technician*, February 1956: 28) and refused to meet with the Producers/Directors section of the ACT and the Art Department in order to discuss the matter. From this, it would appear that stills cameramen were under threat from non-specialized labour at this time. This coincides with ABPC studios listing two sections for 'Stills Department' for a number of film productions in the *Cine Technician* listing: one entry for 'Still Cameraman' and one for 'Unit Publicity Representative'. These double entries only appeared for a period of approximately three months. Lucas makes no direct reference to threats from non-specialized labour either in his autobiographical writings or in interviews. Indeed, the only threats to film stills photography that he acknowledges were connected to the demise of the studio system in Britain. As he put it in a 2005 interview, '[E]arly film moguls were rapidly losing their seats of power, the star system was fading and artists' contracts were not being reviewed. Independent productions outside major studios were being made more frequently, and I could see that changes were inevitable' (Lucas 2005: 6).

The photographers' working day was booked to capacity. In the portrait studio, the day would be organized to make full use of the facilities. Lucas recalled the working day filled with sittings, sometimes up to four or five a day. This type of workload was sustained throughout the year, regardless of the number of films in production at any given time. According to his book *Shooting Stars*, Cornel's 2,500th camera session took place in 1957 when he photographed Shirley Eaton, an indication of the volume of sittings photographers were expected to undertake. The lighting, camera and sitter would have to be carefully arranged and posed, and for Lucas, discussing the sitting with his subject or with the director was often an extra requirement prior to the camera session. Unit stills photographers were equally fully occupied. Images were made constantly during the film production process, as their usefulness to production was wider reaching than just promotion purposes.

## Across the production chain: useful pictures

The studio system of production streamlined processes and maximized the usefulness of each employee, including the stills photographer. Stills were useful commodities across the chain of film production, spanning the entire process of making films. The range of images photographers produced was important for a number of reasons, most of them economic. First, like the Hollywood studios in the 1930s, many British studios in the 1940s and 1950s used photographic portraits as a preliminary to the screen test. Not only did this allow those responsible for casting to see if the subject was sufficiently photogenic and able to work well with the camera, but it also allowed the studios to preserve valuable and expensive film stock. Following the war, Britain was still suffering shortages including the availability of photographic materials and chemicals, and Rank needed to make savings to address their mounting debts. Second, film portraits and head shots were used to promote the star and as material that could be sent to eager fans contacting the star or the studio. According to Geoffrey Macnab (1994), the Publicity Department at Pinewood received more than 60,000 applications per week for portraits of Rank stars in the early 1950s, a figure that compares favourably with the quantities cited for MGM twenty years beforehand. A third type of photograph that proved useful and profitable were the seasonal pictures of stars in Santa suits, or holding Easter bunnies, which were made to maintain audience recognition especially when the stars were not in the process of filming. Timing-wise, these were often shot six months in advance, like fashion images, in order for them to be syndicated internationally. Rank could not afford for their stars to be out of sight and out of mind for long periods. Film stills were also used to create stories for magazines and the proliferation of publications about the movies that readers were eager to buy, as well as for foyer cards, posters and information in campaign books for cinemas. They were valuable tools for continuity departments to be able to check and maintain standards. A cross section of all of these types of images was used for the primary purpose – to sell films and stars to bigger audiences.

This range of image types fits across various stages of the film-making process: pre-production (casting), production (continuity, action shots and industry reflexive work relating to the making of the film), post-production (promotion), sales and distribution (advertising) and out-of-production (maintaining value/visibility). In this way, the photographer occupied a longitudinal role in the film-making process. Although the images were most widely seen in the final stages of the production chain, they were central to production needs as well as profitability in all stages of production. Needs were similar from one film to the next. However, the need for such a large volume of images required the photographer not just to replicate shots but also to use his skills and creativity. Photographs had to remain innovative and fresh in order to keep the magazines interested in printing them and to give the reader something new, whilst at the same time remaining familiar and recognizable. The constraints of the studio system at first glance appear to work in opposition to the idea of creative agency.

## Creative networks

With many photographers undertaking similar roles and the requirements of the studios being relatively repetitive, it was almost inevitable that *types* of image would start to appear. Commentators have tried to classify these types, from the 'inward-gazing and outward looking' conceptual types suggested by John Kobal (1980) to the physical portrait types delineated by Paul Trent (1973): standard head shots, duo portraits, costume, pin-ups, creative, glamour and candid portraits. This reduction to the photograph as 'type' implies a lack of choice, agency and creativity over the images from the photographer's perspective.

Assignments at the Pool were more varied than for some of the smaller studios, but photographers still had to respond to the requirements for the image: speed of production and circulation, appearance, recognizability, clarity and quality. In these terms, the creative autonomy of the photographer could be understood as being restricted by the contradictory requirements of a profit-driven industry. According to Michael Chanan, 'Capitalism has to try and reduce aesthetic labour to the status of ordinary wage labour. In the case of film, it has tried to do this by employing studio conditions ... in order to reduce films to genres and types, which can be made more or less to order' (Chanan 1976: 7). Chanan develops his argument in relation to the production of films under the studio system, but it is just as applicable to the production of film *stills*.

However, Richard Florida's thinking about creative communities provides an interesting counterpoint to this view, and one that seems to correlate with the environment and collaborative situation of the photographic studio in the 1950s. Although he recognizes an 'ongoing tension between creativity and organisation' (Florida 2002: 22), he also points to the creative benefits possible from working as an employee within a larger organization. Constraints can provide a framework or a challenge to creative thinking, often encouraging new solutions or ways of working. A network of people with a range of skills can pull together to overcome difficulties and constraints when working towards a common aim. British film studios in the 1950s provided a working environment for stills photographers in which a variety of contributors (lighting technicians, electricians, printing specialists and, of course, fellow photographers) could work together in developing skills, discussing approaches and learning from other's mistakes. The film studio environment allowed stills photographers access to a creative network of highly skilled workers and gave them the opportunity to experiment, to sometimes make mistakes and to respond to new situations requiring new approaches. This would certainly have been the case in the photographic galleries of the British film studios as well as in MGM in the preceding decades. High volumes of work would mean that it was quickly time to move on to the next job, and that it was possible to try new ways of doing things with the fallback of being able to revert to old ways if unsuccessful.

Lucas, like many other stills photographers of the time, worked within a close network of colleagues. At Pinewood, for example, photographers Norman Gryspeerdt and Ian Jeayes worked with Lucas for the decade of his tenure at the Pool Studio, and their names often appear alongside one another on the reverse of stills. Lucas recognized the contribution of fellow photographers, requesting that their names be placed on the reverse wherever possible. Collaboration between photographers and other technicians would have been a familiar method of working. In his autobiography, Lucas recalled one such example of collaboration with a colleague in his shot of Katherine Hepburn in 1950. He described 'catching the eye of Bill the "Gaffer" [chief electrician] who, anticipating my requirement, shone a light from the gantry onto my unsuspecting subject' (Lucas 1988: 30). The unusual resulting picture is subtle but clearly depicts Hepburn in contemplative pose. When talking of other photographers and technicians, Lucas's comments are inclusive and collaborative, declaring himself as part of the team rather than as part of the hierarchy: 'I was able to persuade management to give me ... a team for make-up and hairstyling, electricians, props and a studio manager to deal with administration' (*Face to Face* 2005: 6). This is reflected in his dedication of *Heads and Tales* to 'the back room boys and girls ... who helped me to capture these images' and his specific appreciation of 'Mrs Joyce Bland, my retoucher over the years' (Lucas 1988: acknowledgements).

It is clear from these types of stories that Lucas considered himself as a working stills photographer and part of a team. However, his elevated position as head of the photographic studio did mean that the attention his work received was wider ranging than that of his colleagues and thus set him apart in terms of status.[8] Lucas occupied a unique position for a British stills photographer within the hierarchy of film production. His behind-the-scenes role places him firmly within the category of technical workers occupied by stills photographers. His status as head of the photographic studio with relative creative agency and authority was in direct opposition with this. This dichotomy is evident in the stories Lucas recounts about his life and work at Pinewood. His reminiscences provide insights into the operation of the studio hierarchies within which behind-the-scenes photographers worked in the 1950s.

## Production cultures and below-the-line working

As a working stills photographer, Lucas took many photographs that could be categorized as formulaic whilst working alongside other photographers in shooting unit stills. Work of this nature reflected the need to produce particular 'types' of images for the studio and located the photographer in a technical, support or 'below-the-line' status within the hierarchy of film production. In many cases, the photographer was told exactly what was required and how the finished image was supposed to look. Many aspects of the work processes in which photographers were engaged, moreover, identified them as technicians. Daily output by photographers clearly involved repetition of many requirements, set-ups and processes, in order to produce the speed and volume of work required by the studio and to meet the needs of the film. The formulaic nature of much of what they produced is highlighted by Macnab in his description of Lucas's photographs of starlets at the Rank Charm School: 'all uniformly good looking, all wearing the same style of clothes, all photographed in identical light and poses' (Macnab 1994: 146).

In his work on production culture, John Caldwell (2008) argues that the types of stories told by production workers are indicators of their place in the production hierarchy. Caldwell identifies two particular types of tale as typical of below-the-line workers. The first, which he terms 'war stories', establish craft expertise and mastery. The second, which he labels 'against all odds allegories', function culturally in order to reinforce labour mystique and establish skill credentials. 'Survival at work establishes value in the first genre', Caldwell asserts, 'acts of anointment or mentoring establish value in the second' (Caldwell 2008: 47). Both types of tales occur in Lucas's reminiscences.

Lucas's 'war stories' include a tale of a near-drowning experience when photographing a night shot of cameramen on a rock out at sea when on location filming *The Blue Lagoon* in 1948. As a photographer, he risked his life but still managed to obtain a fantastic shot. Other, more gentle stories include the difficulties but ultimate successes after struggles in photographing stars who were at best reticent about (Brigitte Bardot) and at worst terrified (Kay Kendall) of having their portraits taken.

Lucas's 'against all odds' stories highlight the importance of the mentoring he received *and* the significance of the breakthrough moment that marked his arrival as a true practitioner. In both *Shooting Stars* (2005) and an interview with Nigel Arthur, Curator of Stills at the British Film Institute, Lucas recounts one particular story of a meeting early on in his career with the influential British portrait and society photographer Cecil Beaton, during the course of which Beaton advised him against taking up photography, describing it as 'an overcrowded profession and very difficult to make a living' (Lucas 2005: x). Lucas states that this incident made him *more* determined to pursue a photographic career, and Beaton later told him that he knew Lucas would ignore his advice and become a photographer anyway. Lucas's account of his experience of photographing Marlene Dietrich also fits the mould of a below-the-line worker tale. Lucas was the relatively unknown photographer seeking to gain approval of his images from a notoriously exacting sitter. Lucas recounts that after her final approval of his images, Marlene welcomed him to 'the club'. He has remarked in a number of re-tellings that this acceptance gave him 'the key to the door' of his photographic career.[9]

The below-the-line status of photographers is also evidenced in power relationships within the studio. Although Lucas was in a position of authority over other photographers, this is rarely made explicit in descriptions of his work. Like his colleagues, Lucas was held responsible for the quality of his own work. On one specific occasion when an image did not reach the standards set by the studio or the relatively powerful stars themselves, Lucas experienced the consequences. His career was nearly cut short after a shoot with actress Yvonne de Carlo in 1952 when he failed to deliver images of the appropriate quality. Negatives of shoots were often circulated quickly for 'global publication' (Lucas 1988: 25). On this occasion, Lucas did not notice that the images were not perfect (de Carlo's mascara had run in the shot), and the following day he was summoned to explain – not to the studio but to the star herself, presumably because it was the content of the image (which would affect the star) rather than the quality of the image (which would affect the studio) which had been compromised. He felt that he needed to resign as a result of this mistake. Although the matter was explained and he retained his job, the incident positioned him as an employee and, as such, someone who was expected to maintain quality standards, meet expectations and apologize or make explanations of his shortcomings.

Public recognition in the form of a credit in publication or distribution is another important indicator of status. This is problematic in the case of photographers as their work does not necessarily appear as part of the film production,[10] but there were other opportunities for the photographers of the 1950s to be credited for their stills work. Lucas was concerned that he, and other photographers at the studio, be credited for their work wherever possible. Photographers' names often appeared on the reverse of the image, but were rarely used in printed material, at the time or subsequently.[11] In some publications, including contemporary ones, the images are titled with the name of the subject or the film, and are given broad provenance such as 'from the Pinewood archives or from private collections' (Bright 2007: 381). Lucas's name appears in publications more often than those of other photographers, primarily due to the nature of his photography – constructed studio portraiture rather than daily 'service' images. These studied portraits are less transient than the publicity stills, and this goes some way towards explaining the perceived higher status of this type of work.

In terms of production cultures, lack of named credit or acknowledgement of the photographer's work firmly situates the role towards the bottom of the studio hierarchy. This is reinforced by a widespread perception that the content of images is dictated by the industrial process rather than creative authorship. However, evidence relating to authorship in the form of copyright legislation provides an explanation for the lack of published accreditation for the photographs. When Lucas was working at Pinewood in the 1950s, legal copyright in the photograph would have rested with the commissioner of the picture (in Lucas's case, the Rank Organisation) or with the employer (also the Rank Organisation in the case of images produced at the Pool Studio). This legal framework helped define the employed photographer as a below-the-line contributor. Although copyright legislation now firmly places the ownership of copyright in the hands of the author of the work, an exemption for employed photographers is still in existence under current UK legislation (Copyright, Designs and Patents Act 1988).

An apparent lack of creative autonomy and an absence of accreditation for their work identify stills photographers as below-the-line workers. There are indicators to situate some aspects of Lucas's work within this category. However, a number of factors indicate that distinctions between some of these below- and above-the-line strata are crossed in relation to Lucas and his work. These factors include ideas of authorship and creative control, networks and relationships within the film industry and the accumulation of career capital.

## Above-the-line indicators

The personal and social networks Lucas built within the studio environment are important indicators of his status as an above-the-line worker. These relationships are revealed partially in Lucas's reminiscences and biography. Perhaps the most notable one during his time as the head of the Pool Studio is his marriage in 1954 to one of the stars he photographed, Belinda Lee,[12] but he also established other social and personal relationships over the period he worked for Rank that he was able to use to increase his creative autonomy. Rank respected Lucas's work and accorded him full creative freedom with his images, requesting only that he comply with foreign censorship regulations required for syndicated images.[13] Similarly, the stars trusted him to make quality images, with only two stars, Marlene Dietrich and Dirk Bogarde, having clauses in their contracts that enabled them to veto any images they did not like.

Lucas was given independence and free rein with his photography. He was able to undertake personally motivated projects such as the sitting with the venerable English actor A. E. Matthews that he describes in *Heads and Tales* (1988). On occasion, he would socialize with his subjects in the bar (Richard Burton, Robert Newton), take them away from the studio in order to relax them (Claudette Colbert, Lauren Bacall), or accompany them on shopping trips (Laurence Harvey). He was entrusted with overseas trips to photograph stars not just on location (Trevor Howard in North Africa 1950, for example) but also at prestigious film events (Diana Dors at the Cannes and Venice Film Festivals). He tells tales of drinking champagne and laughing with Brigitte Bardot in her dressing room and photographing her until she fell asleep.[14] These stories indicate the level of trust, authority and acceptance that Lucas enjoyed within the studio environment. That Lucas had access to his subjects in their dressing rooms and homes as well as on set/location is evidence that the studio saw his ability to interact effectively with his subjects as one of the keys to getting the right photographs. In his autobiographical writings, Lucas talks on a number of occasions about using his skill to put a subject at ease in front of the still lens and of the subject's need to be sympathetically represented. 'To an actress', he observes in *Heads and Tales*,

> the camera has such a critical eye that it demands intense concentration, but at the same time, they require from it just what they want to see. If the results are not to their liking then the performance which they have given has been a poor one. It is up to the photographer to capture that brief moment when satisfaction can be guaranteed. (Lucas 1988: 24)

What is often unclear about the image-making process is whose 'satisfaction' takes precedence. The image itself is a contested site of ownership and control. Lucas's role as head photographer made him pivotal to a number of stakeholders at Pinewood. The still photographer worked for a number of masters: (i) the commissioner of the portrait who has a purpose in mind for the image; (ii) the subject of the image itself, who is central to the success of the photograph; and (iii) the 'end user' of the photograph who, whether an editor, a moviegoer, a cinema manager or a fan, also has expectations and desires invested in the image. There is an 'above-the-line' level of responsibility and creativity attached to delivering results that are satisfactory to all. In remaining faithful to his creative vision and technical standards whilst still producing images that met the requirements of all stakeholders, Lucas was able to meet and often exceed the expectations of everyone who had an investment in the image. I would argue that this contributed to Lucas's view of his work as a collaborative process that required the input of both above-the-line workers such as actors and directors, and below-the-line workers like printers and retouchers.

Caldwell also highlights the significance of what he terms 'genesis stories' – stories that demonstrate 'professional legitimacy' – as a means for above-the-line workers to show how they have risen from the ranks by accumulating skills and expertise. In his autobiographical writings, Lucas asserts his professional legitimacy by describing how he was trained and mentored by 'names' such as Beaton, Hesse[15] and Dietrich. Reinforcing these above-the-line markers are Lucas's 'paths not taken' stories, the best example of which is his account of a plan to emigrate to Hollywood that was abandoned, so he has claimed, because he 'had just come from a country still on terribly strict rationing [and] couldn't face the enormous meals' (Lennon 2001). Caldwell argues that these types of stories are a means for film workers to demonstrate their 'pedigree and industrial ancestry'. In this particular example, Lucas sets out to draw attention to his standing within the industry by simultaneously declaring both his British pedigree and his links with Hollywood.

A tendency on the part of commentators to contrast the permanence of the studio portrait with the transience of the publicity still has also helped to locate Lucas as an above-the-line worker. The portraits Lucas made at the Pool Studio show the development of an autonomous 'style', not replicated by others. Drawing heavily on the conventions of Hollywood portraiture, Lucas operated on the principle that 'light and shade made the image'.[16] Initially criticized by the Publicity Department at Rank, he was unwilling to alter his way of making images, and sought to rise above the industrial process by demonstrating his own creative vision. His work was often reproduced, when cost allowed, as a vision in sepia, another identifier of his individual style. Sepia toning is a post-production chemical process that is labour intensive, expensive and highly skilled. The intensity of the process is reflective of an aesthetic as opposed to an industrial approach to image making. As Michael Chanan points out, 'Aesthetic labour is geared to overreach basic skills, to achieve excellence, literally to excel' (Chanan 1976: 9). Lucas's sense of himself as an artist engaged in aesthetic labour manifested itself in many of his photographic portraits.

The opportunity to learn, collaborate, experiment and then make the images which eventually develop into an identifiable aesthetic points towards a potential for photographic auteurship as a final indicator of above-the-line status for Lucas. Under the studio system, unit stills photographers had very little scope for developing a distinctive vision. Top portrait photographers, in contrast, enjoyed a great deal of creative autonomy and were able to invest their work with a depth and artistic value that marked them out as more than mere technicians. Hollywood portrait photographers such as George Hurrell have subsequently gained recognition as artists in their own right. Lucas meets two of the criteria that Andrew Sarris uses in his classic work on cinema and authorship to determine whether a director can be considered a cinematic auteur: heightened technical competence and evidence of a personal style and vision. Sarris's third criterion – 'interior meaning' or 'élan of the soul' (Sarris 1992) – is more subjective. The purpose of Lucas's star portraits is to connect subject and audience beyond the frame of the photograph and, for many seeing his work, they certainly achieve this purpose. If we also throw into the mix the idea of auteurship as a deliberate commercial strategy related to audience reception (see Corrigan 1991), then Lucas can certainly be considered an auteur.

Towards the end of Lucas's time at the Pool Studio, his work received its first marker of cultural recognition and wider professional legitimacy in the form of a major exhibition of his photographs. *Portraits of the Stars: An Exhibition of Photographs by Cornel Lucas* was held from 8 May to 24 May 1958 at the Kodak Gallery in London. The exhibition was pivotal in placing Lucas's work in contexts other than those related to film production and distribution. A year later, the creative partnership of Cornel Lucas and the Rank Organisation at Pinewood studios came to an end. In 1959, Lucas resigned from his position as head of the stills studio. Pinewood had announced 400 redundancies in the previous year.[17] Styles, fashions and technologies were changing rapidly, cinema attendances were falling, and the work of the stills photographer was becoming more and more freelance as studios again started cutting costs. It was on an extended holiday from the studio in 1959 that Lucas decided to resign from Rank. According to his account in *Shooting Stars*, Lucas was prompted to send the telegraph tendering his resignation by David Niven, 'an International Sales Director from Rank, and plenty of wine' (Lucas 2005: xiii). This incident is a further indication that Lucas's social network extended further than that of other photographers or workers in similar roles. In resigning from Rank and setting up an independent photographic studio as his next career move, Lucas demonstrated that he had achieved as much as he could achieve working within the studio hierarchy. His move allowed him ultimate photographic control based on his name and reputation. The networks he built, and continued to build throughout the subsequent decades, remained largely connected to the film industry. He photographed stars, stunt men and set painters, and prominent producers, directors and behind-the-scenes workers with their film awards. These images, I would argue, reflect his view that film-making is a collaborative enterprise that depends upon the contribution of a wide range of workers both above and below the line.

## Seeing the unseen

Examining the work of one of the most visible members of a group of behind-the-scenes photographers reveals much about the production environment and the workplace experience of stills photographers in the British film industry at a key point in its development. As a member of the stills camera section at Pinewood, Lucas felt very much part of a team, and this is reflected both in his willingness to acknowledge the work of other photographers and in his desire to ensure that their contributions were recognized. It is clear that the position Lucas occupied was an unusually privileged one in comparison with the photographers he worked alongside, who rarely received credit for their work. But even if his experiences were atypical, they do give us an insight into the working practices of the behind-the-scenes photographers who enticed film-goers into the cinemas and whose work is still very much in circulation. Issues of recognition, reputation, creative control and independence are problematic for behind-the-scenes workers. The difficulty with stills photographers in particular is how to place them within the structure of production practices in the film industry. Although the images made by photographers are visible to large audiences, the role of the photographer is mostly hidden behind the camera and out of the spotlight. Such is the nature of photography: the photographer allows others to see the unseen. As a consequence, many accounts of the history of the film industry overlook the contribution of photographers whilst at the same time exploiting or making use of the products of their creativity and skill.

At Pinewood in the 1950s, production of these images relied on a model similar to that of the Hollywood studio system in the 1930s and 1940s, which defined the photographer as a below-the-line technician. Public recognition of the contributions of leading photographers like Lucas has subsequently created the potential for a reclassification of the photographer as an above-the-line practitioner. Lucas's recollections of his time at the Pool Studio illustrate both the degree of autonomy that was available to the creative practitioner working within the studio system *and* the constraints under which he operated. His role was one that demonstrated both above-the-line and below-the-line traits. Like all the other behind-the-scenes stills photographers of the time, his position was paradoxically outside the network of film, whilst at the same time being central to its production. As David Puttnam pointed out in his foreword to Lucas's collection of portraits published in 1988,

> Whenever I ask a photographer to take on the responsibility of shooting the stills for a picture, I always make a point of reminding him (or her) that from ten to one hundred times as many people will see their work as will *ever* see the movie itself. Add to this the fact that many of those who *do* see the film will make their decision based solely on the appeal of the photographs they've seen, and you begin to get some idea of the imagination and skill that's expected of the 'stills man'. (Puttnam in Lucas 1988: foreword)

## Notes

1 Chris Beetles Fine Photographs Gallery 'specialises in photographic prints by the world's most sought-after photographers, with an emphasis on 20th century and British masters of the medium'. http://www.chrisbeetlesfinephotographs.com/ [accessed 22 June 2011].

2 Government Papers. Cabinet Meeting 22, (49). Conclusions of a Meeting of the Cabinet held at 10 Downing Street on Thursday 24 March 1949.

3 That is not to say that there were not many very highly skilled and renowned photographers in Britain, but his decision to visit and work on some skills in the United States is attributed in *Shooting Stars* to 'his combined love of the movies and photography' (Lucas 2005: x).

4 This is the date displayed on the brass front-plate of Cornel's camera, held at the National Media Museum in Bradford.

5 The union changed its name in 1956 when it incorporated television workers, becoming ACTT (the Association of Cinematograph, Television and Allied Technicians). It is currently known as BECTU (Broadcasting Entertainment Cinematograph and Theatre Union).

6 Email correspondence with retired ACTT Union official Brian Shemmings. 2 July 2010.

7   For further information on archive content, see http://www.bectu.org.uk/advice-resources/history-project [accessed 8 July 2011].

8   A few stills photographers achieved acclaim outside of their stills work – in particular Norman Gryspeerdt, who worked at Pinewood and was admired for his artwork and skill with the Bromoil photographic process.

9   See the short film *Cornel Lucas: A Portrait* (2008), directed by Nigel Arthur [TV]. See also Lucas (1988, 2005).

10  There are some exceptions to this. One example is that of photographic images made by John Cowan in the 1960s which appeared in the Antonioni film *Blow Up* (1966).

11  An early example of publication of these credits appears in a double-page spread for the film *The Reluctant Widow* published in *Picture Post*, 28 January 1950. (*Sabres Out at High Noon*, byline 'Photographed by Cornel Lucas and Norman Gryspeerdt'.)

12  He was divorced from Lee in 1958. In 1960 he married another of the beautiful stars he photographed, Susan Travers. At the time of writing, they have celebrated more than fifty years of marriage.

13  An example of these restrictions is the 'no zips showing on the back of garments' for Italian audiences (*The Guardian*, 9 April 2001).

14  All anecdotes appear in *Heads and Tales* (Lucas 1988).

15  Paul Hesse was an American commercial, fashion and advertising photographer who moved to Hollywood in 1940. He photographed film stars and made many successful advertising campaigns using Hollywood stars, pioneering techniques for photographic lighting and colour glamour images.

16  *Cornel Lucas: A Portrait* (2008).

17  Also termed 'sackings' in *Cine Technician*, February 1958: 195.

## Bibliography

Bright, M. (2007), *Pinewood Studios: 70 Years of Fabulous Filmmaking*, London: Carroll and Brown.

Caldwell, J. (2008), *Production Culture: Industrial Reflexivity and Critical Practice in Film and Television*, Durham and London: Duke University.

Campany, D. (2007), 'Introduction', in C. Schifferli (ed.), *Paper Dreams: The Lost Art of Hollywood Still Photography*, Gottingen: Steidl.

Chanan, M. (1976), *Labour Power in the British Film Industry*, London: BFI.

*Cornel Lucas: A Portrait* (2008), Film, Directed by Nigel Arthur [TV].

Corrigan, T. (1991), *A Cinema without Walls: Movies and Culture after Vietnam*, New Brunswick, NJ: Rutgers University Press.

Eyles, A. (2005), 'Photographed by Cornel Lucas'. *The Veteran*, 107 (summer): 17–19.

*Face to Face*. Summer 2005, Issue 13, National Portrait Gallery.

Fahey, D. and Rich, L. (1998), *Masters of Starlight: Photographers in Hollywood*, London: Columbus Books.

Finler, J. (1995), *Hollywood Movie Stills*, London: Batsford.

Florida, R. (2002), *The Rise of the Creative Class*, New York: Basic Books.

Kobal, J. (1980), *The Art of the Great Hollywood Portrait Photographers*, London: Allen Lane.

Lennon, P. (2001), 'Rank Insider', *The Guardian*, 9 April, p. 15.

Lucas, C. (1988), *Heads and Tales*, Luton: Lennard Publishing.

Lucas, C. (2005), *Shooting Stars*, Bath: The English Group.

Macnab, G. (1994), *J. Arthur Rank and the British Film Industry*, London: Routledge.

Political and Economic Planning (PEP) (1952), *The British Film Industry: A Report on Its History and Present Organisation, with Special Reference to the Economic Problems of British Feature Film Production*, London: PEP.

Sarris, A. (1992), 'Notes on Auteur Theory in 1962', in M. Cohen, G. Mast and L. Braudy (eds), *Film Theory and Criticism. Introductory Readings*, New York, Oxford: Oxford University Press.

Stollery, M. (2009), 'Technicians of the Unknown Cinema. British Critical Discourse and the Analysis of Collaboration in Film Production', *Film History*, 21 (4): 373–93.

Trent, P. (1973), *The Image Makers: Sixty Years of Hollywood Glamour*, London: Octopus Books.

Vieira, M. A. (1997), *Hurrell's Hollywood Portraits*, New York: Harry N. Abrams.

Warren, P. (2001), *British Film Studios: An Illustrated History* (2nd edition), London: BT Batsford.

# Making faces

## Competition and change in the production of Bollywood film star looks

chapter

# 11

CLARE M. WILKINSON-WEBER

## Introduction

It is scarcely possible to talk about Indian film, certainly popular Hindi film made in Mumbai,[1] without reference to the upheavals produced by the liberalization of the Indian economy in the early 1990s. A mere two to three years after the removal of restrictions on private businesses and relaxation of import controls, Hindi films – always vehicles for the depiction of material wealth and consumerist novelty – began to be filled with the consumer goods, fashions and furnishings that were becoming available for purchase at home. Adjustments to the corporate framework for media production have taken longer to fall into place, but now are increasingly evident, as it seems that periodic calls to 'professionalize' and 'corporatize' the film industry are finally being answered (Bose 2006; Ganti 2004; Prasad 1998). While familial networks remain critical to the forging of film careers, the entry of major global and national corporations into film-making is prompting financing, planning and marketing to be organized according to a business calculus.

The influence of media imagery on ideologies of the body, and in particular upon the disciplinary practices that aim to improve or enhance it, has drawn comment in recent South Asian scholarship (Cullity 2002; Derné 2008; Li et al. 2008). The interpenetration of advertising and film worlds is apparent from the growth of in-film marketing and the aggressive recruitment (and, arguably, the equally aggressive volunteerism) of Bollywood film stars as endorsers of such things as hair and skin care products (Wilkinson-Weber 2010). Less remarked upon is how the growth of beauty and personal grooming products and services has affected the ways in which professional services within the film industry itself are supplied and articulated. This chapter redresses this imbalance by returning a focus that habitually directs itself towards consumption back onto production, in this case the production of the actor's look via make-up and hairstyling. The changed economy has had important implications for the industry's ways of working, in particular for practices like doing make-up

183

or creating hairstyles, that developed in the decades before economic liberalization. The greater weight of commodities and services that can be offered outside the film set drive not just the way in which heroes and heroines are depicted (as men and women who don't simply conform to but actually define what is considered 'stylish' in the world outside film). They also affect what is and is not done in the make-up room as the actors prepare to go on set. Processes and products for the making of film illusions, in this case the transformation of one's appearance, are displaced onto realms outside the film setting, and new forms of knowledge need to be mastered by make-up and hair artists in order to achieve contemporary film looks.[2]

## Industry, actors and the technicians of 'look' in Hindi film

The Indian film industry is one of the biggest and oldest in the world, and its influence reaches into diasporic South Asian and non-South Asian audiences throughout Asia, Africa, parts of Europe, North America and the Caribbean. Of the various regional industries, the one based in Mumbai has the highest national profile and greatest global appeal, despite being outstripped in total output by production houses in South India (Dwyer and Patel 2002: 8; Ganti 2004: 3). Film in India is almost as old as in Europe and the United States. The first Lumière short was exhibited in 1896, followed within a few years by the first Indian-made short film (Ganti 2004: 7). The fundamental techniques of film-making were borrowed along with its technology, and the industry has continued, through collaboration, homage or straight lifting, to adopt themes and effects from film industries to the west and the east. Nevertheless, Hindi film-making has maintained a stylistic as well as a practical distinctiveness in the way in which narrative is constructed and how films are made. Many on-screen characteristics (the unique mélange of melodrama, singing, dancing and action, for example) as well as customary behind-the-scenes practice can be traced to Mumbai's Parsi theatre, named for the educated and prosperous Zoroastrian community that formed and supported it (Hansen 2001, 2002; Rajadhyaksha 1996a: 398).

Owing to the industry's firm sexual division of labour, film make-up was, and remains, a male specialty. Its basic practice came from theatre with the use of heavy greasepaint designed to give colour and definition to the actor's face under strong lights. Some older make-up artists even started out as actors, applying their own make-up according to theatrical tradition. The oldest accounts I have gathered come from make-up artists who entered the industry, some as young as thirteen years old, between 1941 and 1949 (Ganti 2004: 20; Mukherjee 2010; Rajadhyaksha 1996b: 679). They received no formal training, but rather learned their craft by working as assistants to established make-up artists. Opportunities to refine and develop make-up skills were few and far between. Veteran make-up artist Jagat Kumar related stories of visiting a Max Factor shop by the Regal Cinema in the Colaba area of South Bombay, remarking, 'They [make-up artists] used to go once a week to buy make-up, people at Max Factor demonstrated the make-up, advised the make-up, they did make-up. From there I picked up how to make a beautiful face.' (In a recent interview, another senior make-up artist Ram Tipnis also refers to the Max Factor shop; Mukherjee 2010.)

Several described reading books for make-up tips and, in a lone instance, make-up artist Pandhari Jukar went to Moscow for a year-long course in colour make-up at the instigation of the Hindi film star Nargis. (In a 2005 interview, Jukar adds that he was working on the Indo-Soviet film *Pardesi* (1957) at the time; Bajaj 2005.) Other sources of technical innovation have been Western collaborators and employees on Indian film sets. The first film shot in Technicolor, *Jhansi-ki-Rani* (1952), employed several foreign specialists to whom various Indian assistants were deputed and from whom they learned vital new techniques. Special-effects make-up, also very much a matter of trial and error for make-up artists, could best be picked up by novices who happened to work in studios famous for producing either 'mythologicals' (films that retold tales of the deities) or films in the distinct Hindi horror genre.

After Indian independence in 1948, big studios with permanent in-house production staff began to give way to smaller production houses and freelance producers using mercantile capital (Kabir 2001: 13; Rajadhyaksha 1996a: 409, 1996b: 679). Thereafter came the rise of a star system in which lead actors became valuable commodities, perceived as the chief selling point of the film (Dwyer and Patel 2002: 20; Rajadhyaksha 1996b: 679). Over the next few decades, actors increased their load of films per year, and the time to completion of a film extended as actors had fewer and fewer dates on which to finish any one of them. With the rise of the post-independence film star came the differentiation of company versus personal make-up artists and hairdressers. Some make-up artists stuck to working for the company their entire careers, attending to character artists and actors in smaller roles and major actors if the need arose. Others took up the opportunity to develop careers as personal make-up artists to stars (although working for stars exclusively and distancing oneself from make-up responsibilities for the rest of the cast became more common from the 1980s onwards). Attachments to stars might, for some make-up artists, last for years. In other cases, make-up artists acquired star clients one after another in rapid succession. As much as this might be (and was) attributed to the fickleness of the stars, the ability to jump to new artists was a necessity given the normal waxing and waning of film acting careers. As actors aged, their roles would become less central, their shooting dates fewer, and with this fewer work shifts for which the make-up artist (and hairdresser) would be paid. Some make-up artists switched between company and personal employment depending upon circumstance and opportunity.

Hairdressers, all of them female, begin to appear in credits by 1950, and increased in number as hairstyles took on more dramatic form in the late 1950s and early 1960s. Most interviewees had come to film work with some background, even a brief one, in beauty parlour work. Their appearance in film is therefore an indication of the increasing importance of visiting hair salons in the personal grooming practices of female actors for it was there that a prospective film hairdresser might be spotted and cultivated, either by the actor or by production staff. Personal hairdressers and company hairdressers have always by convention been women who work only with female actors (whether stars or character actors) and not male actors (whose hair is attended to by the make-up artist). As with make-up, the line between personal work for stars and company work for character actors was not clearly drawn at first, although it did become so as time went on. Early hairdressers were disproportionately drawn from the Catholic Christian or Anglo-Indian communities, as can be discerned by names in film credits such as Miss Flory, Mrs Charlotte, Miss Connie and the occasional addition of surnames like Rodriguez or d'Souza.[3] These communities had always been more inclined towards the acquisition of Western styles because of a common Christian identification and sharing of non-Indian tastes with colonial authorities. They often grew up making Western hair styles on themselves or their friends, and as bouffants and beehives came into vogue for heroines, young Christian women's familiarity with the techniques and looks of styled hair was naturally an aspect of their appeal to film-makers. Chinese immigrants and their descendants are well-known proprietors of beauty parlours in many urban centres throughout India, and Mumbai is no exception. Among my informants, the hairdresser with the longest film experience, Connie Rodricks, had begun working in a Chinese beauty parlour around 1960 (very much against the wishes of her parents, who were scarcely mollified by the reassurance that hairdressing was more respectable than dancing). The only ethnic Chinese hairdresser I interviewed had come to Mumbai for film work directly from parlour work in Calcutta. I have no other information on the role of Chinese beauty parlours for film heroines. While Chinese beauty parlours still form a distinct subset of parlours in Mumbai today, others run by non-Chinese began to spring up as the 1960s progressed.

The make-up artist for the hero and the make-up artist and hairdresser for the heroine remain today the first line of support, the practical core of the star entourage. Make-up and hair, along with costume, together form the actors' look and the three elements are traditionally managed together in the same backstage space of the dressing room. In addition, hairdressers, as fellow females in the otherwise male world of the set, are able to assist the heroine with her dress. Dressmen (costumers) are not dressers to women because of cultural rules circumscribing the forms of contact between males and females. Dressmen, make-up artists and hairdressers are all part of the same labour association, the Cine Costume, Make-up Artistes and Hair Dressers' Association that since the 1940s has nominally guaranteed basic wages and set the conditions of entry into the industry.[4]

## The art of 'making do'

Before I go on to describe the most recent shifts in make-up and hair practices, it is worth recapping what we can learn from the accumulated experiences of the producers of look in cinema up until the 1990s. The peculiar art world of Indian cinema was, until very recently, one in which a set of well-defined handicraft and technical skills were brought to bear in circumstances that were not always the easiest or most comfortable. Understanding how make-up and hair was done requires appreciation of an environment in which material scarcity was routinely compensated for with artisanal ingenuity. The challenges of adapting make-up to black and white film, like having to replenish it in hot studios under hot lights, faced film-makers in other parts of the world. But for such a large and successful industry, it is startling to discover the degree to which Hindi film-makers were constantly forced to make do with old, temperamental equipment, antiquated film stock, and little in the way of materials that could be acquired ready to use. Make-up artists tell stories handed down from their fathers and grandfathers of how they would manufacture their own make-up supplies: 'During my grandfather's times, there used to be powder which they used to mix with castor oil or jasmine oil or some other oil to make the base. This they had to mix for a long time for two to three hours and then make the base according to skin type. Now we get sticks and packs ready.' Or,

> In old times we used to make the base in our hands, mixing in our hands but now all is ready. Even when we used [to] apply eyeliner we used to apply with stick. We had to boil the stick so that infection does not occur. Again we used to cut the stick ourselves. Today we get the ready-made mascara but in old times we used to heat the *kajal* (kohl) and then apply it. Now everything is in sticks.

The production of illusion, using the limited materials of pre-1990s India, was the outcome of ingenuity, will and, according to some, a very different work environment from the one that prevails currently. Connie Rodricks, whose film career began in 1964, showed me some of the tools of her trade: bendable frames on which to build hair into vertiginous styles; hanks of human hair to make wigs; combs, ties and lots of pins. The glossy, two-foot-long tresses from which wigs could be made are much sought after for hair extensions by Western actors and celebrities today (Taylor 2006). They have been used for decades as raw material by wig makers and hairdressers in Bombay film. As she related stories about the hair effects she had created, the hairdresser was in effect describing a form of mental labour, meshed closely with manipulative, tactile skills, that was at a premium in the industry before economic liberalization. Along with her peers, she stressed the importance of creativity in her work, the ability to make hairstyles that looked 'correct', that could appear 'realistic' no matter how they happened to have been constructed. In the most striking example of the kind of thing I am talking about, a retired make-up artist recalled his invention, after many hours of thought (and a glass of beer), of a piece of special effect make-up intended to show an acid-burned face. He macerated pieces of mutton in vinegar, rolled them out 'like *chapatis*' (flat breads) in the morning to make them thin and ragged, then cut them according to the actor's facial measurements. After he had added colour, and masked the odour with lashings of perfume, he glued a piece to the actor's face. This went on for months without the actor having any idea of how the effect was created. Other veteran designers, make-up artists and hairdressers talk nostalgically about the collaborative work environments of the mid-century, emphasizing that 'all eat together, no big man, no small man' and 'whole unit will sit for script, in that we come to know till what age does an artist go, what is the family status of the actor, nowadays the system is not there'.

In attempting to explain similar accounts from senior cinematographers, Shuddhabrata Sengupta speculates that stable work groups, organized in studios, facilitated forms of inventiveness that were thwarted once the production team was subordinated to the film star. '[A]ctors, directors, technicians and production staff were part of an integrated unit in which everyone knew one another, had a modicum of respect for one another's professional skills and had the time to spend with one another on a regular basis. Once the studio system collapsed and films became vehicles for stars, the importance of the team diminished' (Sengupta 2005: 129–30). In other words, the 'shift'-based system that allowed film stars to juggle their participation in several films broke up the integrity of work groups. Sengupta's thesis is compelling in many respects, and is confirmed by several concurring recollections of dressmen whose careers began in the 1940s. However, it does not explain the warm memories of personal designers, make-up artists and hairdressers whose employment was predicated on the pre-eminence of the same film stars who, according to Sengupta, helped bring an end to collaborative, studio-based practices. I do not think that the positive sentiments of the latter about their work are to be explained solely by their close contact with celebrity. Indeed, these personal make-up and hair artists speak just as firmly about the value of their knowledge, the seriousness with which their opinions were listened to and the respect they were given. Arguably these nostalgic statements indirectly reflect the bitterness of professionals in a mercurial and uncertain industry who find their skills unwanted in the present. But I also believe that they point to a recent, dramatic shift in conventions from long-established theatrical models towards fashion, one that is even greater than that represented by the introduction of film hairdressers. This can be seen in the increasing importance of advertising and magazine work, and the rise of a set of practices associated with the new economic and material regime.

## Commerce and commodity in the construction of the body

The distinction of company make-up and hair stylists from those who work exclusively for a star continues into the present. And now, with the ever-growing importance of advertising in a commodity-rich economy and the attractiveness of Hindi film stars as product endorsers, advertising work has become as absorbing for personal make-up and hair artists as film. According to William Mazzarella (2003), advertising was set on its contemporary course slightly before liberalization took hold, with the newest generation of joint Indian and foreign advertising operations dating from the mid-1980s. New standards of professionalism and creativity, as well as a renewed commitment to discerning and eliciting what was distinctly Indian in a campaign, propelled advertising in print, visual and eventually electronic media in unprecedented directions. Participation in the consumer economy soon became as emblematic of Indianness as devout parsimony had been in a more Gandhian conception of the nation (Kripalani 2006: 208; Mazzarella 2003: 14). Amidst breathless paeans to new Indian consumerism, scholars have cautioned that many remain excluded from participation in the consumer economy because of lack of means (Fernandes 2000), and there are arguably few signs that rampant consumer capitalism in film or real life has revolutionized social relations (Derné 2008). However, if one considers that involvement with branded commodities extends beyond the mere purchase of them into the various commodity chains and forms of provisioning that bring them to the marketplace and put them in the hands of buyers, the shift in the economy has clearly had quite a broad impact (Fine and Leopold 1993; Foster 2005). This is certainly true for anyone working in the film industry, whether they are confident, adept consumers or not. Make-up artists and hairdressers, for example, ignore or withdraw from the commoditization of beauty and grooming services at their peril. There are three strands to these recent developments: first, the use of professional products in set make-up and hairdressing; second, stars' own patronage of brands and services to craft and discipline of the body; and third, the appearance of stars in advertisements as brand endorsers. All three have implications for the work of film make-up artists and hairdressers.

In both make-up and hairdressing for film, there is an important distinction between professional products and commercial ones. In film, temporary hairpieces, wigs and accessories are used that would not be used in off-screen life, and screen make-up must accommodate the effects of set lighting (even if faster film, location shooting and the shift to new digital formats have reduced the artificiality of film conditions in at least some circumstances). Here, too, high-profile brands are finding a foothold. The most highly regarded products are foreign made and as recently as 2002 (when I conducted my first interviews) were unobtainable inside the country. Make-up artists either had to pick them up abroad or ask someone else to do so on their behalf. Names like Bob Kelly (now defunct) and Kryolan come up in conversation as ideal choices, particularly in contrast with Indian brands. By 2010, MAC was emerging as the brand of choice at the highest levels. The problem with MAC, and with other foreign brands, was the difficulty in replacing particular colours and shades once they had run out. However, every indication is that supply problems will be solved as brands realize the wealth of commercial opportunities that await. MAC, for example, has a new tie-in with Mickey Contractor, one of the best known of the high-profile make-up artists in the industry (Bronfman 2011).

The aesthetics of make-up have also changed as both film technology and prevailing tastes have changed. All of the currently working make-up artists I interviewed remarked upon the shift away from heavy, pancake make-up and striking effects, which could be summed up in the words of one of them as 'moving away from a filmi (glamorous, associated specifically with films) look and towards a natural, subtle look'. Thick layers of foundation and powder, darkly defined brows on both males and females, dramatic eye shadow shades and exaggerated colour contrasts of any kind are very much in disfavour (see also Bronfman 2011). Not only this, but the actors, male and female, now take on a greater burden of self-care compared to the past, as they are expected to follow the cosmetic industry's recommendations for taking care of skin and hair. More intrusive modifications are now within reach, such as cosmetic surgery, hair weaves and especially coloured contact lenses which, one designer assured me, are so popular that some heroines rarely take them out. The contrast between foreign products, training and the abandonment of long-held practices is summed up in a statement by a young hair salon owner: '[T]oday each and every one of them [actors and actresses] has, like best make-up artists, trained abroad, who are using good products, they have fantabulous skin, and for years actresses had acne that they dealt with stuff that was used for donkey's years.'

Full wigs, commonplace for female actors for many years either to give them longer hair or to make elaborate constructions upon hidden frames, are now generally disliked. They are, in one hairdresser's terms, 'artificial', whereas part wigs (which give body and shape to the hair) can appear 'natural'. A hairstylist with a strong salon background who now works as a hair designer for films complained that the quality of Indian wigs was poor, even though the quality of hair exported for wig-making was quite high. As a result she was loath to use full wigs to cover up the heroine's hair entirely. If the film is a period one in which the hairstyles are elaborate, there may be no choice in the matter. If, however, the hairdresser can exercise close control over the wig-making process, the results can be very satisfactory. Maria Sharma, one of the most experienced hairdressers in the business, supervised the construction of several wigs for Kangna Ranaut in *Once Upon a Time in Mumbai* (2010) (personal communication; see also 'Maria Sharma Creates 12 Hairdos' 2009). As far as the heroine is concerned, part wigs are acceptable to create innovative styles or add volume to hair, but only because they can be applied and removed quickly. A hairdresser whose career has spanned this transition noted the emphasis of contemporary heroines upon convenience: '[N]ow the artist thinks us[ing] your own hair is best; once pack up comes you can leave immediately.' Unless very complex or period styles are required, women's hairstyles now tend to be what stylists call 'open', or loose, straight hair that can be trimmed, coloured and highlighted at the salon and simply brushed out and lacquered at the set. Male stars too are now opting for fashionable cuts at salons, rejecting more traditional barbering services.

Although there has been relatively little change in the preference for heroines to wear their hair long, more techniques and innovations have gradually become available, from colouring to highlights, styling via haircutting, adding layers or texturizing and, most recently, adding length through extensions.[5] Stars turn to modern hair and beauty salons not just for hair care but for a range of beauty treatments, including pedicures, manicures, skin treatments, laser keratotomy and so on. Those in the very top ranks of the industry, however, still prefer to get what services they can overseas (one star reportedly got her hair conservatively but expertly cut for a film role at Frederic Fekkai in New York City). For years, the beauty parlour was either a modest neighbourhood affair providing periodic skin care, depilation, hair treatments and so on or a more westernized yet still somewhat sober entity housed in exclusive hotels (Dwyer and Patel 2002). Hairdressers who emerged when these salons were the rule describe them as places where women went for 'party' styles or for wedding makeovers. Nowadays, however, the salon is not simply an exotic source of grooming for special occasions like weddings or parties, but is also a critical resource for young, upper-middle-class women (and men also) to maintain a fashionable business or leisure look (Bhattacharya 2006). The first high-street salons date roughly from the later 1970s, with the now iconic Nalini and Yasmin salon in Bandra a benchmark of sorts (conveniently located in the heart of a residential area filled with the creative classes of Bollywood cinema).

Trendy studios and stylists whose shopfronts are practically indistinguishable from those found in the West are located in more prestigious areas of the city and its suburbs, and offer younger, more adventurous clientele services like cutting, styling, colouring, make-up and makeovers. Rock, pop and Indi pop play in the background and the interior use of space and decoration deviates little from what one might find in Europe or North America.

Actors are enthusiastic product endorsers, appearing in advertisements in magazines, newspapers, television and online. One sure sign of success in the commercial salon world is being able to boast of movie stars as clients or to be first in line to be able to promote a global brand (Nashrulla 2008). Another crucial outlet for promoting actors as personalities and style leaders includes photo spreads in film magazines like *Stardust*, *Filmfare* and *Cineblitz*. *Filmfare* was until the 1980s a publication that meshed film gossip and photo galleries with film reviews, analysis and discussion of world cinema. It now more closely resembles a version of *People*, with star interviews, celebrity gossip, behind-the-scenes stories and lavish photo spreads of stars in designer clothes. *Cineblitz* and *Stardust* follow the same format. The photo shoots that are at the core of the magazines are key showcases not just for the stars but for designers, make-up artists and hairdressers whose names appear in the photo credits. In fact, many make-up artists and hairdressers working today say that their work is moving substantially into the advertising or photo shoot domain, where they can make a name for themselves and guarantee future employment. The top echelons of the personal artists, including Bharat and Dorris Godambe, Mickey Contractor and Adhuna Akhtar (founder and proprietor of b:blunt salon), are sufficiently diversified, essentially running their own make-up and hair corporations, that their positions are secure. The lower-level personal artists must always be ready to cultivate new heroes and heroines as their patrons age and get fewer roles, or decide to hire new talent. The fashion and pageant worlds have provided the launch pad for many contemporary actors, and even those actors who lack a modelling background are recruited by fashion designers (who also work as costume designers for films) to promote their clothing collections. Make-up artists and hairdressers then may go along to prepare their stars in ramp shows.

It is important to qualify these observations with the point that Hindi film has been linked to fashion and advertising for decades. The connection of stars with commodities in the public imagination dates back to the late 1930s, when Devika Rani was the first film star to appear in a print advertisement, endorsing Palmolive soap (Weinbaum *et al.* 2008: 34). Given that the recent enthusiastic embrace of product endorsement by stars is not at all unprecedented, what is new is the trend towards showcasing Indian media celebrities instead of white models, linking desirability to a clear-cut Indian ideal. In addition, the sheer range and diversity of products that are available for a star to become attached to has increased dramatically. In beauty products related to make-up and hair care alone, the scant diversity of brands a mere twenty years ago (Lux, Lifebuoy, Sunsilk and a few Indian name brands) has now been augmented with international brands like Head and Shoulders, Garnier, L'Oreal, Revlon, Maybelline, Clarins and Paul Mitchell, to name but a few.

Heroes and heroines, following the injunctions of the brand advertising they help create, take on more responsibility for forms of bodily improvement and consider that their own authority in matters of appearance outstrips that of the hairdresser or make-up artist. Several of my informants stated matter-of-factly that heroines regarded hairdressing in film as a form of personal rather than professional service. Indeed, one went so far as to say that 'nowadays an actress thinks [the] hairdresser is her slave'. The film hairdresser implicitly competes for the attention and loyalties of the actor with the salon and her hairstylist there; the same is true of the make-up artist and the makeover consultant. In the salon stylist's view, the actor merely has to find a film hairdresser who

> will work with her, and they're the ones who do the put-ups, the styling and that. *They just finish up* [emphasis added], what we do is that we do the cut, and then we call them in, and we train them that this is how it is to be worn, how it is going to be falling, this is how we cut it, so the stylist comes in.

In other words, the core style of the actor's look in a film comes from the salon, not the make-up room.

Film hairdressers had depended until very recently upon stars who travelled abroad to bring back any products that could give them an advantage in producing innovative looks for their patrons. They have also continually tried to improve their own knowledge of brands through reading film and fashion magazines, and by taking as many opportunities to work on magazine shoots and ramp shows as possible. These latter opportunities are, though, far more open to the personal artists who attend to particular stars than to company personnel. A close relationship with a salon is advantageous since new products, like curl boosters, alight there instead of on the film set. Not only do salons provide the base of training for more and more hairdressers, but the space that separated the salon from the set has narrowed. The b:blunt salon is owned and run by Adhuna Akhtar, who happens to be the wife of actor and director Farhan Akhtar. Unsurprisingly, stylists from this salon are key hairdressers on films on which Akhtar works, some of them taking a leading role in deciding hairstyles for characters in the entire film.

Another consequence of the influence of the salon in film work is that the strict gender divide between make-up men and hairdresser women is coming into question. A significant number of openly gay men with salon training question and contest the exclusivity of hairdressing as a women's domain. Meanwhile, women outnumber men significantly in enrolment in make-up and hairstyling courses, and they predominate in salons. Since the work of the salon affects a film's look, it is hardly surprising that women from that world have become as interested in handling stars' make-up as well as their hair – and not just female stars but male stars as well. At the same time, women who do training courses abroad specifically in film make-up find that their skills are in demand back in India, but they are perpetually frustrated in their attempts to work openly in what is a man's occupation by mandate (to the extent that they might have to hand over to a male assistant or make themselves scarce if an official of the Cine Costume, Make-Up Artistes and Hairdressers' Association comes on set for an inspection to check that only card-carrying members are working). I have heard older, traditionally minded make-up artists explaining that men monopolize make-up because, as men, they understand what makes a woman beautiful more than women do. By this heterosexist logic, women should do men's make-up since they must be uniquely attuned to male beauty, but the very thought of women working in close, private contact with men is unthinkable to the senior generation. Patriarchal attitudes in the industry are by no means restricted to older practitioners: in a recent interview, make-up superstar Mickey Contractor startlingly proclaimed that industry sexism was evident in the refusal to allow men to do women's hair, with no mention whatsoever of women's desire to do make-up on both men and women (Bronfman 2011).

## Differentiation and resistance

The heightened responsibilities and privileges of top-rank personal hairdressers and make-up artists have driven an ever larger wedge between them, the more modest personal artists, and the rest of the company. The differences are concretized in the higher wages and better treatment that the loftiest personal artists receive compared to everyone else. This discrepancy among hair and make-up artists was among the factors that drove the Cine Costume, Make-Up Artistes and Hair Dressers' Association to join with twenty-two other technical and acting associations in industrial action in October 2008 over pay and conditions.

At least officially, a crew member has to get an association card to work in films. Obtaining a card involves an initial expense of around Rs 12,000.[6] Other conditions include a minimum age of eighteen, five years' residence in the state of Maharashtra, proof of identity and educational status, and two reference signatures from current association members in good standing. The association is maintained on the basis of annual membership fees. On a production, a head dressman, make-up artist and, if needed, hairdresser are appointed who typically bring with them two assistants each. Assistants' pay is meagre but there is no lack of people eager to get into the business, and some question whether the admission of new members should be under stricter control. The first child of an association member is eligible to pay a lower fee for their card if and when he or she follows their parents into the business, but younger children must pay the full fee.

Company labour is hired for a fixed period on salary. If more time is needed to complete the film, remuneration is made in daily wages. If more employees are needed (for, say, crowd scenes), those are hired at a rate established by the association, also on daily wages. Money (which is considered to include wages plus expenses) is disbursed by production to the head make-up artist or hairdresser who in turn gives it to his or her assistants and daily wage workers. Wage rates are established in agreement with the Federation of Western India Cine Employees (FWICE), which negotiates with the Indian Motion Pictures Producers' Association (IMPPA) on member associations' behalf. The Cine Costume, Make-Up Artistes and Hair Dressers' Association does not negotiate directly with producers.

The 2008 action was long in coming. In 2002, I heard many complaints about the undercutting of wages, preferential treatment for personal make-up and hair artists, and delays in payment. Some pointed to the extension of the working day in TV from twelve hours up to fourteen and fifteen hours as a development originating in the mid-1990s. The association had hitherto done little to address these problems, for, as most film workers recognize, the most important relationships are between the technician and the producers and director, not their relationship with their association. From the point of view of the old hands, the pressure on wages was considerable from newcomers eager to get into the business by working for far less than the agreed association rates. 'If the style is open hair, then they will get someone cheaper to do it', explained one hairdresser. 'If you ask Rs 2,000 per day there is someone standing behind who will ask only Rs 1,500 then someone who has 1,000. ... You might even get someone who will do the job [for] Rs 500.'

It is assistants who are in the worst position, since they must depend upon the head make-up artist or hairdresser to pay them. Their pay may be, I was told, as little as Rs 200 per shift as a result. If a card-carrying member of the association were prepared to work for less than the negotiated amount, there would be very little the association could do to sanction such behaviour. At the other end of the pay scale, personal artists typically charge far more than the daily wage per shift established by the association, from at least double to in excess of five times as much. 'If we do personal then it depends upon the status of the artist. For like Aishwarya's make-up artists will demand and producer has to pay because it's her make-up.' For their part, the personal make-up artists heartily concur that the association rates are ludicrously low, but feel there is nothing wrong with using their prestigious position to stake a claim to an appropriate reward.

> See, the association rate is there, but it is very negligible – you cannot survive on that rate because make-up artist is working since morning only, he has to be there, he has to make ready all artists, and after the shoot only, before the pack up, the cleaning of the make-up, the make-up materials; he learns at the end of the day that period of work is not shown in the association arrangement. Suppose he has earned his name, people call him because we do a good job, so they invite you for a job, so then he starts taking extra money for that because he knows he has reached a certain level. Because when you've reached on a certain level, you can't ... on a higher level he can demand more, and producers also do not argue on that.

Not only do the people who work for stars get paid more, they get paid on time because the star can intercede with the company to ensure they get their compensation. It is a very different story for company workers. In 2005 I was told, 'Money matter has become very bad, very bad, they may pay all the stars and all that, but they don't want to pay the technician, and sometimes our money gets stuck. We really need to call them [the producers] up to the office [when] we don't get our money. It's happening in lots of places.'

A crisis point was reached in the latter half of 2008, after the associations collectively determined that the annual agreements over pay struck in January with the producers' association were not being honoured. The FWICE called for a 'non-cooperation movement' involving extras, dancers, carpenters, grips, gaffers and camera operators (Dore 2008), with the key points of contention the low rates of pay, protracted delays in receiving it, unapproved extensions to the working day and use of labour not sanctioned by the associations (Ramesh 2008). Some members had waited for months in vain for pay; others were regularly working twenty-hour shifts and being supplanted by non-association workers (Dore 2008). Conditions were particularly difficult in television. An estimated 147,000 workers stayed away from the studios for the three-day stoppage, with some above-the-line workers joining them in solidarity. Dinesh Chaturvedi, the head of FWICE, said, 'A film worker gets 600 rupees (around £8 or $13 at time of writing) per day and a television worker gets paid 500 rupees per day. The least the producers can do is pay them on time' (Ramesh 2008). I was told independently that payment was not being made by the shift, at best only once a month. Hours were being extended without any increase in wages. However, as much as the reluctance of production houses to pay decent wages on time was aggravating workers, the glaring disparities in pay between celebrity personnel and themselves were especially grating. The strike ended when producers agreed to hike pay between 7.5 and 35 per cent for more than a dozen crew categories and promised to create new contracts replacing daily pay with monthly hires that included life insurance. However, a *Variety* story reports that some association members, make-up artists among them, rejected the agreement as insufficiently generous (Frater 2008). At that point, the agreement was allegedly frozen, although every indication is that work essentially returned to normal. In 2010, no apparent stoppages were taking place and make-up artists had no information to offer about the frozen agreement.

## Conclusions

As technical skills in film-making settle into their post-liberalization forms, the authority of objects in the production of look – in this case commodities and the services they are part of – is striking: 'If we say to any artist I will put on moustache [by hand] they will not like it, they want ready-made. They will not go into the detail of the work. Now[adays] the make-up artists give order and get it done [by an outside contractor].' Branded commodities are the currency of professionalism, as argued by one hairdresser whose career began in the late 1970s: 'I only had to create in that time. Today if I don't have something with me then I am not a good hairdresser. My daughter is new but if I give her each and every material she will be a good hairdresser whether she knows her job or not. This is the difference.' Other hairdressers were in agreement that the present-day hairdresser must be ready to come armed, so to speak, with all the materials and tools she may expect to use, from gels to curlers to straighteners, and so on.

Industrial production has for centuries used products of one labour process as the factors or instruments of another. What has changed for film-makers in Mumbai is that the balance of finished products entering production as factors have begun to outweigh the incomplete, yet-to-be modified materials upon which the costume designer, dressman, tailor and embroiderer had to work previously (Marx 1976: 288–9). The world of film, as fantastic as it is in Bollywood, is now opened up to increasingly interpenetrating scapes (Appadurai 1990). Where elaborate hair designs and make-up effects done backstage used to depend relatively little upon the efforts of salons and the uses of consumer cosmetics, now 'open hair' and subtle make-up depend on the world outside the film set almost exclusively. Present-day make-up artists and hairdressers amplify appearances constructed outside the sets – they rarely create new ones.[7]

The salon owners stress the benefits of a more sophisticated approach to hair and make-up, fuelled by a fashion rather than a theatrical sensibility. This approach appeals most obviously to youth, but it also ties film looks to the broader context of a global cinema and a global fashion world. It is keyed also to notions of realism and the desire to construct cinematic heroes and heroines who interact with and participate smoothly in the world outside film. This means, on the one hand, that grittier films using more naturalistic visual and narrative conventions are more common than they used to be, but it also means that seductive and beautiful looks from films travel directly and overtly into fashion activities (working the ramps, appearing in magazine shoots dressed in designer clothing). Fashionable film clothing is targeted precisely at the consumers in the audience who have the ready means to look like the stars. For these viewers, 'realism' is merely the confirmation that their emulative behaviours are normal and not unusual. Whereas copying used to involve convoluted instructions to tailors, begging beauty products from visiting foreigners and trips to the old-style beauty parlour, now a panoply of anti-aging, anti-acne, moisturizing, plumping, defining products, just to name a few, are no farther away than the nearest chemist's shop or the growing numbers of department stores.

Not only has film-making become more defined by the kinds of commodities that it uses, the commodities themselves have altered the experience of time. Speed is regarded by those with the greatest investment in the 'new' industry (fashion designers, top make-up artists, hairdressers etc) as a sign of the improvement of film from its inefficient, haphazard past to a slick and no-nonsense present. The laborious work of a mid-century make-up artist has been transformed into the fast-paced preparation, shooting and pack up of films and ads. Not only that, but integration of newcomers into the industry is now much faster. The old head make-up artist and hairdresser could take their time with their assistants, letting them in on their secrets sparingly, slowly, so that mastery was acquired – as in any apprenticeship system – by stages, and not always without some struggle. But as the hairdressers' comments at the beginning of this section demonstrate, having things, or knowing about things, propels their owner into a job far faster than ever before. Knowledge spreads in new ways via listservs and chat rooms, as well as in the training programmes now cropping up in cities as sidelines of salon businesses. 'Everything is now fast', says one make-up artist who rode the wave from the early 1970s to become a major provider of training, salon services and ad make-up.

> We used to do lot of things [by] hand. Before when we had to straighten the hair we used to use blow-dryer and comb continuously to give that look and now we take only five minutes to that same job. If we had to do

curls previously we used our hands to do the curls and then pin up, then blow-dryer if they used [it] to dry it – for two hours.

Just as the processes and regimes of beauty have tended to impose disciplines upon the body (to which subjects willingly acquiesce), so they entail disciplines assimilated and enacted by those who must put those regimes into practice. The beneficiaries, at this point, are distinct in terms of their relative youth and higher class, imbibing and now passing on the techniques and rhetoric of the production of beauty to film clients and their imitators. Within film, some must adapt to the shift of disciplinary practice to locations and businesses outside; others must shift their practice in part to arenas where the production of images has become equally critical.

## Notes

1  Bombay is now officially known as Mumbai but is still referred to in film circles by its old name.
2  The present chapter is based on several months' fieldwork in Mumbai between 2002 and 2008 collecting interviews and ethnographic data among film craftspeople and technicians.
3  Many names have variant spellings. Thus, Connie Rodricks, a recently retired senior hairdresser whom I interviewed in 2002, has her name spelled Connie Rodrigues, Miss Connie, Connie, Cony, Kony and Koni, among other variations, on film credits. Happily, these variations are all grouped together under a single name on the Internet Movie Database (IMDB) so that her accomplishments can all be seen, but other hair and make-up professionals are not so lucky.
4  Before hairdressers were recognized in the industry, the association was named simply the Cine Costume and Make-Up Artists Association.
5  The most up-to-date extensions using keratin bonds came in around 2002–3.
6  Between 2006 and 2011 a dollar ranged in value from approximately 44 to 50 rupees, and a pound sterling from 70 to 75 rupees. Of course, wages in the Indian context have to be understood in terms of the overall lower cost of living in that country.
7  Special effects and period make-up, of course, are the exceptions. Foreign make-up specialists are frequently brought in for this kind of work, although there are wig and prosthetic make-up artists who have been working for decades in the industries using their own ingenious methods to produce unusual effects. Latex for prosthetics was almost completely unobtainable until fairly recently, and even in 2005 I was told it had to be bought overseas and brought back to India, where it had to be kept in the refrigerator. By this point, make-up artists were adept in its use.

## Bibliography

'Maria Sharma Creates 12 Hairdos for Once Upon a Time in Mumbaai' (2009), *Images: Business of Beauty*, http://www.imagesbusinessofbeauty.com/News.aspx?Id=195&topic=1 [accessed 9 August 2011].

Appadurai, A. (1990), 'Disjuncture and Difference in the Global Cultural Economy', *Public Culture*, 2 (2) (April): 1–24.

Bajaj, R. (2005), 'Vanity Box: Pandhari Juker', *Harmony Magazine*, http://www.harmonyindia.org/hportal/VirtualPageView.jsp?page_id=910 [accessed 9 August 2011].

Bhattacharya, P. (2006), 'Paradigm Shift for India's Hair Care', *GCI Magazine*, http://www.gcimagazine.com/marketstrends/regions/bric/27779339.html [accessed 9 August 2011].

Bose, D. (2006), *Brand Bollywood: A New Global Entertainment Order*, New Delhi: Sage.

Bronfman, M. (2011), '10 Minutes with Makeup Magician and MAC Maverick Mickey Contractor', *Huffington Post*, http://www.huffingtonpost.com/marissa-bronfman/mac-mickey-contractor_b_891820.html [accessed 9 August 2011].

Cullity, J. (2002), 'The Global Desi: Cultural Nationalism on MTV India', *Journal of Communication Inquiry*, 26 (4) (1 October): 408–25.

Derné, S. (2008), *Globalization on the Ground: Media and the Transformation of Culture, Class, and Gender in India*, Thousand Oaks, CA: Sage.

Dore, S. (2008), 'Bollywood Strike Ends with Deal', *Variety*, 6 October, http://www.variety.com/article/VR1117993449?refCatId=1066&query=strike+bollywood [accessed 9 August 2011].

Dwyer, R. and Patel, D. (2002), *Cinema India: The Visual Culture of Hindi Film*, New Brunswick, NJ: Rutgers University Press.

Fernandes, L. (2000), 'Restructuring the New Middle Class in Liberalizing India', *Comparative Studies of South Asia, Africa, and the Middle East*, 20 (1–2): 88–112.

Fine, B. and Leopold, E. (1993), *The World of Consumption*, New York: Routledge.

Foster, R. J. (2005), 'Commodity Futures: Labour, Love and Value', *Anthropology Today*, 21 (4) (August): 8–12.

Frater, P. (2008), 'Strike Up in the Air', *Daily Variety*, 24 November, p. 18.

Ganti, T. (2004), *Bollywood: A Guidebook to Popular Hindi Cinema*, New York: Routledge.

Hansen, K. (2001), 'The Indar Sabha Phenomenon. Public Theatre and Consumption in Greater India (1853–1956)', in R. Dwyer and C. Pinney (eds), *Pleasure and the Nation: The History, Politics and Consumption of Public Culture in India*, Delhi: Oxford University Press.

Hansen, K. (2002), 'A Different Desire, A Different Femininity: Theatrical Transvestism in the Parsi, Gujarati, and Marathi Theatres, 1850–1940', in R. Vanita (ed.), *Queering India: Same-Sex Love and Eroticism in Indian Culture and Society*, New York: Routledge.

Kabir, N. (2001), *Bollywood: The Indian Cinema Story*, London: Channel 4 Books.

Kripalani, C. (2006), 'Trendsetting and Product Placement in Bollywood Film: Consumerism through Consumption', *New Cinemas: Journal of Contemporary Film*, 4 (3): 197–215.

Li, E. P. H., Min, H. J., Belk, R. W., Kimura, J. and Bahl, S. (2008), 'Skin Lightening and Beauty in Four Asian Cultures', *Advances in Consumer Research*, 35: 444–9.

Marx, K. F. B. (1976), *Capital: A Critique of Political Economy/Uniform Title: Kapital. English*, New York: Vintage Books.

Mazzarella, W. (2003), *Shoveling Smoke: Advertising and Globalization in Contemporary India*, Durham, NC: Duke University Press.

Mukherjee, D. (2010), 'A Material World: Notes on an Interview with Ram Tipnis', *Bioscope*, 1 (2): 199–205.

Nashrulla, T. (2008), 'Beauty: A Profile of Young Star Asif Rajan', *Hindustan Times*, 9 March, Section: Fashion and Beauty, http://www.hindustantimes.com/Entertainment/Fashion/Beauty-a-profile-of-young-star-Asif-Rajan/Article1-280881.aspx [accessed 20 April 2012].

Prasad, M. M. (1998), *Ideology of the Hindi Film: A Historical Construction*, Delhi: Oxford University Press.

Rajadhyaksha, A. (1996a), 'Indian Cinema: Origins to Independence', in G. Nowell-Smith (ed.), *The Oxford History of World Cinema*, New York: Oxford University.

Rajadhyaksha, A. (1996b), 'India: Filming the Nation', in G. Nowell-Smith (ed.), *The Oxford History of World Cinema*, New York: Oxford University Press.

Ramesh, R. (2008), 'International: Strike by 100,000 Film Workers Brings Bollywood to a Standstill', *The Guardian*, 2 October p. 25.

Sengupta, S. (2005), 'Reflected Readings in Available Light: Cameramen in the Shadows of Hindi Cinema', in R. Kaur and A. J. Sinha (eds), *Bollyworld: An Introduction to Popular Hindi Cinema*, New Delhi: Sage.

Taylor, J. (2006), 'Religious Offering: Faith, Hope – and Western Vanity', *The Independent*, December 16.

Weinbaum, A. E., Thomas, L. M., Ramamurthy, Priti, Poiger, U. G., Dong, M. Y. and Barlow, T. E. (2008), 'The Modern Girl Around the World: Cosmetics Advertising and the Politics of Race and Style', in A. E. Weinbaum et al. (eds), *The Modern Girl Around the World: Consumption, Modernity, and Globalization*, Durham, NC: Duke University Press.

Wilkinson-Weber, C. M. (2010), 'From Commodity to Costume: Productive Consumption in the Production of Bollywood Film "Looks"', *Journal of Material Culture*, 15 (1): 1–28.

# Appendix

## List of France-based female DPs with at least one feature film credit (source: Unifrance professional directory, Internet Movie Database)

Names in **bold** indicate AFC members, names * indicate the most significant non-AFC DPs with:

    A – indicates high-profile or numerous assistantships
    D – indicates a move to directing
    TV – high-profile or numerous TV credits

1   Nathalie Abensour – two credits 1993–4
2   Muriel Abourrouse/Aboulrous – three credits + TV 2005–10
3   Sonia Armengol – one credit 2008
4   Patrizia Atanazio – two credits 2004–8
5   *Nurith Aviv – forty-five credits 1969–2008. Several well-known for Varda, Allio, Gitai *et al.*
6   Gertrude Baillot – three credits 2003–7, TV 2009
7   *Claire Bailly du Bois – six credits 1983–2009, mostly documentaries. A
8   **Diane Baratier – eighteen credits 1993–2009**
9   Brigitte Barbier, three credits 2000–5. A
10  Nedjma Berder – four credits 2003–9
11  Cécile Bodènes – one credit, 2010
12  Margaux Bonhomme – two credits 2002–4. A
13  Isabelle Bourzat – one credit 2008 and substantial TV
14  **Céline Bozon – twenty credits 2002–10**
15  Prune Brenguier – one credit 2009
16  Sophie Cadet – four credits 1999–2009
17  Sylvie Calle – one credit 2002. TV

18   **Caroline Champetier – fifty-one credits 1981–2010**

19   Claire Childéric – two credits 1998–2008

20   Emmanuelle Collinot – three credits 2001–8. TV

21   Sara Cornu – three credits 1994–2005. A

22   Isabelle Czajka – one credit 2000. D

23   Ariane Damain – one credit 1995

24   Meryem de Lagarde – one credit 2006

25   *Josée Deshaies – seventeen credits 1998–2010. Partnership with Bonello. Canadian origins

26   Isabelle Dumas – two TV

27   *Nathalie Durand – ten credits 2000–11 (*La Faute à Fidel*) + five TV

28   Isabelle Fermont – one credit 2006

29   Francine Filatriau – TV (4 x series). A

30   **Chrystel Fournier – fifteen credits 2001–10**

31   Anne Galland – one credit 2005

32   Arlette Girardot – two credits 1997–2010 + three TV

33   **Agnès Godard – twenty-eight credits 1991–2011**

34   *Pascale Granel – six credits 2001–8 (*Le Souffle*) + seven TV

35   Julie Grünbaum – five credits 1995–2010

36   Elin Kirschfink – one credit 2004. A

37   Marion Koch – three credits 2002–10

38   *Sabine Lancelin – twenty-two credits 1994–2010

39   **Jeanne Lapoirie – thirty credits 1983–2010**

40   *Emmanuelle Le Fur – five credits (*Souviens-toi de moi* 1996: co-credit) 1996–2010

41   Valérie Le Gurun – three credits 1995–8 (*Etat des lieux* co-credit, *Ma 6-T va crack-er*). TV (Canada currently)

42   **Dominique Le Rigoleur – twenty-seven credits, 1981–2005**

43   Florence Levasseur – six credits 2000–10

44   **Hélène Louvart – forty-seven credits, 1990–2011**

45   Irina Lubtchansky – seven credits 2004–10 (*L'Enfer d'Henri-Georges Clouzot* co-credit; *36 vues du Pic-Saint-Loup*). A

46   Pascale Marin – one credit 2007

47   Claire Mathot – nine credits 2006–10 (*Plein Sud*). A

48   Corinne Maury – one credit 2005

49   *Béatrice Mizrahi – eight credits 1994–2010 (*Jacques Rivette, le veilleur*; *Profils paysans, l'approche*, both co-credits). TV

50   Julia Muñoz – two credits (*Salvador Allende* co-credit) 2002–4

51   Claudine Natkin – two credits 2005–11

52   Dominique Perrier – two credits 1996. (*Reprise, Comment je me suis disputé … ma vie sexuelle* co-credit). D

53   Pénélope Pourriat – two credits 2000–7

54   Elizabeth Prouvost – three credits 1984–94. TV

55   *Catherine Pujol – eight credits 1999–2008 (*Le Petit Voleur, Jean-Philippe, Entre les murs*, all co-credits). TV

56  Elsa Quinette – one credit 2005
57  Tessa Racine – two credits 1995–7. A
58  Isabelle Razavet – fourteen credits 1991–2009 (*Hauts les coeurs* co-credit). TV
59  Léna Rouxel – two credits 2004–7
60  Donné Rundle – one credit 1999
61  *Virginie Saint-Martin – twenty-one credits 1991–2011. (*La Séparation* co-credit, *Une liaison pornographique, Le Tango des Rashevski, La Femme de Gilles*). Works mostly in Belgium
62  Nathalie Sarles – two credits 1999–2004 (*La Révolution sexuelle n'a pas eu lieu*)
63  Marie Spencer – nine credits 1999–2008 (*La Faute à Voltaire* co-credit, *Je pense à vous*). TV
64  Flore Thulliez – four credits 1989–2007. TV. A
65  **Myriam Vinocour – ten credits, 1996–2011**

# Index